Space:
A Children's
Encyclopedia

A DORLING KINDERSLEY BOOK

**LONDON, NEW YORK,
MELBOURNE, MUNICH, and DELHI**

Consultant Peter Bond

Project editor Wendy Horobin
Project designer Pamela Shiels
Editors Fleur Star, Holly Beaumont,
Lee Wilson, and Susan Malyan
Designers Rachael Grady, Lauren Rosier,
Gemma Fletcher, Karen Hood, Clare Marshall,
Mary Sandberg, and Sadie Thomas
Proofreaders Lorrie Mack and Penny Smith
Indexer Chris Bernstein
Picture researchers Ria Jones, Harriet Mills,
and Rebecca Sodergren
Production editor Sean Daly
Jacket designer Natalie Godwin
Jacket editor Matilda Gollon
Publishing manager Bridget Giles
Art director Martin Wilson

Packaging services supplied by **Bookwork**

First published in Great Britain in 2010 by
Dorling Kindersley Limited,
80 Strand, London, WC2R 0RL

Copyright © 2010 Dorling Kindersley Limited
A Penguin Company

10
048-175938-05/10

A CIP catalogue record for this book
is available from the British Library

ISBN: 978-1-40535-375-5

Colour reproduction by Media Development
and Printing Limited, United Kingdom
Printed and bound in China

Discover more at
www.dk.com

Contents

Introduction

Only about 500 people have left Earth behind to explore
the wonders of outer space. Now you, too, can voyage
through space and time, and enjoy an experience that is
out of this world.

As you turn the pages of this lavishly illustrated encyclopedia,
you will learn about how rockets and telescopes work, discover
what it is like to work and live in space, and unravel the
mysteries of the final frontier. You'll travel from our small,
blue planet to strange worlds with poisonous atmospheres,
hidden oceans, and huge volcanoes. Then head out into the
Milky Way to discover the multicoloured clouds, stars, and
galaxies that lie scattered throughout the Universe.

Packed with beautiful images from the world's most powerful telescopes and full of amazing facts, this encyclopedia is invaluable as a reference book for researching projects or perfect for just dipping into.

For anyone who has ever stared up at the night sky and wondered what the Universe is really like, this book is an essential read.

Peter Bond

O When you see this symbol in the book, turn to the pages listed to find out more about a subject.

▲ GENERAL ARTICLES *focus on particular topics of interest (* O *p72–73). Many have fact boxes, timelines that chronicle key stages in development, and picture features.*

▲ DETAILED PROFILES *accompany features about our solar system (* O *p128–129). These are packed with facts and figures about the structure, composition, and features of each planet.*

▲ FACT FILES *take an in-depth look at one topic, such as telescopes (* O *p18–19). They detail all you need to know about the subject.*

▲ PHOTO SPREADS *capture items of special interest within each chapter, such as exploding stars (* O *p216–217).*

OBSERVING
THE UNIVERSE

We live on one tiny planet in the vast Universe. Finding out what else is "out there" has been one of our biggest challenges, and it started with people simply staring at the sky.

What is *space?*

We live on a small, blue planet called Earth. It has a surface of liquid water and rock, and is surrounded by a blanket of air called the atmosphere. Space begins at the top of the atmosphere. It is an unimaginably vast, silent, and largely empty place, but it has many amazing properties.

FACT FILE

- In the US, anyone who flies above an altitude of 100 km (62 miles) in a rocket or spacecraft gets a special badge called "astronaut wings".
- Our most common name for people who travel into space is "astronauts", meaning star travellers. The Russians call them "cosmonauts", meaning travellers through the Universe, and the Chinese name is "taikonauts", from their word for space.
- A person who stepped out into space without a protective suit would quickly die. He or she would be unable to breathe, but would still have around 10 seconds to reach safety before losing consciousness.

Blacker than black
In photos taken from space, our planet is surrounded by blackness. This shows how empty outer space is. Planets like Earth shine because they reflect light from the Sun. Stars shine because they produce huge amounts of energy by burning fuel. Most of space looks black because there is nothing there to produce or reflect light.

OUTER SPACE...

10,000 km

100 km

◄ OUTER SPACE *Even in places far from stars and planets, space contains scattered particles of dust or a few hydrogen atoms.*

THE EDGE OF SPACE

Earth's atmosphere does not end suddenly – it gets gradually thinner and thinner as you travel up from the ground. Most experts agree that outer space starts at a height of 100 km (62 miles). Yet even above this height, there is a layer of very thin air called the exosphere. Hydrogen and other light gases are slowly escaping into space from this outermost part of Earth's atmosphere.

◄ EXOSPHERE *This top layer of the atmosphere extends up to 10,000 km (6,000 miles) above Earth.*

◄ THE ATMOSPHERE *protects Earth's surface from harmful radiation and the full heat of the Sun. At night, it stops heat escaping into space.*

IN A VACUUM

A place without any air or gas is called a vacuum. On Earth, air transfers heat from one place to another. In space there is no air to distribute heat, so the sunlit side of a spacecraft gets very hot, while the other side is in darkness and gets very cold. Spacecraft have to be tested in a thermal vacuum chamber before they are launched to make sure that they can survive these extreme space temperatures.

Sun

📷 **WATCH THIS SPACE**

Anything that travels through space at a steady speed is weightless. This is why things inside a spacecraft float, and astronauts are able to lift huge satellites using just their hands. The weightlessness disappears if the spacecraft either slows down or speeds up.

Hot

▶ BARBECUE ROLL *This is a slow, rotating movement, used to stop any part of a spaceship getting either too hot or too cold.*

Cold

▲ ESCAPING GRAVITY
The space shuttle uses up all the fuel in its two booster rockets just to overcome gravity and reach outer space.

Getting off the ground

It is difficult to get into space because Earth's gravity holds everything down. To overcome gravity and go into orbit, a rocket has to reach a speed of 28,000 km/h (17,500 mph), known as escape velocity. This requires a lot of fuel to provide energy. To reach the Moon and planets, spacecraft have to travel at an even higher speed – 40,000 km/h (25,200 mph).

9

Our place in space

Planet Earth is our home, and to us it seems a very big place. Flying to the other side of the world takes an entire day, and sailing around the world takes many weeks. Yet in the vastness of the Universe, Earth is just a tiny dot. In fact, an alien flying through our galaxy would probably not even notice our little planet.

EARTH AND MOON

Earth's nearest neighbour is the Moon, our planet's only natural satellite. The Moon is a lot smaller than Earth. Its diameter is only about one-quarter the diameter of Earth, and 50 Moons would fit inside Earth. Although it looks quite close, the Moon is actually about 384,000 km (240,000 miles) away. It takes a manned spacecraft three days to travel from Earth to the Moon.

THE SOLAR SYSTEM

Earth is just one of many objects that orbit the star we call the Sun. The Sun's "family" consists of eight planets, five dwarf planets, hundreds of moons, millions of comets and asteroids, and lots of gas and dust. All these things together are called the solar system. The four small planets closest to the Sun are made of rock, while the four outer planets are much larger and made mostly of gases. The solar system is big – the Voyager spacecraft took 12 years to reach Neptune, the outermost planet.

THE LOCAL GROUP

The Milky Way is one of the largest galaxies in a cluster of about 45 galaxies, known as the Local Group. Most of these galaxies have no particular shape and are much smaller than the Milky Way. The two closest galaxies to the Milky Way are called the Large and the Small Magellanic Clouds. They lie about 200,000 light years away and are easily visible with the naked eye from Earth's southern hemisphere. The biggest galaxy in the Local Group is the Andromeda Galaxy – a great spiral galaxy, much like the Milky Way. It lies about 3 million light years away, in the constellation of Andromeda.

THE UNIVERSE

The Universe is everything that exists – all the stars, planets, galaxies, and the space between them. There are millions of galaxy clusters in the Universe: in fact, wherever we look with telescopes, the sky is full of galaxies. Scientists estimate that there must be about 10 thousand billion billion stars in the Universe – more than the number of grains of sand on all the beaches on Earth.

THE MILKY WAY

Our solar system is located in a large spiral-shaped galaxy called the Milky Way. The Sun is just one of at least 100 billion stars in this galaxy, and lies about 30,000 light years from the centre. The Milky Way is vast – it measures about 100,000 light years across. A spaceship travelling at the speed of light (300,000 km or 186,000 miles per second) would take 100,000 years to fly from one side of the galaxy to the other. The Milky Way is so big that the stars in it are usually a long way apart. The nearest star to our Sun is more than 4 light years away.

FAST FACTS

■ It would take a modern jet fighter more than a million years to reach the nearest star.
■ A light year is the distance that light travels in one year. It is about 9.5 trillion, or 9.5 million million km (6 trillion miles).
■ How big is the Universe? No one knows, because we cannot see the edge of it – if there is one. All we do know is that the visible Universe is at least 93 billion light years across.
■ The Universe has no centre.

A CIRCLE OF STARS

This time-exposure photograph was taken in
late summer in British Columbia, Canada.
The circular lines of light are the trails of
northern polar stars. However, the stars are not
moving – the trails appear because the camera

Early ideas

Compared with everything else around us, Earth seems incredibly large. Ancient peoples believed it was the biggest and most important place in the Universe, and that everything revolved around it. These ideas only began to change very slowly after the introduction of the telescope in the early 1600s.

EARTH-CENTRED UNIVERSE

Ancient peoples watched the Sun, Moon, and stars very carefully. They saw that all of them travelled from east to west across the sky. Clearly, they were all going around a stationary Earth. For several thousand years, almost everyone believed that Earth was at the centre of the Universe. The main problem with this idea was that it did not explain the movements of some of the planets – sometimes Mars or Jupiter appeared to stand still or even move backwards.

Earth

Sun

FLAT EARTH OR ROUND EARTH?

Stand on the seashore and look at the horizon. It seems to be flat. For a long time, people thought that Earth was flat and that, if you went too far, you would fall off the edge. However, it was gradually realized that Earth was round, like a giant ball. Nature provided several clues:

■ The shadow that Earth casts on the Moon during a lunar eclipse is curved, not straight.
■ A sailor travelling due north or south sees stars appear and disappear over the horizon. On a flat Earth, he would always see the same stars.
■ A ship sailing over the horizon should simply get smaller and smaller if Earth is flat. In fact, the hull disappears first, and the top of the sails last.

▼ LAND AHOY! *As the boat gets closer to the island, the sailor sees the tops of the mountains first. Then, as the boat moves over the curve, lower land comes into view.*

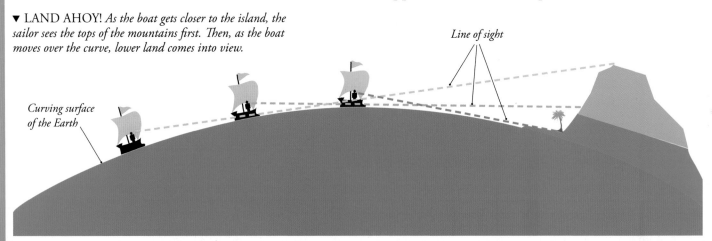

Line of sight

Curving surface of the Earth

ORBITS

The ancient Greeks taught that the circle was the perfect shape. So it seemed logical to believe that all of the planets travelled in circles. Unfortunately, measurements showed that this did not fit their movements across the sky. One way around this was to add small circles to the larger circles, but even this did not work. The mystery was solved in 1609 when a German mathematician, Johannes Kepler, realized that the planets move along elliptical (oval) orbits.

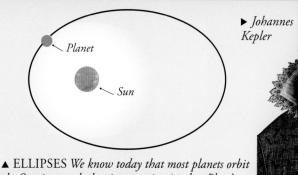

Planet

Sun

▶ *Johannes Kepler*

▲ ELLIPSES *We know today that most planets orbit the Sun in a path that is not quite circular. Pluto's orbit is a very stretched circle known as an ellipse.*

📷 WHAT A STAR!

Polish astronomer Nicolaus Copernicus (1473–1543) was the first person of more modern times to realize that the Sun, not Earth, is at the centre of the solar system. His ideas were extremely unpopular.

◀ *A lunar eclipse*

▶ HE SAW IT COMING
Hipparchus was the first person to develop a way of predicting solar and lunar eclipses.

Astounding astronomer

One of the greatest early Greek astronomers was Hipparchus of Nicaea (190–120 BCE). He discovered many things, including that Earth rotated on a tilted axis, which caused the seasons. He worked out the distance from Earth to the Moon by comparing views of a partial and total solar eclipse. He found that the Moon had an elliptical orbit and that its speed varied. He also catalogued all the stars in order of brightness and plotted their positions in the sky on the first star chart.

THE CALENDAR

Although ancient civilizations did not have telescopes, they did have instruments to measure angles, and could measure the positions of the Sun and the stars. They used the movement of the Sun as their calendar, and built monuments and temples that reflected the calendar. The Toltecs of Central America built the Pyramid of Kukulcan with 365 steps, one for each day of the year.

▲ PYRAMID OF KUKULCAN *This temple is built in honour of Kukulcan the serpent god. When the Sun is in the right place it creates a shadow in the shape of a serpent.*

Telescopes

Telescopes are instruments for looking at things that are far away. Almost everything we know about space has been discovered by looking through telescopes. Optical telescopes can capture light from the deepest parts of space, but are limited by the size of their mirrors and lenses.

▶ THE YERKES OBSERVATORY *was funded by business tycoon Charles T. Yerkes, who had made his fortune developing Chicago's transport system.*

REFRACTING TELESCOPE

The first telescopes were refracting telescopes, which used lenses to bend and focus light. The biggest refracting telescope is at Yerkes Observatory in Wisconsin, USA. Built in 1897, it is still used for looking at stars and tracking their movements through space.

▼ THE YERKES TELESCOPE
Built in 1897, the Yerkes telescope has a lens diameter of 100 cm (40 in) and weighs 5.5 tonnes (6 tons) – as much as an adult African elephant.

Eyepiece

Objective lens

Lenses magnify the image

Refracting telescopes

A refracting telescope uses a convex (outwards curving) glass lens to collect and focus incoming light. An eyepiece is used to magnify the image. One problem with using lenses is that they are heavy. If they are too big they will start to sag, distorting the image. This limits the size and power of the refracting telescope.

Eyepiece

Small mirror

Objective mirror

Reflecting telescopes

A concave (inwards curving) mirror focuses light towards a smaller mirror. This sends the beam of light to an eyepiece, which magnifies the image. Because mirrors are lighter than lenses, reflecting telescopes can be much bigger and more powerful than refracting telescopes.

EVEN BIGGER TELESCOPES

Although reflecting telescopes can be built much bigger than refracting telescopes, they too will have problems if the mirror is more than 8 m (27.5 ft) across. Astronomers solve this problem by using a number of smaller mirrors that can be fitted together to make one big mirror. Each mirror section is controlled by a computer that can adjust its position by less than the width of a human hair.

Mirror, mirror...

Not all telescopes use glass mirrors – some use liquid metal instead. A shallow bowl of mercury or silver is spun at high speed until it forms a thin reflective surface. Liquid mirrors can only be used to look straight up. If they are tilted the liquid will fall out!

TAKE A LOOK: EARLY TELESCOPES

The first telescopes were made by Dutch spectacle-maker Hans Lippershey, in 1608. These were simple refracting telescopes made from a pair of glass lenses set into a tube. When the Italian astronomer Galileo Galilei heard about Lippershey's invention he quickly set about building an improved telescope with a greater magnification.

▲ HANS LIPPERSHEY *is said to have come up with his invention while watching two young boys playing with lenses.*

▶ GALILEO'S DRAWINGS
By 1610, Galileo had developed a much more powerful telescope. He used this to study the Sun (👁 p208), recording his observations in a series of drawings.

◀ NEWTON'S TELESCOPE
Isaac Newton made the first working reflector telescope in 1668.

Giant *telescopes*

The Hale telescope caused quite a stir when it was completed in 1948. Equipped with a 5 m (16 ft) mirror, it was the largest and most powerful telescope ever built. As technology has improved, telescopes have been built with mirrors up to 10 m (33 ft) across. Even larger telescopes are now planned, with mirrors of 30 m (98 ft) or more.

TELL ME MORE...

To get the best images, telescopes are placed at high altitude so they are above the clouds and most of the atmosphere. Remote mountains are ideal as there is little light interference from nearby towns. Mauna Kea, an extinct volcano in Hawaii, is home to many telescopes.

Keck Telescopes

- **Size of primary mirror** 10 m (33 ft)
- **Location** Mauna Kea, Hawaii
- **Altitude** 4,145 m (13,600 ft)

Until 2009 the twin Keck telescopes were the world's largest optical telescopes. The Keck II telescope overcomes the distorting effects of the atmosphere by using a mirror that changes shape 2,000 times per second.

Gemini Telescopes

- **Size of primary mirror** 8 m (26 ft)
- **Location** North: Mauna Kea, Hawaii. South: Cerro Pacho, Chile
- **Altitude** North: 4,213 m (13,822 ft). South: 2,722 m (8,930 ft)

The twin Gemini telescopes are located either side of the equator. Between them they can see almost every part of both the northern and southern skies. The two telescopes are linked through a special high-speed internet connection.

Very Large Telescope (VLT) Array

- **Size of primary mirror** 8.2 m (27 ft)
- **Location** Mount Paranal, Chile
- **Altitude** 2,635 m (8,645 ft)

The VLT array consists of four 8.2 m (27 ft) telescopes and four movable 1.8m (4 ft) telescopes. The telescopes work together by combining the light beams from each telescope using a system of underground mirrors.

Large Binocular Telescope (LBT)

- **Size of primary mirror** 8.4 m (28 ft)
- **Location** Mount Graham, Arizona, USA
- **Altitude** 3,260 m (10,700 ft)

The LBT has two 8.4 m primary mirrors mounted side-by-side, which collect as much light as one mirror measuring 11.8 m (39 ft) across. The LBT is currently the largest and most powerful single telescope in the world.

Hale Telescope

- **Size of primary mirror** 5 m (16 ft)
- **Location** Palomar Mountain, California, USA
- **Altitude** 1,700 m (5,580 ft)

Even today, more than 60 years after it was built, the Hale telescope is the second-largest telescope using mirrors made of a single piece of glass. Mirrors much larger than this tend to sag under their own weight, distorting the image received.

European Extremely Large Telescope (E–ELT)

- **Size of primary mirror** 42 m (138 ft)
- **Location** Chile
- **Altitude** 3,060 m (10,040 ft)

This revolutionary telescope should come into operation in 2020. The primary mirror will be 42 m (138 ft) across and will collect 15 times more light than the largest telescopes in use today. One of its main objectives is to find Earth-like planets orbiting other stars.

Thirty Meter Telescope (TMT)

- **Size of primary mirror** 30 m (98 ft)
- **Location** Mauna Kea, Hawaii
- **Altitude** About 4,000 m (13,000 ft)

The $300 million TMT is expected to be completed in 2018. At its heart will be a primary mirror measuring 30 m (98 ft) in diameter, made up of 492 hexagonal segments. It will collect almost 10 times more light than one of the 10 m (33 ft) Keck telescopes. Astronomers will use the TMT to observe the formation and development of new galaxies.

Seeing *light*

Light, the fastest thing in the Universe, is an energy wave moving at just under a billion km/h (about 670 million mph). That means it can travel from New York to London in just two-hundredths of a second – faster than the blink of an eye!

Now you see it
If you look at a beam of light, it appears to be white. However, when white light hits a shaped piece of glass, called a prism, it splits into a rainbow. We call these colours, or wavelengths, of light the visible spectrum, because our eyes can see them.

▲ WHITE LIGHT contains a mixture of all the wavelengths of light in the visible spectrum.

▲ WHEN A BEAM *of white light strikes the surface of a prism, it is bent. But each different wavelength is bent by a slightly different amount, and this splits the light into its spectrum of colours.*

WAVES OF ENERGY

There are many types of energy wave. Scientists arrange them according to their wavelength. This is the distance between the peak of one wave and the next. The higher the energy of the wave, the shorter the distance between its peaks. The complete range of waves is known as the electromagnetic spectrum.

GAMMA RAYS

▲ *Gamma rays have the shortest wavelengths. They are released in an intense burst when a massive star collapses and explodes in a supernova.*

X-RAYS

▲ *The bright white areas around the rim of the Cartwheel Galaxy are thought to be neutron stars and black holes emitting powerful X-rays.*

ULTRAVIOLET (UV)

▲ *The blue areas in this image of the NGC 300 galaxy are regions of star formation. New stars give off mainly ultraviolet light.*

▶ WE CAN USE *light energy to measure the composition and heat of things. This is how we know that the Boomerang Nebula is the coldest object in space at 1K.*

Spectroscopy

This technique uses colour to determine what stars are made from and how hot they are. Every chemical element produces its own pattern of coloured or dark lines when passed through a special prism. By looking at the patterns, scientists can tell which elements are present and how much energy the atoms have.

Using the spectrum

Even though we can't see all the wavelengths, we can detect them and use them to discover things that are usually invisible. All types of matter radiate some form of energy, which means they can be picked up by telescopes that are sensitive to different parts of the electromagnetic spectrum.

▶ LIKE *all other stars, our Sun has its own unique spectral fingerprint.*

ABSORPTION SPECTRA

EMISSION SPECTRA

Absorption spectra show patterns of black lines.

Emission spectra show patterns of coloured lines.

Lines are caused by atoms that absorb or emit radiation at specific wavelengths.

WAVELENGTH

The colours we see are all part of the visible spectrum.

VISIBLE RAYS

▲ *The Sun's visible light is only a tiny part of the energy that it radiates. Our eyes can't see the other wavelengths, but we can feel infrared heat.*

INFRARED

▲ *Using infrared enabled astronomers to see through the dust of the Milky Way. It revealed three baby stars that had not been seen before.*

MICROWAVES

▲ *The left-over heat from the Big Bang was detected using microwaves. It is only 2.7K above absolute zero, which is as cold as you can get.*

RADIO WAVES

▲ *These have the longest wavelengths. The massive black hole at the centre of the galaxy Fornax A is a powerful source of radio waves, shown in orange.*

21

Infrared *astronomy*

We are all familiar with the colours of the rainbow – red, orange, yellow, green, blue, indigo, and violet. These colours are part of what is known as the visible spectrum. Beyond the red end of the spectrum is infrared light, which we call heat. Although we cannot see infrared light, we can detect it using special telescopes, which reveal things usually hidden by clouds of dust.

SATURN'S HOT SPOT

Infrared images of Saturn reveal that it has a "hot spot" – the first warm polar cap to be discovered. This is the hottest part of Saturn and is 8–10 degrees warmer than at the equator. A huge storm, thousands of kilometres across, constantly rages over Saturn's south pole.

◄ *Infrared image of Saturn. The paler areas show where Saturn is warmest.*

A GALAXY FAR, FAR AWAY...

Messier 81 is a spiral galaxy located in the northern constellation of Ursa Major (the Great Bear). Messier 81, or "Bode's Galaxy" as it is also known, is about 12 million light years from Earth. M81 is easily visible through binoculars or small telescopes. In infrared light the spiral arms are very noticeable because they contain dust that has been heated by hot, massive, newly born stars.

SPITZER SPACE TELESCOPE

Infrared light from space is almost completely absorbed by Earth's atmosphere, so infrared telescopes are placed on high mountains, on aircraft, or on satellites. NASA's Spitzer Space Telescope is one of the most powerful infrared observatories. Spitzer took 18 hours and over 11,000 exposures to compose this image of the Andromeda Galaxy (below).

▲ THE EYE IN THE SKY
Resembling a giant eye in space, this infrared view of the Helix Nebula reveals a bright cloud of dust surrounding a dying star.

WHAT A STAR!

Frederick William Herschel (1738–1822) was a German astronomer and musician. Using a prism to split sunlight and a thermometer to detect heat, Herschel proved that there are invisible forms of light that occur beyond the visible colour spectrum. This invisible heat was later called "infrared" – meaning "below red".

▲ THIS IS HOW *we usually see the Andromeda Galaxy, in visible light. The main infrared image (above) has revealed its spiral arms in greater detail. Their structure is very uneven, which suggests that Andromeda may have been affected by collisions with its two satellite galaxies in the past.*

TAKE A LOOK: CONSTELLATION ORION

Looking up at the constellation Orion you should be able to make out the stars that form its outline. You should also be able to see the bright patch of the Orion Nebula beneath Orion's Belt. This nebula is a stellar nursery where new stars are being born. If you were to look at the Orion constellation through an infrared telescope you would see a huge dust cloud with bright patches where young stars heat the surrounding dust. The stars themselves are too hot to be seen in infrared light.

▲ VISIBLE LIGHT
The stars of the constellation Orion.

▲ INFRARED LIGHT
Bright dust clouds surrounding Orion.

Messages from the *stars*

American engineer, Karl Jansky, was the first to discover radio waves coming from space, using a home-made aerial in 1931. Today, scientists use radio waves to learn about all kinds of objects in space and have even attempted to contact alien life.

RADIO ASTRONOMY

Radio astronomy is the study of objects in space that produce radio waves. Radio waves are like waves of light but are beyond the visible end of the spectrum. Invisible radio waves are detected by radio telescopes and can then be converted into images for us to see.

Numbers, from one to ten, showing how we count.

Symbols representing important chemicals found in life on Earth.

The DNA molecule – the blueprint for life on Earth.

A human form and the population of Earth.

Earth's position in the solar system.

A symbol representing the Arecibo telescope.

▲ IS THERE ANYBODY THERE?
Arecibo was used to transmit this coded message into space in 1974. So far, we haven't had a reply.

Movie star
The Arecibo telescope has featured in *Contact*, a film about first contact with extra-terrestrial life, and the James Bond film *Goldeneye*.

Arecibo
The largest single radio telescope in the world is Arecibo, on the Caribbean island of Puerto Rico. The telescope measures 305 m (1,000 ft) across and its dish is built into a dip in the hillside, with the radio receiver suspended 137 m (450 ft) above like a giant steel spider. Although Arecibo's dish doesn't move, its location near the equator means it can see a wide region of the sky.

TELESCOPE NETWORKS

MERLIN

- **Dish** various sizes
- **Location** various sites, UK

MERLIN is a network of seven dishes across the UK. Operated from Jodrell Bank, it includes the 76.2 m (250 ft) Lovell telescope. Altogether, the network forms a telescope equal to a single dish 217 km (135 miles) wide. It is so powerful it can detect a coin up to 100 km (62 miles) away.

VLBA

- **Dish** 25 m (82 ft)
- **Location** Hawaii, Mainland USA, West Indies

The Very Long Baseline Array (VLBA) is a system of 10 radio telescope antennas. The combined effect is equal to that of a single dish more than 8,000 km (5,000 miles) wide. The VLBA can see things in such fine detail that it is equivalent to a person standing in New York reading a newspaper in Los Angeles!

In this radio image, Jupiter is shown to be encircled by a belt of radiation.

The parabolic dish reflects the signal to the subreflector.

The subreflector focuses the signal into the receiver.

Jupiter calling Earth…
The first radio signals from a distant planet were detected from Jupiter in 1955. Since then, all of the giant gas planets have been shown to produce radio waves. Radio signals can also be bounced off the rocky planets and asteroids.

Very Large Array
One of the most important radio astronomy observatories in the world is the Very Large Array (VLA) in New Mexico, USA. The VLA has 27 dishes arranged in a Y shape. Each arm of the Y is almost 21 km (13 miles) long. When the radio signals from each dish are combined, the whole array is equal to a giant antenna 36 km (22 miles) wide.

The 25 m (82 ft) wide dishes can be moved along tracks to change their positions.

Invisible *rays*

Ultraviolet (UV) light, X-rays, and gamma rays are types of electromagnetic radiation emitted by extremely hot objects. They are invisible and most are absorbed by Earth's atmosphere, so the best way to view them is with telescopes on high-flying balloons, rockets, or spacecraft.

WATCH THIS SPACE

Some gamma ray bursts are so incredibly bright that they can actually be seen with the naked eye. One was spotted in March 2008 in the constellation Bootes, even though it was an astonishing 7.5 billion light years away.

◄ THE BALLOON *was made of thin plastic and was 110 m (360 ft) wide – big enough to fit two Boeing 767 planes inside!*

▲ THIS *telescope was lifted by a balloon into the sky over the Arctic Circle. As the Sun never sets there in the summer, the scientists could monitor the Sun all day.*

Flying high

Although only in the air for six days, this helium balloon, part of a project called Sunrise, helped astronomers to get a unique look in UV light at how the Sun's magnetic fields form. It lifted a large solar telescope 37 km (121,000 ft) into the sky, high above the obscuring effects of Earth's atmosphere.

GAMMA RAY BURSTS

Gamma rays are the most energetic form of light. Gamma ray bursts, known as GRBs, are caused when massive stars run out of fuel and collapse to form a neutron star or black hole.

Gamma rays   *Invisible rays*

INTEGRAL

The INTEGRAL space observatory is equipped with highly sensitive detectors that can view objects in X-rays, gamma rays, and visible light all at the same time. Sent into space in 2002, it circles Earth every three days on the lookout for explosive GRBs, supernova explosions, and black holes.

▶ USING EARTH *as a shield to block emissions from distant black holes, INTEGRAL has discovered both strong and faint gamma ray and X-ray signals coming from our galaxy, possibly signals from neutron stars and black holes.*

SDO

The Solar Dynamics Observatory (SDO) studies the Sun at many different wavelengths, particularly those at the extreme end of UV. Scientists use the data that it collects from its continuous observations to learn more about how solar activity affects life on Earth.

THE X-RAY MOON

Scientists were surprised when they found that even fairly cold objects, like the Moon, can give off weak X-rays. Here the visible Moon is compared with an X-ray image of the same area. The X-rays are produced when solar X-rays from the Sun bombard the Moon's surface and excite the atoms in the rocks.

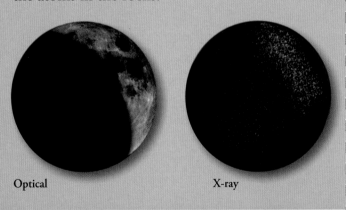

Optical   X-ray

THE SUN

With an optical telescope, we just see a scattering of dark sunspots on the Sun. When these spots are viewed with an ultraviolet-light telescope, hot, explosive solar flares can be seen.

Optical

Ultraviolet

Extreme ultraviolet

X-rays   **Ultraviolet (UV) rays**   *Visible rays*

Hubble *Space* Telescope

The Hubble Space Telescope (HST) is the most famous space observatory. Since being placed in a low Earth orbit by space shuttle Discovery in April 1990, Hubble has sent back a huge amount of scientific data and incredibly detailed images of objects in space.

📷 WHAT A STAR!

Edwin Hubble (1889–1953) was the first person to realize that there are other galaxies beyond the Milky Way, and that these galaxies are moving away from each other as the Universe expands.

Almost every part of HST has been replaced during its lifetime. Once repaired and upgraded, it is released back into orbit.

SERVICING MISSIONS

Hubble is the only telescope designed to be serviced in space. A space shuttle flies alongside the telescope, takes hold of it with a robotic arm and places it within the shuttle's cargo bay. Astronauts can then carry out repairs and replace old instruments.

Blurred vision of space

The HST mission met with a major setback when it was launched and the first images it sent back were blurry. The cause was eventually tracked down to a mirror that had been incorrectly polished, and was too flat at the edges by about one-fiftieth of the width of a human hair! The problem was finally solved three years later when astronauts added lenses to correct the focus.

▲ *Before repair*   ▲ *After repair*

The picture on the right is of the Butterfly Nebula, a cloud of gas and dust ejected by a dying star. The image was taken by the HST's newest and most advanced camera, installed in 2009.

Secondary mirror

Path of light

Hubble's aperture door can be closed if it is in danger of letting light from the Sun, Earth, or Moon into the telescope.

Primary mirror: problems with the shape of the mirror were solved using corrective "eyeglasses".

Instrument module

Solar panels: power generated by the panels is also stored in six batteries and used to power Hubble when it flies through Earth's shadow.

▲ SATELLITES
Hubble communicates with the ground via NASA's Tracking and Data Relay Satellite System (TDRSS).

📷 **WHAT A STAR!**

Lyman Spitzer (1914–1997) developed the idea of a telescope in space and was instrumental in the design and development of the Hubble Space Telescope.

HST FAST FACTS

- **Length** 13.2 m (43.3 ft)
- **Diameter** 4.2 m (13.8 ft)
- **Weight** 11,110 kg (24,490 lb)
- **Launch date** 24 April 1990
- **Cost at launch** $1.5 billion
- **Orbit** 569 km (354 miles) above Earth
- **Speed** 28,000 km/h (17,500 mph)

▲ SIGNALS *from TDRSS are received at the White Sands Ground Terminal in New Mexico, USA.*

▲ GROUND CONTROL
Hubble is controlled from the Goddard Space Flight Centre in Maryland, USA.

WITCHES AND GIANTS

The man in the Moon may be fiction, but there is a witch in space! The Witch Head Nebula is in the constellation Eridanus, a safe distance of 900 light years from Earth. With her hooked nose and pointed chin, she glows blue in the reflected light of Rigel, a bright supergiant star (not seen in this picture).

▲ EYE SEE YOU *Shown in infrared light, the centre of spiral galaxy NGC 1097 looks like an eye. A small companion galaxy is caught up in its arms on the left.*

▲ STAR LIGHT *Pismis 24 is an open cluster of stars. It contains three of the most massive stars ever observed. Stars are still forming in the glowing nebula (bottom).*

▲ F-ANT-ASTIC *The "body" of the Ant Nebula is actually two lobes of fiery gas ejected from a dying star at speeds of up to 1,000 km (600 miles) per second.*

▲ BUBBLE BLOWER *Young star HH 46/47 blows out two jets of warm gas. The jets have crashed into the dust and gas around the star, forming huge bubbles.*

▲ SQUARE-EYED *The Retina Nebula has an unusual cylinder shape, appearing square from the side. Hot gas escapes from each end, and dust darkens the walls.*

▲ JUMBO JET *Looking like a tornado in space, HH 49/50 is a jet of churned-up dust and gas ejected from a young star (off the top of the picture). It is 0.3 light years long.*

31

Observatories in *space*

Most of the high-energy particles and radiation emitted from objects in space are filtered out by the blanket of air around Earth. The moving atmosphere also causes shimmering or twinkling, making it hard to obtain sharp images. To study these objects it is much easier to observe them from space observatories.

XMM-Newton can pick up faint X-rays that Chandra cannot detect.

Chandra
NASA

■ **Named in honour of** the Nobel Prize-winning scientist Subrahmanyan Chandrasekhar
■ **What is it?** X-ray observatory
■ **Launched** July 1999
■ **Equipped with** four cylindrical mirrors nested inside each other.
■ **Orbit** Circles Earth every 65 hours in an elliptical orbit 10,000–139,000 km (6,200–86,500 miles) high.

Chandra can detect X-rays from hot regions of the Universe, such as exploded stars, galaxy clusters, and the edges of black holes. It can even observe X-rays from particles just before they fall into a black hole. The first X-ray emission it saw was from the supermassive black hole at the centre of the Milky Way.

▲ *Chandra flies 200 times higher than Hubble.*

XMM-Newton
European Space Agency – ESA

■ **Named in honour of** the famous 17th-century scientist Sir Isaac Newton. XMM stands for X-ray Multi-Mirror.
■ **What is it?** X-ray observatory
■ **Launched** December 1999
■ **Equipped with** three X-ray telescopes, each containing 58 concentric mirrors that are nested inside each other.
■ **Orbit** Circles Earth every 48 hours in an elliptical orbit between 7,000 km (4,350 miles) and 114,000 km (70,800 miles) high.

Since X-rays pass through ordinary mirrors, X-ray telescopes are equipped with curved mirrors fitted inside each other. The X-rays glance off these mirrors and reach the detectors.

▲ *Starburst galaxy M82, the Cigar Galaxy.*

Spitzer Space Telescope
NASA

■ **Named in honour of** the famous US scientist, astrophysicist Lyman Spitzer
■ **What is it?** Infrared telescope
■ **Launched** August 2003
■ **Equipped with** 85 cm (33 in) wide main mirror and three supercooled science instruments.
■ **Orbit** Spitzer is in an unusual Earth-trailing orbit. As time goes by, it gradually drifts further away from our planet. This allows uninterrupted viewing of a large part of the sky.

This telescope takes images and studies the infrared light coming from some of the coolest objects in the Universe, including dust clouds around stars where stars and planets are forming, and dusty galaxies.

▲ *Spitzer's solar shield protects it from the Sun's heat and Earth's infrared radiation.*

TAKE A LOOK: A CLOUD OF MANY COLOURS

Each space observatory highlights different aspects of celestial objects, such as Cassiopeia A, the youngest known supernova remnant in our Milky Way galaxy. It lies about 10,000 light years away. The rapidly expanding cloud is thought to be the remains of a massive star that exploded as a supernova around 1680.

▲ OPTICAL IMAGE FROM HUBBLE *The visible light image shows huge swirls of debris glowing with the heat generated by a shockwave from the blast.*

▲ INFRARED IMAGE FROM SPITZER *Hot gas (green and blue) and cool dust (red) combine in the yellow areas, showing both were created in the explosion.*

▲ X-RAY IMAGE FROM CHANDRA *The ever-expanding cloud of hot gas from the explosion is clearly visible – in fact, it is 10 light years in diameter!*

▲ MULTICOLOURED *Combining images from Hubble (yellow), Spitzer (red), and Chandra (green and blue) can help explain how supernovas evolve.*

Fermi Gamma-ray Space Telescope
NASA

- **Named in honour of** the Nobel Prize-winning Italian scientist, Enrico Fermi, a pioneer in high-energy physics
- **What is it?** Gamma-ray observatory
- **Launched** June 2008
- **Equipped with** Large Area Telescope (LAT) and a Gamma-ray Burst Monitor (GBM).
- **Orbit** Circles Earth every 95 minutes, 550 km (340 miles) high.

This telescope was developed by the USA, France, Germany, Italy, Japan, and Sweden. The satellite can turn to observe new gamma rays without commands from the ground.

▶ *This telescope has discovered many new pulsars* (👁 p228).

Herschel Telescope
European Space Agency – ESA

- **Named in honour of** William Herschel, the German-British astronomer who discovered infrared light and the planet Uranus
- **What is it?** Infrared telescope
- **Launched** May 2009
- **Equipped with** 3.5 m (11 ft) wide main mirror and three supercooled science instruments.
- **Orbit** Herschel operates from an area in space located 1.5 million km (930,000 miles) from the Earth in the direction opposite from the Sun.

Able to detect a wide range of wavelengths, Herschel will investigate how the first galaxies were formed and evolved and be able to probe cold, dense clouds of dust in more detail than ever before.

▲ *Instruments are supercooled using helium.*

James Webb Space Telescope
NASA

- **Named in honour of** NASA's former chief
- **What is it?** An optical and infrared space telescope. Considered to be the successor to the Hubble Space Telescope.
- **Launch date** 2014
- **Equipped with** 6.5 m (21¼ ft) primary mirror, the largest mirror ever flown in space.
- **Orbit** 1.5 million km (932 million miles) away on the night side of Earth.

The USA, Europe, and Canada are currently building the telescope. Once launched, it will be able to study the farthest and faintest objects in the Universe.

Sunshield

▲ *The sunshield is the size of a tennis court.*

Unusual observatories

Scientists today use all sorts of strange instruments to observe the Universe. Here are a few of the more unusual ones from around the world.

▲ *THESE unassuming white containers contain highly sensitive equipment that monitors the Sun.*

GONG
The Global Oscillation Network Group

■ **Location** Six stations around the world (California, Hawaii, Australia, India, Canary Islands, and Chile).
■ **Function** Studies sound waves from the Sun.

These observatories study sound waves moving inside the Sun by detecting small quakes on its surface. These quakes excite millions of sound waves, each one carrying a message about the Sun's interior.

LIGO
The Laser Interferometer Gravitational-Wave Observatory

■ **Location** Three detectors in Washington and Louisiana states, USA
■ **Equipped with** L-shaped observatory with 4 km (2½ mile) long tubes containing laser beams and mirrors.
■ **Function** Searches for gravity waves.

Gravity waves are thought to be ripples in space–time, possibly produced when black holes collide or supernovas explode. They may also have been generated in the early Universe. Detecting them is so difficult that none have yet been found.

▲ *If a gravity wave passes through Earth it will affect the light from the laser beams in the tubes.*

South Pole Telescope (SPT)
The Arcminute Cosmology Bolometer Array Receiver

■ **Location** Amundsen-Scott Research Station, South Pole
■ **Equipped with** 10 m (33 ft) telescope
■ **Function** Observes microwave background radiation.

In the Antarctic winter, sunlight doesn't reach the South Pole so it is dark night and day. The extremely dry air makes it a perfect location to search for tiny variations in the radiation left over from the Big Bang.

▼ *The telescope has to be supercooled to ¼ of a degree above absolute zero, −273°C (−459°F).*

▶ *SOFIA 747SP is able to keep its telescope pointing steadily at an object in space even if the aircraft is struck by turbulence.*

SOFIA
The Stratospheric Observatory for Infrared Astronomy

- **Location** The left-hand side of the fuselage of a modified Boeing 747SP
- **Equipped with** A 2.5 m (100 in) diameter reflecting telescope.
- **Function** To observe the sky in visible and infrared light.

The aircraft will fly above the clouds and most of the atmosphere at altitudes of between 11 and 14 km (7 and 8½ miles) for up to eight hours at a time. It is hoped that SOFIA's observations will answer questions about the creation of the Universe. It is expected to be in use for 20 years.

SNO
Sudbury Neutrino Observatory

▼ *The rock shields the detectors from cosmic rays.*

- **Location** 2 km (6,800 ft) underground in a working nickel mine, Sudbury, Ontario, Canada
- **Equipped with** "Heavy" water in a 12 m (39 ft) diameter tank, surrounded by 9,600 sensors.
- **Function** To study high-energy particles (neutrinos) from the Sun's core and exploding stars.

Neutrinos usually pass undetected through Earth, but when they collide with the heavy water atoms they produce light flashes, which are picked up by the sensors surrounding the tank.

ALMA
Atacama Large Millimeter/submillimeter Array

- **Location** A 5,000 m (16,400 ft) high plateau in the Atacama desert, Chile
- **Equipped with** At least 66 antennas across 200 pads over 18.5 km (11½ miles).
- **Function** To observe the gas and dust of the cool Universe.

ALMA is a collection of 66 dishes up to 12 m (39 ft) across that can operate together as a single, giant telescope. The dry climate, together with the thin atmosphere at such a high altitude, is perfect for clear views of infrared and microwave radiation from space.

▲ *TRANSPORTERS are used to move the giant antenna dishes to different positions.*

THE VIOLENT UNIVERSE

Ever-changing and full of action, the Universe contains everything that exists: all matter from the smallest atom to the largest galaxy cluster, the emptiness of space, and every single second of time.

What is the *Universe?*

The Universe is everything that exists – planets, stars, galaxies, and the space between them. Even time is part of the Universe. No one knows how big the Universe is, or where it starts and ends. Everything is so far away from our own little planet that light from stars and galaxies can take billions of years to reach us – so we see the Universe as it looked billions of years ago. But we can use the information this light provides to discover how the Universe began and how it might end.

LIGHT YEARS

◄ WE CAN *find out what the Universe was like early in its history by using different types of telescope.*

Telescopes are like time machines. They detect light that has travelled from distant stars and galaxies. This means that we see them as they were when the light started on its journey – thousands, or even billions of years ago. Astronomers measure the size of the Universe in light years. A light year is the distance light travels in one year – about 9.5 trillion km (6 trillion miles). Light from the furthest galaxies we can see has taken about 13 billion years to reach us. We see them today as they were long before the Sun and Earth came into existence.

Now you see it…
Light travels through empty space at 300,000 kilometres a second (186,000 miles a second). At this speed light waves could travel around the world seven times in a single second.

FUTURE UNIVERSE

For many years, scientists believed that the pull of gravity from the stars and galaxies would gradually slow down the expansion of the Universe. However, recent observations suggest that this expansion is accelerating. If it is true, the galaxies will get further and further apart. No more stars will form, black holes will disappear, and the Universe will end as a cold, dark, lifeless, and empty place.

We can see and measure three
dimensions of space – height, width,
and depth. Time is a fourth dimension.
Scientists believe the Universe may
have at least six other, hidden,
dimensions. These are all curled up on
each other and are infinitely tiny.

▲ AS OBJECTS *move away from
us their light spectrum changes. By
measuring the change we can work
out how fast they are moving.*

Star

Earth

Measuring distances

Measuring distances in the Universe
is tricky. Many galaxies are so far
away, the only thing we can use is
light. Because the Universe is
expanding and stretching space, the
wavelengths of light from an object
also become stretched. Any dark
lines in its spectrum move towards
the red end, which astronomers call
a "redshift". By measuring the size
of this redshift, astronomers can
calculate the distances of the galaxies
and how fast they are moving away
from us. The oldest and fastest-
moving galaxies are those with the
biggest redshifts.

Shape of the Universe

Since we live inside the Universe it is hard to
imagine that space has a shape. Scientists,
however, think that it does have a shape, and
that this depends on the density of its matter.
If it is greater than a critical amount then the
Universe is said to be closed. If it is less, then
it is described as open (saddle-shaped).
However, spacecraft observations have shown
that the Universe is very close
to the critical density, so
scientists describe it as flat.
A completely flat Universe
has no edge and will go on
expanding forever.

Closed

Open

Flat

◄ ALL *the stars, dust, and gas we can
see in the sky make up only a small part
of the Universe. Most of the Universe is
made of mysterious, invisible dark matter
and dark energy (* ○ *p62–63).*

MULTIPLE UNIVERSES?

Is our Universe alone, or are there other Universes that
we cannot see? No one knows, but some scientists
believe that there might be many other Universes. This
structure may resemble an enormous bubbly foam, in
which some Universes have not yet inflated. Some may
have different physical laws and dimensions to ours. In
theory, it may even be possible to connect one Universe
to another through a spinning black hole. However, no
other Universes can affect anything in our Universe, so
it is impossible to prove that they exist.

Birth of the *Universe*

Scientists believe that the Universe was born in a huge fireball about 13.7 billion years ago. This "Big Bang" was the beginning of everything: time and space, as well as all the matter and energy in the Universe.

INFLATION

At the instant it began, the newborn Universe was incredibly small and unimaginably hot and dense. Inside the fireball, energy was being turned into matter and antimatter. Then it began to expand and cool. For a tiny fraction of a second the expansion was quite slow, but then the Universe shot outwards. It has been expanding steadily ever since, and might even be speeding up.

1 The Universe begins to expand from infinitely tiny to the size of a grapefruit. The huge amount of energy this releases kick-starts the formation of matter and antimatter.

BIG BANG

Time 1. 0 seconds

Temperature Fireball

▼ THE BLUE AND PURPLE *colours show X-rays being given off by matter and antimatter collisions as high-energy particles stream away from the white pulsar at the centre of the image.*

Quarks   Electrons

▲ THE MOST COMMON *particles in the Universe today include quarks and electrons. They are the building blocks of all atoms.*

Matter and antimatter

Immediately after the Big Bang, huge amounts of energy were turned into particles of matter and mirror-image particles of antimatter. When the two types meet they destroy each other in a flash of radiation. If equal numbers of both had been created they would have wiped each other out. However, everything we can see in the Universe today consists mainly of matter. The only explanation seems to be that, for some unknown reason, the Big Bang created slightly more matter than antimatter.

Which came first?

There was no "before" the Big Bang because time and space did not exist. After the Big Bang, space began to expand and time began to flow. But neither could start until the other one began. It took scientists years to figure out this mind-boggling fact!

FIRST THREE MINUTES

During the first three minutes the Universe cooled from being unbelievably hot to less than one billion degrees Kelvin. In the same period, it expanded from an area billions of times smaller than an atom to the size of our Milky Way galaxy.

2 By now the Universe is the size of a football field. Huge numbers of matter and antimatter particles collide and destroy each other, creating more energy.

3 The Universe suddenly inflates and starts to cool. A new range of exotic particles form, including quarks and electrons.

4 The Universe is still too hot to form atoms, but quarks begin to group together and form heavier particles, particularly protons and neutrons.

2. 10^{-43} seconds	3. 10^{-35} seconds	4. 10^{-7} seconds	3 minutes
10^{32} K	10^{27} K	10^{14} K	10^{8} K

▲ *K stands for Kelvin, a temperature scale used by astronomers. 0 K equals –273°C (–459°F). It is the lowest possible temperature anything can reach in the Universe.*

BUILDING UP TO ATOMS

Proton   Neutron   Helium nucleus

Protons and neutrons are particles that each contain three quarks. Once the expanding Universe had enough protons and neutrons, they began to form very simple atomic nuclei, the basis of hydrogen and helium atoms. Most stars are made of these two types of atoms. Within three minutes of the Big Bang, almost all of the hydrogen and helium nuclei in the Universe had been created.

It took hundreds of millions of years for stars, galaxies, and planets to start filling the Universe. If the Universe hadn't begun to cool, the atoms they are made from would never have formed.

THE FOGGY UNIVERSE

Around 300,000 years passed before the first atoms started to form. This process began when the temperature of the Universe dropped to about 3,000 K. In this cooler Universe, protons and atomic nuclei were able to capture extremely tiny particles called electrons and become atoms. Until this point, the Universe was very foggy – light could not travel far because it was constantly bouncing off atomic particles. This fog is why we cannot see anything that was happening at that time – even with the most powerful telescopes.

300,000 years

3,000 K

WHAT IS AN ATOM?

An atom is the smallest piece of matter that can exist on its own. Atoms have a central core (the nucleus) made up of protons and neutrons. Circling the nucleus are electrons. The number of protons, neutrons, and electrons an atom has determines which element it is. When the first stars exploded as supernovas, the energy they released created new, heavier elements, such as carbon, oxygen, and iron. This process continues today.

FIRST STARLIGHT

About 200 million years after the Big Bang huge clouds of hydrogen and helium gas began to build up. The pull of gravity made the clouds collapse into dense clumps of atoms. As these clouds shrank and became hotter they ignited and formed the first stars. These stars didn't last long before they exploded and helped produce new stars.

BEGINNINGS OF GALAXIES

Galaxies also began to form fairly soon after the first stars. Dense clouds of gas and young stars were pulled together by gravity and dark matter to form small galaxies and new stars. Gradually these galaxies began colliding with each other to make larger galaxies.

The Big Bang also created four fundamental forces that affect the Universe. These are gravity, the electromagnetic force, the weak nuclear force, and the strong nuclear force. Gravity is what keeps planets in orbit around stars. Electromagnetism is linked to electricity and magnetism. The weak force governs how stars shine, while the strong force holds together the protons and neutrons in the nuclei of atoms.

The Moon is held in orbit around Earth by the pull of gravity.

200 million years	500 million years	Present day
100 K	10 K	2.7 K

▲ THE CMB *provides the best evidence for the Big Bang. It marks the point at which the temperature dropped enough for atoms to form.*

Glowing embers of the Big Bang

We cannot see any light from the Big Bang. However, we can detect a faint glow of radiation – known as the Cosmic Microwave Background (CMB) – that still covers the sky. This leftover radiation shows what the Universe was like 300,000 years after it began. The map shows slightly warmer and cooler ripples. The first galaxies probably grew from the slightly cooler and denser (blue) patches of gas.

THE BIG BANG MACHINE

Scientists cannot see what the Universe was like immediately after the Big Bang. But they are trying to learn more by building huge machines on Earth. The latest and most advanced of these is the Large Hadron Collider in Switzerland. This $4 billion instrument will attempt to re-create the Big Bang by crashing beams of protons together 800 million times a second. The beams that collide are expected to create many new particles and possibly provide a reconstruction of the Universe in its very first moments.

100 billion *galaxies*

Wherever we look in the sky, the Universe is full
of galaxies – huge star systems that are tied together
by gravity. The first galaxies were born less than
one billion years after the birth of the Universe
in the Big Bang.

GIANTS AND DWARFS

There are at least 100 billion galaxies in the Universe. Some
are enormous, containing hundreds of billions of stars.
Others are much smaller, sometimes containing fewer than
a million stars. There are many more small galaxies than
giant galaxies, even though the dwarf galaxies tend to be
swallowed by their larger neighbours over time. We live in
a galaxy of about 100 billion stars called the Milky Way.

M51 GALAXY

▲ M51, *the Whirlpool Galaxy, is about 30 million light years from Earth.*

Seeing the light

There are many features of galaxies that do not show up in visible light. To find out the true nature of a galaxy, you have to look at it at different wavelengths with different instruments. The above image of M51 combines images taken by four space telescopes. One showed up X-rays given off by black holes, neutron stars, and the glow from hot gas between the stars (shown in purple). Infrared and optical instruments revealed stars, gas, and dust in the spiral arms (in red and green). Young, hot stars that produce lots of ultraviolet light are blue.

TAKE A LOOK: WHIRLPOOL

By the mid-19th century, astronomers had discovered many fuzzy patches in the night sky, which they called nebulas. To find out more about them, Lord Rosse built what was then the world's largest telescope – the 1.8 m (72 in) Birr telescope. With it, he made the first observation of what is now known as the Whirlpool Galaxy (M51). His drawing of the galaxy is dated 1845.

This Hubble Space Telescope image is of Zwicky 18, a dwarf galaxy about 60 million light years away.

ZWICKY 18

HUBBLE DEEP FIELD *For 10 days in October 1998, the Hubble Space Telescope stared at a tiny region of space, revealing a view never seen before – thousands of galaxies up to 12 billion light years away. It features many spiral galaxies like our Milky Way, as well as elliptical galaxies and peculiar-shaped galaxies that are involved in collisions.*

GAS GALAXIES

Some galaxies are very large, yet contain very few stars. These faint galaxies are made almost entirely of gas, so in photos they appear as a smudge in the sky. One example, Malin 1, contains enough gas to make 1,000 galaxies like the Milky Way. It seems to have just begun to make stars. Its vast, but faint, disc is six times bigger than the Milky Way. A much closer, normal galaxy can be seen at the bottom of the picture.

The arrow points to Malin 1.

It can be seen better in this treated image.

Galaxies have existed for many billions of years – but where did they come from? Astronomers today use observatories to look back to the very early Universe. These distant views show fuzzy galaxies involved in violent collisions. Could this be how the first galaxies formed?

▲ THEORY TEST *This computer model shows matter clumping into strands under the influence of gravity. The first galaxies form inside these strands.*

WHAT HAPPENS?

There are two main theories of how galaxies form. In one version, huge clouds of gas and dust collapse to form galaxies. In the other version, stars form into small groups and then merge to form larger groups, then galaxies, and finally clusters of galaxies.

Changing shape

Many galaxies begin life as small spirals before becoming larger ellipticals, often as the result of a collision. This doesn't mean that the galaxies crash into each other – the gaps between the stars in a galaxy are large enough for the galaxies to pass through each other. However, it does change the galaxy's shape.

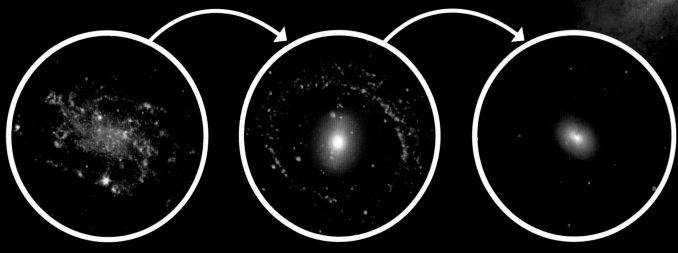

▲ YOUNG SPIRAL *NGC 300 is a young spiral galaxy with lots of star formation*

▲ TEENAGE TRANSITION *As the galaxy grows older, there is less star formation*

▲ OLD ELLIPTICAL *Large, gas-poor elliptical galaxies contain old stars*

Odd one out

Hoag's Object is a very unusual galaxy. It does not look like other irregular, spiral, or elliptical galaxies. Instead, it has a circle of young blue stars surrounding its yellow nucleus (core) of older stars.

▲ BLUE RING *Clusters of hot blue stars dominate the ring. They may be the remains of another galaxy that came too close.*

◄ SMOKIN'! *The Cigar Galaxy is an irregular galaxy with a lot of star formation. More stars are formed in young galaxies than in older ones.*

STARTING A SPIRAL

Most scientists believe that the early Universe was filled with hydrogen and helium. Some suggest that clouds of gas and dust, collapsing and rotating under the influence of gravity, formed spiral galaxies.

▲ COME TOGETHER *Clouds of dust, gas, and stars are pulled together by gravity.*

▲ TURN AROUND *Gravity makes the collapsed clouds rotate. New stars form and rotate around the centre of the mass.*

▲ SHRINK DOWN *The spinning action flattens the cloud, forming a galactic disc of dust, gas, and stars.*

▲ TAKING UP ARMS *The disc continues to rotate, causing spiral arms to form.*

TYPES OF GALAXIES

There are three main types of galaxy. These are classified according to their shape and the arrangement of stars inside them.

■ **Irregular** galaxies contain a lot of gas, dust, and hot blue stars, but have no particular shape. They are often the result of a collision between two galaxies.

■ **Elliptical** galaxies are round, oval, or cigar-shaped collections of stars. They usually contain very old red and yellow stars with little dust or gas between them.

■ **Spiral** galaxies are huge, flattened discs of gas and dust that have trailing arms.

▲ IRREGULAR *These galaxies sometimes have the beginnings of spiral arms.*

▲ ELLIPTICAL *There is no gas in an elliptical galaxy so no new stars can form.*

▲ SPIRAL *Spirals rotate very slowly, about once every few hundred million years.*

47

A SOMBRERO IN SPACE

Around 28 million light years from Earth, in the constellation Virgo, lies a spiral galaxy with a very bright nucleus. It has an unusually large central bulge, and is surrounded by a dark, inclined lane of dust (shown here in a side-on view). Named for its hat-like appearance, this is the Sombrero Galaxy.

The Milky Way

We live on a small planet that circles an insignificant star in a tiny part of a huge, spiral star system – the Milky Way galaxy. The Milky Way was born more than 10 billion years ago, and is likely to exist for many more billions of years.

Norma arm

Carina-Sagittarius arm

Crux-Scutum arm

Galactic centre

Galactic bar

Perseus arm

Orion arm

Our Sun

The laser points to the exact centre of the Milky Way.

Seeing stars

If you live far away from bright city lights, you may be lucky enough to see a faint band of light that crosses the night sky. Ancient observers called it the Milky Way because it looked like a stream of spilt milk in the sky. They had no idea what it was, but the puzzle was solved in 1610 when Galileo turned his telescope on the Milky Way and discovered that it was made up of thousands of stars.

Solar system

Globular cluster of millions of stars

Central bulge

Dark halo

Galactic disc

▲ HOW BIG IS OUR GALAXY? *The Milky Way is about 100,000 light years across but only 2,000 light years thick towards its outer edge. Most of the Milky Way's mass seems to come from mysterious, invisible dark matter (◉ p62–63).*

A SPIRAL GALAXY

The Milky Way is a barred spiral galaxy, which means it is shaped like a giant Catherine wheel, with curved arms trailing behind as it turns. The stars in our galaxy all move around the centre as the galaxy spins. Our Sun, which is about 28,000 light years from the centre, goes around the galaxy once every 220 million years. Stars near the centre take less time to orbit than the Sun.

X-ray binary system

Possible binary system with black hole

Cold gas cloud

Centre of galaxy containing black hole (Sagittarius A*)

The Sun is just one of about 200 billion stars in the Milky Way. Most stars lie in the galaxy's central bulge, but younger stars and dust clouds are found in the five spiral arms. A supermassive black hole lies at the centre.

THE HEART OF THE MILKY WAY

The centre of the Milky Way is a mysterious place about 600 light years across. While this is just a tiny part of the galaxy, the core contains one-tenth of all the gas in the galaxy, along with billions of stars. These include the remains of supernovas and bright sources of X-rays, such as binary systems (pairs of objects) that are thought to contain a black hole.

SGR A*

▲ ACTIVE PAST *SGR A* seems to have been active in the past. Light echoes from an outburst of X-rays 300 years ago can be seen passing through nearby dust clouds.*

The hidden monster

At the centre of our galaxy lies a monster: a giant black hole that contains about four million times more material than our Sun. This is Sagittarius A* (or SGR A*), named after its location in the constellation Sagittarius. At the moment it is a sleeping giant, creating billions of times less energy than giant black holes in other galaxies.

Ancient star streams

Not all of the material in the Milky Way lies in a flat disc. Three narrow streams of stars have been found arcing high above the galaxy. They are between 13,000 and 130,000 light years from Earth and extend over much of the northern sky. The largest stream is thought to be the scattered remains of a dwarf galaxy that collided with the Milky Way.

Baby stars

The heart of our galaxy is cluttered with stars, dust, and gas surrounding the black hole. Conditions there are harsh, with fierce stellar winds – powerful shock waves that make it difficult for stars to form. We don't yet know how stars form there because, until recently, no one could peer through the dust to find newborn stars. However, in 2009 the Spitzer Infrared Observatory found three baby stars, all less than one million years old, embedded in cocoons of gas and dust.

The Magellanic *Clouds*

The Milky Way is not the only galaxy visible in our skies. In the southern hemisphere you can also see the two Magellanic Clouds. They are generally thought to be satellite galaxies linked by gravity to the Milky Way, but recent research suggests they may be just passing through our neighbourhood.

▶ UP IN THE CLOUDS *The Large Magellanic Cloud is about 170,000 light years away from the Milky Way. The Small Magellanic Cloud is about 200,000 light years away.*

MILKY WAY

LARGE MAGELLANIC CLOUD

SMALL MAGELLANIC CLOUD

◀ LMC CLOSE-UP *Nearly one million objects are revealed in this detailed view from the Spitzer Infrared Observatory, which shows about one-third of the whole galaxy. Blue represents starlight from older stars. Red is from dust heated by stars.*

LARGE MAGELLANIC CLOUD

The Large Magellanic Cloud (LMC) lies in the constellations Dorado and Mensa. It is about 25,000–30,000 light years across and contains about 100 billion solar masses. The LMC is classed as an irregular galaxy, although it has a bar in its centre and some signs of spiral arms. It may have once been a spiral galaxy that was pulled into a new shape by the gravity of the Milky Way.

Colourful clouds

The Magellanic Clouds contain many supernova remnants. These are the remains of massive stars that exploded thousands of years ago, leaving behind colourful expanding clouds of hot gas.

▼ NAME GAME *The Magellanic Clouds are named after the 16th-century explorer Ferdinand Magellan. He was one of the first Europeans to see the Clouds in the southern skies.*

▶ STAR NURSERY *This false-colour image shows a part of the Tarantula Nebula near the star cluster NGC 2074. It shows a "nursery" where new stars form. The area has dramatic ridges, dust valleys, and streams of gas that glow in ultraviolet light.*

Small Magellanic Cloud

The Small Magellanic Cloud (SMC) is one of the most distant objects that can be seen with the naked eye. This irregular dwarf galaxy is a smaller version of the LMC. It contains less dust and gas, but it still has a number of star-forming regions (the red regions shown above). The SMC has a visible diameter of about 15,000 light years and contains several hundred million stars. Its mass is about seven billion times the mass of our Sun.

Tarantula Nebula

30 Doradus is a vast star-forming region in the LMC. The region's spidery appearance gives it its popular name, the Tarantula Nebula. It is about 1,000 light years across, and 170,000 light years away. If it were as close as the nearest star nursery to Earth (the Orion Nebula, 1,500 light years away), it would be visible during the day and cover a quarter of the sky. The nebula contains very hot stars that are among the most massive stars we know.

 TAKE A LOOK: MAGELLANIC STREAM

The Magellanic Clouds and the Milky Way are connected by an unusual, extended ribbon of hydrogen gas – the Magellanic Stream. Visible only at radio wavelengths, the Stream extends more than halfway around the Milky Way. It may have been created when material was stripped off these galaxies as they passed through the halo of our Milky Way. Another theory suggests that the two Clouds passed close to each other, triggering massive bursts of star formation. The strong stellar winds and supernova explosions from that burst of star formation could have blown out the gas and started it flowing towards the Milky Way.

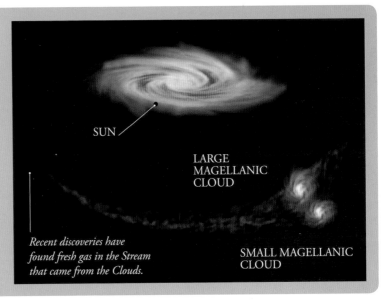

SUN

LARGE MAGELLANIC CLOUD

Recent discoveries have found fresh gas in the Stream that came from the Clouds.

SMALL MAGELLANIC CLOUD

The Local *Group*

The Milky Way is not alone in space, but is a member of a cluster of galaxies called the Local Group. The Local Group contains at least 45 galaxies plus several more lying on its borders.

ANDROMEDA

The Andromeda Galaxy (M31) is our largest galactic neighbour, and is more than two and a half times the size of the Milky Way. The entire disc of the spiral galaxy spans about 260,000 light years, which means that it would take 260,000 years for a light beam to travel from one end of the galaxy to the other.

OUR NEIGHBOURS

The galaxies in the Local Group all lie less than 3 million light years from the Milky Way. They are arranged into two smaller groups based around the two largest galaxies: the Milky Way and Andromeda. It is possible that, in several billion years, the Milky Way and Andromeda will collide and merge to form one huge galaxy.

▶ GROUPED TOGETHER
Some of the largest galaxies in the Local Group are shown here.

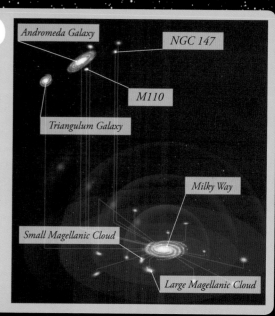

Andromeda Galaxy

NGC 147

M110

Triangulum Galaxy

Milky Way

Small Magellanic Cloud

Large Magellanic Cloud

Hot-hearted Andromeda

In the middle of Andromeda is a cloud of hot gas that gives out X-rays. The X-rays are thought to come from a binary system (a pair of stars) that contains a neutron star or a black hole that is pulling material away from a normal star. As matter falls towards the neutron star or black hole, friction heats it up to tens of millions of degrees and produces X-rays.

▶ CHANDRA'S VIEW
This image from NASA's Chandra X-ray Observatory shows the centre of Andromeda. Low energy X-rays are red, medium energy X-rays are green, and blue indicates high energy X-rays.

▲ ANCIENT COLLISION
Dust rings inside Andromeda provide evidence that the galaxy was involved in a violent head-on collision with the dwarf galaxy Messier 32 (M32) more than 200 million years ago.

Dwarf galaxies

The Local Group contains several dozen dwarf galaxies, and probably many more that are waiting to be discovered. Most are very small and faint, containing up to a few hundred million stars. Lurking behind dust and stars near the plane of the Milky Way is the closest known starburst galaxy – an irregular dwarf galaxy known as IC 10. Although its light is dimmed by dust, you can see the red glow of the star-forming regions.

WATCH THIS SPACE
This ultraviolet and infrared image of M33 shows a mix of dust and young stars in the galaxy. In some of the outer regions of the galaxy, there are many young stars (glowing blue) and very little dust.

Triangulum Galaxy

M33, or the Triangulum Galaxy, is the third largest galaxy in the Local Group. It is also known as the Pinwheel Galaxy because of its face-on spiral shape, which is more than 50,000 light years wide. M33 is thought to be a satellite of the Andromeda Galaxy. Like Andromeda, M33 is used as a cosmic ruler for establishing the distance scale of the Universe.

A look at the centre of our galaxy reveals hundreds of thousands of stars packed into an area of sky the width of a full Moon. Near-infrared light (yellow) shows regions where stars are being born. Infrared light (red) reveals dust clouds, while X-rays (blue) show ultra-hot gas and emissions from black holes.

▼ BRILLIANT BINARY *This binary star is a major source of X-rays. It is probably a massive star being orbited by either a neutron star or a black hole.*

▲ PISTOL STAR *The brightest known star in the Milky Way may be 10 million times brighter than the Sun.*

▲ SAGITTARIUS A*
This supermassive black hole is the centre of our galaxy. Its eruptions in the past have cleared the surrounding area of gas.

When galaxies collide...

Like islands in a vast sea of space, most galaxies are millions of light years apart. However, some galaxies are close enough to be pulled by gravity into clusters. Members of galaxy clusters can pull on each other so strongly that they collide.

STEPHAN'S QUINTET

Stephan's Quintet is a group of galaxies that appear to be smashing into each other. Four of them are about 280 million light years away from Earth, but the fifth is closer to us. NGC 7318b is passing through the main group at nearly 320 million km/h (200 million mph). This creates a shock wave that causes the gas between the galaxies to heat up and give out X-rays (the light blue region in the middle).

The NGC 7319 spiral galaxy contains a quasar (👁 p60–61).

NGC 7318a (right) is in front of NGC 7318b (left).

NGC 7320 is much nearer to Earth than the other galaxies.

COLLISION COURSE

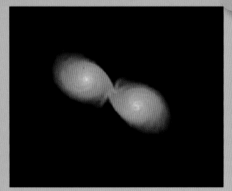

▲ VIRTUAL COLLISION *In real life, galaxy collisions take billions of years, so computers are used to see what might happen.*

▲ 6 BILLION YEARS *Since the spiral galaxies first met, gravity has begun to pull long tails from the galaxies.*

▲ 24 BILLION YEARS *In the time gap, the galaxies had separated again... until they rejoin as one slices through the other.*

This image shows gas temperature. Red is coolest, blue is hottest.

▲ ARP 194 *The top part of group ARP 194 contains two galaxies that are in the process of merging (top left in the image). The blue "fountain" running down looks as if it connects to a third galaxy, but this galaxy is much further away and not connected at all. The fountain contains stars, gas, and dust.*

Cluster collision

The ultimate crashes occur when several clusters of galaxies collide. The biggest collision astronomers have seen so far is a pile-up of four clusters called MACS J0717. This filament (stream) of galaxies, gas, and dark matter is 13 million light years long. It is moving into an area already packed with matter, causing repeated collisions. When the gas in two or more clusters collides, the hot gas slows down. Galaxies don't slow down as much, so they end up moving ahead of the gas.

▲ THE MICE *Named after their long "tails" of stars and gas, the two interacting galaxies known as The Mice (officially called NGC 4676) will eventually join together to form one huge single galaxy. The Mice are 300 million light years away from Earth, in the constellation Coma Berenices.*

A distorted view

Some galaxy clusters act as magnifying lenses in the sky. Their powerful gravity distorts the space around them. This means that light from more distant galaxies or quasars is bent on its way to us. We see multiple arcs and distorted images of the distant object, like a mirage in space.

▲ THE ANTENNAE *This is the nearest and youngest pair of colliding galaxies. Early photos showed them to look like insect antennae. These "tails" were formed when the two spiral galaxies first met around 200–300 million years ago. Billions of new stars will be born as the galaxies continue to collide.*

▲ 26 BILLION YEARS *The central regions fall together and the two galaxies eventually join together.*

▲ 30 BILLION YEARS *The two spiral galaxies finally merge and form one massive, elliptical galaxy.*

Active galaxi

There are many active galaxies in the Univ
While our own is quiet at present, others a
generating huge amounts of energy. In the
of each is a supermassive black hole with a
gravitational pull. This is the galaxy's power

Powerful magnetic field drives high-speed jets away from the black hole.

The disc of hot gas sends out radiation such as X-rays.

SPINNING WHEEL

An active galaxy is like a wheel. At the hub is a black hole. Its gravity pulls in dust, stars, and gas, making a spinning disc with an outer "tyre" of dust and gas. A strong magnetic field around the black hole blasts out jets of particles, looking like an axle for the wheel.

Active types

There are four main types of ac
galaxies: radio galaxies, Seyfert
galaxies, blazars, and quasars (sl
for quasi-stellar objects). Radio
galaxies (such as Cygnus A show
above) are the source of the stro
radio waves in the Universe. Rac
galaxies appear all over the Unive
but blazars and quasars are founc
only billions of light years away.

Dusty radio

The nearest radio galaxy to Earth is Centaurus A (Cen A). The central regions of this elliptical galaxy are hidden behind an unusual dark, thick band of dust. It was one of the first objects outside the Milky Way to be recorded as a source of radio waves, X-rays, and gamma rays. The two huge plumes of radio signals (in pale blue) are 200 million light years long. They were created by a collision with a spiral galaxy.

📷 WATCH THIS SPACE

This image of the elliptical radio galaxy M87, taken with the Hubble Space Telescope, reveals a brilliant jet of high-speed electrons sent out from the nucleus. The jet is produced by a black hole with the mass of three billion Suns.

Seyfert galaxies

A Seyfert galaxy is powered by a central black hole, hundreds of millions of times the mass of the Sun. Trapped material spirals into the hole, and jets are created where some of the material is blasted out at high speed. This image of NGC 4151, the brightest Seyfert galaxy, shows a side-on view of the jets being blasted into space.

Spiralling Seyfert

M106 looks like a typical spiral galaxy, with two bright spiral arms and dark dust lanes near its nucleus. However, in radio and X-ray images, two additional spiral arms of gas can be seen between the main arms. The core of M106 also glows brightly in radio waves and X-rays, and twin jets have been found running the length of the galaxy. M106 is one of the closest examples of a Seyfert galaxy, powered by vast amounts of hot gas falling into a central massive black hole.

TAKE A LOOK: BLAZARS

A blazar is built around a supermassive black hole in a host galaxy, but the amount of energy it gives out changes over time. Our view of a blazar is different to the other active galaxies. From Earth we look down on the jets and disc, just like looking at a hole in a ring doughnut.

▲ THIS SET *of images shows the movement of matter given out by blazar 3C 279. It seems to move faster than the speed of light, but this is an illusion.*

Quasars

Quasars are the brilliant cores of faraway galaxies. They are similar to Seyfert galaxies, but much brighter – so bright that their light hides the fainter galaxy around them. Quasars are powered by supermassive black holes fuelled by interstellar gas sucked inside. They can generate enough energy to outshine the Sun a trillion times.

Dark matter

Dark matter is the Universe's biggest mystery. Astronomers can tell that there is something invisible in the spaces between stars, as it's creating enough of a gravitational pull to bend starlight as it travels towards Earth. However, no one knows what dark matter looks like or what it is made from.

▲ MISSING PIECES *At the moment we know next to nothing about dark matter, but scientists are looking for subatomic particles that might help us complete our picture of the Universe.*

MAPPING IT OUT

This computer simulation shows how dark matter is spread throughout the Universe. The yellow areas show the highest concentrations of dark matter. These regions have enough gravity to pull together visible matter, creating galaxies.

IT'S A MYSTERY

Five percent of the visible Universe of stars and planets is normal matter. However, this matter would not have enough gravitational pull to hold the galaxies together, so

ATOM

astronomers know that there must be another kind of matter, even if it's invisible. Dark matter isn't made of atoms, and doesn't reflect light or any other kind of radiation, but it appears to make up a quarter of the matter in the Universe.

Dark energy

As well as dark matter, astronomers think the Universe is full of dark energy. In fact, about 70 percent of the Universe is made of this stuff, although no one has ever seen it. Scientists suspect it's there because something is making the Universe expand at an ever-increasing rate. However, no one is sure what this energy is or where it came from.

The Bullet Cluster

The Bullet Cluster was formed when two galaxy clusters collided, one tearing through the middle of the other like a bullet. The cluster's normal matter (which appears pink here) has been slowed down in the collision by a drag force. However, the dark matter has continued to move outwards without slowing, creating a light-bending aura (shown in blue).

What's the matter?

This image of a distant galaxy cluster shows a ring of dark matter around its centre. The ring would not normally be visible, but we can tell where it is from the way that the gravity of dark matter bends the light of distant galaxies.

◄ *Astronomers believe that this ring of dark matter could have been created by a collision between two galaxy clusters.*

LIFT-OFF!

The first successful suborbital flight was made by a V-2 rocket in 1942. But how do these huge, heavy machines take off, and what else have we sent into space?

How rockets *work*

A rocket is a launch vehicle used to carry astronauts or a payload (such as a satellite) from Earth into outer space. It must reach a speed of around 28,000 km/h (17,500 mph) to overcome the pull of Earth's gravity and enter orbit. This is done by burning chemicals to create thrust.

Third stage delivers crew or payload to Earth orbit

Second stage takes over when the first stage is released

First stage includes the engines and fuel to launch the rocket

UNITED STATES

THRUST

GRAVITY

◄ IN PARTS *Each stage of a multi-stage rocket carries its own engines. When the fuel is used up, the stage is made to fall away.*

▲ NEWTON'S LAW *Isaac Newton's Third Law of Motion says, "To every action there is an equal and opposite reaction".*

LIFTING OFF

All objects on Earth are pulled down by gravity. So how does a huge, heavy rocket take off? When hot gases exit from a rocket's engines they push against the downward pull of gravity, which propels the rocket upwards. This is called thrust. Isaac Newton explained that this works because every action (gases pushing down) has an equal, opposite reaction (rocket moving up).

ROCKET REGISTER

■ **R-7 Semyorka** (Russian) Originally a missile, this was modified to launch Sputnik 1, the first artificial satellite.
■ **Vostok** (Russian) In 1961 this was used for the first manned space flight of cosmonaut Yuri Gagarin.
■ **Saturn V** (American) The world's largest and most powerful rocket took the first men to the Moon in 1969.
■ **Titan** (American) 368 Titans were used on manned flights and to take probes to five planets including Mars.
■ **Soyuz** (Russian) This family of rockets, first used in 1966, services the International Space Station.
■ **Ariane** (European) Five types of Ariane have been used to launch satellites and probes into space.

ENGINES AND FUEL

■ **There are two types** of rocket engine: those that use solid propellant (fuel) and those that use liquid propellant. Many small rockets use solid propellant. Larger rockets may use a combination of solid fuel and liquid fuel in different stages.

■ **Boosters** are additional engines used to provide extra thrust for takeoff and are then jettisoned (thrown off).

■ **Solid fuel boosters** (shown below) are like fireworks: once they are lit, they cannot be shut down until all the propellant is used up.

Propellant

Casing

Burning surface

Liquid oxygen needed to burn the fuel

Nozzle

Liquid hydrogen

■ **Engines that use** liquid fuels (shown left) are much more complicated than solid-fuelled boosters. This is because the fuel and propellant have to be stored in separate tanks, then brought together in a combustion chamber. This is where the fuel burns, creating hot exhaust gases.

Combustion chamber

Bring your own oxygen

To fly in space, rockets not only have to carry their own fuel, they also need to carry a source of oxygen, called an oxidizer. This is because chemicals (the fuel) need oxygen to burn, or combust. On Earth, oxygen is present in the air, but there is not enough oxygen in space for combustion. The combustion process generates hot gases that are directed out of nozzles at high speed, producing thrust.

▲ TESTING *The RS-68 rocket has liquid-fuel engines. Its exhaust gases are nearly transparent.*

Nozzles can be angled to change the direction of flight.

Booster

▲ REAR VIEW *Soyuz has four boosters around its core stage. The faster the hot gas escapes through the nozzles, the faster the rocket will fly.*

3, 2, 1...

...And Soyuz TMA-16 blasts off on a mission to the International Space Station. Its four boosters burned for 118 seconds, producing blinding fire and deafening noise – but inside the tightly sealed capsule, the three crew members just heard a dull drone. It took around eight and a half minutes for the rocket stages to separate and the Soyuz spacecraft to reach low Earth orbit, 200 km (125 miles) above Earth.

The space *shuttle*

The space shuttle was the world's first reusable spacecraft. It takes off like a rocket, but lands back on Earth like a glider. The shuttle was launched for the first time in 1981 and has since flown on more than 130 missions. It carries a crew and cargo, and its missions have included launching satellites and building space stations.

WHAT IS IT?

The shuttle consists of three main parts: a winged orbiter that carries the crew and the cargo, two white booster rockets, and a huge orange fuel tank. The fuel tank and the boosters are discarded, or jettisoned, during the ascent – only the orbiter actually goes into space. The fuel tank is the only part of the shuttle that cannot be reused.

The robotic remote manipulator arm is used in space to lift things in and out of the payload bay.

Payload bay doors

The orbiter transports cargo, known as the payload, in this large bay and can carry loads up to 25,000 kg (55,250 lb). Doors open right along the top of the bay, allowing large satellites, such as the Hubble Space Telescope, to be carried.

These flaps on the edges of the wings are called elevons. They help control the descent and landing.

◄ ENGINES
The three main engines at the back of the orbiter swivel up and down and from side to side to steer the shuttle.

The crew

On a typical mission, the shuttle carries five to seven crew members: a commander, a pilot, several scientists, and sometimes a flight engineer. They travel in the crew compartment at the front of the orbiter, which contains the flight deck and their living quarters.

DISASTERS

There have been two major disasters involving the space shuttle:

▲ CHALLENGER *disintegrated 73 seconds after launch in 1986, killing the crew. The explosion was caused by hot gas escaping from a booster rocket.*

▲ COLUMBIA *broke apart during re-entry into the Earth's atmosphere in 2003, due to damage to the heat protection system on one of the wings. All seven crew members were killed.*

Start of the journey

The space shuttle is launched from the Kennedy Space Center in Florida, USA. Lift-off is powered by the two booster rockets and the three main engines on the orbiter, which are fuelled by liquid hydrogen and liquid oxygen from the fuel tank. About two minutes after lift-off, the booster rockets are jettisoned and fall back to Earth. When the shuttle reaches its orbit, the main engines are shut down, and the empty fuel tank is jettisoned and burns up in the atmosphere.

▼ HOME AGAIN *Atlantis deploys its drag chute as it lands in 2009.*

▲ SPLASHDOWN
The two booster rockets land in the Atlantic Ocean, off the coast of Florida. They are recovered by ships, so that they can be used again.

FAST FACTS

- The orbiter is 37 m (122 ft) long and has a wingspan of 24 m (78 ft).
- Only five space-worthy orbiters have ever been built: Columbia, Challenger, Discovery, Atlantis, and Endeavour.
- A typical mission lasts 12 to 16 days.
- The shuttle's main fuel tank holds about 2 million litres (526,000 gallons) of fuel.
- During re-entry, the outside of the orbiter heats up to more than 1,500°C (2,730°F).
- The shuttle can go from 0–27,500 km/h (0–17,000 mph) in less than eight minutes.

Touchdown

To leave orbit, the orbiter fires its thrusters and decelerates from hypersonic speed. It drops down through Earth's atmosphere underside first, generating enormous heat through friction with the atmosphere. The shuttle lands on a long runway, usually at the Kennedy Space Center, using a drag chute to help it slow down.

Launch *centres*

The very first launch sites were located on military bases in the USA and the USSR, and these have remained the main US and Russian launch centres ever since. Today, launch sites have been built or are under construction in many countries, including China, French Guiana, India, and South Korea.

▲ THE FIRST *launch pad built at Baikonur in the USSR was used to launch both Sputnik 1 and Yuri Gagarin (shown above) into orbit.*

▼ THIS ROCKET, *shown in the vehicle assembly building at the Kennedy Space Center, was the first Saturn V to be launched. It was used on the Apollo 4 mission.*

AN IDEAL SITE

Rockets are not permitted to take off over highly populated areas, so launch sites are always located in remote places. A site near the sea, such as Cape Canaveral on the Florida coast, works well. Rockets launch eastwards, over the Atlantic Ocean, and any jettisoned stages fall into the water.

Cape Canaveral (USA)

This launch centre started life as a missile test centre, located on the site of an old air base. The first rocket was launched there in 1950. Since 1958, the site has been the main centre for US launches, and the only one for manned missions. Launch Complex 39, located on an island to the north of Cape Canaveral, was added in the 1960s for Saturn V launches. This area is known as the Kennedy Space Center. In total, more than 500 rockets have been launched from the Cape.

Baikonur (Russia)

All Russian manned flights and planetary missions are launched from Baikonur, a centre situated on the flat, deserted plains of neighbouring Kazakhstan. The Baikonur "cosmodrome" includes dozens of launch pads, nine tracking stations, and a 1,500 km (930 mile) long rocket test range. Missile and rocket tests started there in 1955.

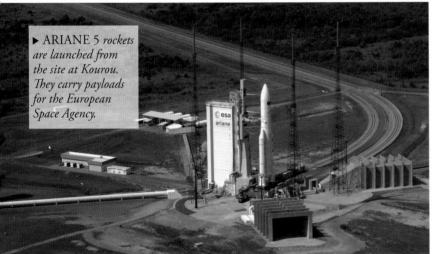

▶ ARIANE 5 *rockets are launched from the site at Kourou. They carry payloads for the European Space Agency.*

Jiuquan (China)

This launch centre is situated in the Gobi Desert, 1,600 km (1,000 miles) west of Beijing, and was first used in 1960. In 1970 a Long March-1 rocket launched the Mao-1 satellite from Jiuquan, making China the fifth nation to launch an artificial satellite into orbit. Today, Jiuquan is the launch site for China's manned Shenzhou spacecraft, but it is limited to south-eastern launches, to avoid overflying Russia and Mongolia.

Plesetsk (Russia)

More missiles and rockets have been launched from Plesetsk than from any other launch site in the world – over 1,500 of them. The centre is located close to the Arctic Circle, about 800 km (500 miles) north-east of Moscow. Plesetsk has been a leading missile testing and space launch centre since 1957. For many years, it was a top-secret site and the Soviet government only admitted its existence in 1983.

LIFT-OFF!

▲ THE PLESETSK *launch site is situated in an area of forest and lakes. About 40,000 service personnel and their families live in the nearby town of Mirnyy.*

Kourou (European Space Agency)

The location of this launch site in French Guiana is one of the best in the world. It is near the equator, which gives the maximum energy boost from the Earth's rotation for launches into equatorial orbits, and weather conditions are favourable throughout the year. The site has been used as the main European spaceport since July 1966. A new pad has recently been built for use by the Russian Soyuz launcher.

The Odyssey (Sea Launch company)

The most unusual launch site is the Odyssey platform, which launches rockets from the middle of the Pacific Ocean. A satellite is prepared onshore in California, USA, attached to a Zenith rocket, then transferred to the Odyssey platform. The platform sails to a site near the equator, a journey of 11 to 12 days, then the rocket is launched.

Launching *Ariane 5*

Launched from the Kourou spaceport in French Guiana, the Ariane 5 rocket is capable of lifting two satellites weighing almost 9 tonnes (10 tons) into orbit. The rocket and its satellites are assembled and prepared for launch in special facilities at the Ariane launch complex.

THE LAUNCH COMPLEX

The ELA-3 launch complex was built in the 1990s especially for the European Ariane 5 rocket. Between 8 and 10 rockets can be launched there each year, and each launch campaign lasts 20 days. The control centre is located in a protected enclosure, designed to withstand the impact of any falling rocket pieces, and has two independent launch control rooms.

▼ TECHNICIANS *load the Philae lander onto the Rosetta probe ready for its journey to comet Churyumov-Gerasimenko (👁 p157).*

▼ A SOLID *rocket booster arrives for integration with an Ariane 5 rocket at the assembly building.*

Rocket stages
The 58 m (190 ft) high launcher integration building is where the stages of the Ariane 5 rocket are joined together. The rocket's core stage is positioned on a mobile launch table and the two solid boosters are attached on either side. The core stage is topped off with one of three available upper stages. The launch table and the rocket are then transferred to the final assembly building.

▲ THE MAIN STAGE, *which will contain the liquid propellant, is hoisted into position and the nozzle is attached.*

Preparing the payload
Satellites are prepared for launch in the vast payload processing building. It is so big that several satellites can be handled at once. The building also has two areas for hazardous activities, such as loading the highly inflammable propellant (fuel). The finished payload, now ready for launch, is then taken to the assembly building to be attached to the rocket.

◀ AN ARIANE 5 *rocket consists of a central core stage, two solid boosters, and an upper stage. It is almost 52 m (170 ft) high.*

▶ WATER TOWER *This supplies the water that is showered into the flame trenches and around the launch table. It holds about 1.5 million litres (400,000 gallons) of water.*

LIFT-OFF!

▲ THE PAYLOAD *is hoisted by a special mobile crane and placed on top of the rocket.*

Final assembly

Inside the final assembly building, the satellite is installed on top of the rocket. It is covered with a shell, known as the payload fairing, which protects the satellite during the launch. Then the rocket's upper stage and the attitude control system are fuelled. About 12 hours before the launch, the mobile launch table and the completed rocket are rolled out to the launch zone.

▶ THE ROCKET *is slowly moved out on a crawler tractor.*

Launch zone

This area is where the most dangerous operations take place, so it is located 2.8 km (1.7 miles) from the other buildings. The rocket's core stage is filled with liquid hydrogen and liquid oxygen propellant, then the main engine and solid booster stages are ignited and the rocket lifts off. The launch zone has a concrete foundation with three flame trenches that catch the rocket's exhaust. During lift-off, the area is showered with water to reduce the effects of noise and heat.

Artificial *satellites*

In astronomy, a satellite is a body that orbits a planet. There are natural satellites, such as moons, and artificial (man-made) satellites such as communications satellites and space stations. The first artificial satellite was very simple, but modern ones are much more complicated.

Four aerials on Sputnik transmitted radio signals.

IT'S GOOD TO TALK

Many artificial satellites are designed for communication – sending data such as TV broadcasts, mobile phone signals, pictures of clouds and land use, and scientific information. The owners of a satellite also need to be able to keep track of it. This is mainly done using dish-shaped antennas on the ground and on the satellite.

Sputnik 1

Launched on 4 October 1957, the Russian satellite Sputnik 1 was the first artificial satellite to successfully be placed in orbit around Earth. The 58 cm (23 in) diameter aluminium ball carried four wire antennas up to 3 m (10 ft) long. Sputnik's beeping signals continued for 21 days, but it survived in orbit for 92 days before burning up during re-entry on 4 January 1958.

◄ LASER LOCATOR
The precise orbits of some satellites are checked by bouncing laser pulses off the satellite.

I'VE GOT THE POWER

■ Satellites have to power themselves. This is usually done by using large solar arrays ("wings") crammed with light-sensitive solar cells. The arrays are many metres long and have to be folded during launch.
■ The solar cells can provide several kilowatts of power, although they become less efficient as they get older.
■ The arrays can be turned so that they always collect as much sunlight as possible. When the satellite goes into shadow, it gets its power from rechargeable batteries.

DON'T MISS THE BUS

Most commercial satellites are built on the same basic model, designed to be as strong and light as possible. A platform called a bus contains all the main systems, including the batteries, computer, and thrusters. Attached to the bus are antennas, solar arrays, and payload instruments (such as cameras, telescopes, and communications equipment that the satellite uses to do its job).

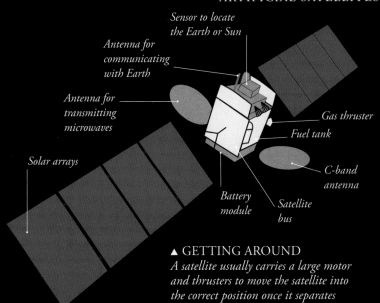

Sensor to locate the Earth or Sun

Antenna for communicating with Earth

Antenna for transmitting microwaves

Solar arrays

Gas thruster

Fuel tank

C-band antenna

Battery module

Satellite bus

▲ GETTING AROUND
A satellite usually carries a large motor and thrusters to move the satellite into the correct position once it separates from its launch vehicle.

Super solar satellite
Vanguard 1 holds the record for being the oldest man-made object in space. Launched in 1958, it was the fourth artificial satellite to successfully reach orbit, and the first to be powered by solar panels. Communication with Vanguard stopped in 1964, but the satellite still circles the Earth among a cloud of space debris.

Satellites can be affected by many things. Small meteorite impacts, the solar wind, solar radiation, and minor changes in gravity can all alter its position or even cause damage.

◄ POINT IT RIGHT
Many satellites need to point in the right direction to line up their antennas and communicate with Earth. Getting the correct position, or "attitude", can be a tricky job!

Hot and cold
The side of a satellite facing the Sun gets very hot, while the shaded side becomes very cold. This causes problems because most satellite equipment is sensitive to extreme heat or cold. Ways of protecting equipment include using layered insulating blankets that look like foil to keep heat in, and adding radiators to release heat from electrical equipment.

NASA's Lunar Reconnaissance Orbiter (LRO) is a robotic spacecraft sent to study the Moon's surface from an orbit 50 km (31 miles) away.

Satellites *in orbit*

Thousands of satellites have been sent into space since Sputnik 1 in 1957. There are many different types and sizes, and many different uses. Most are placed in low Earth orbit, between 200 and 2,000 km (125 and 1,250 miles) above Earth. These take about 90 minutes to make one orbit of Earth.

WEATHER WATCHER

Some weather satellites, such as the European Space Agency's Meteosats, are in geostationary orbit – they stay above the same place on Earth. Orbiting 36,000 km (22,370 miles) above Earth, they take 24 hours to go once around the planet. By staring at a fixed point, they can study the changing weather.

Weather forecasting
Satellites, especially those in low polar orbits, can take amazingly detailed images of weather. They are used to forecast the weather – but we don't always get it right! The image below, taken by NASA's Terra satellite, is of tropical cyclone Gonu passing over the Gulf of Oman. The storm was predicted to travel inland, but it didn't.

▲ STAYING POWER *This Meteosat stays above West Africa, on the equator. As Earth turns, the satellite follows.*

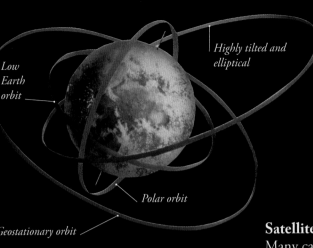

Low
Earth
orbit

*Highly tilted and
elliptical*

Polar orbit

Geostationary orbit

SAT NAV FAMILIES

- There are several families of satellites that provide navigation information. The best known, and most widely used, is the American Global Positioning System (GPS).
- GPS has 24 satellites in 6 orbits that criss-cross 24,000 km (15,000 miles) above Earth. There are nearly always three or four satellites above the local horizon at any one time.
- Russia's Glonass system is similar to GPS.
- Europe's Galileo satellite constellation is planned to start in 2014.

Types of orbit

Different orbits are used for different missions. Many communications and weather satellites stay above the equator, either in a near orbit called low Earth orbit, or much further out, in a geostationary orbit. Satellites can survey the entire planet in great detail from low polar orbits as Earth spins beneath them. Earth observation satellites and astronomical observatories can be found in highly elliptical (oval-shaped), tilted orbits.

Satellite navigation

Many cars, lorries, and aircraft are fitted with satellite navigation equipment (sat-nav) that acts as an electronic map and route finder. They work by picking up signals from four satellites at the same time, which locates your precise position on the planet.

▶ GALILEO GUIDE *A European sat-nav system called Galileo is currently being planned. It will have 30 satellites in three inclined (tilted), circular orbits.*

Observing Earth

Many satellites are used to study Earth's surface. From their images we can learn about many subjects, including changing land use, ocean currents, and air pollution. By taking pictures of the same place from different angles, they can produce 3-D images. Some satellites can see objects smaller than 50 cm (20 in) across, and may even be able to read headlines on a newspaper. Radar satellites can see the ground even at night or when an area is covered by cloud.

Telecommunications satellites

Radio, TV, and telephone communications have been transformed by satellite technology. The first live TV signals were relayed from America to Britain in 1962. Today, satellites can transmit hundreds of digital TV channels to rooftop dishes. We can watch live events and sports tournaments from around the world, and satellite phones make it possible to call someone in the middle of a desert or on top of a mountain.

SATELLITE SHOT

This detailed view of Russia's Lena River delta was taken by NASA's Landsat 7 satellite while in orbit about 700 km (430 miles) above Earth. Landsat's image sensor picks up eight different wavelengths of visible and infrared light, which combine to create spectacular false-colour images of surface features.

LUNA 3's CAMERA *took 29 photographs over 40 minutes, imaging 70% of the previously unseen far side.*

Space *probes*

In the 1950s and 1960s, the Soviet Union and the USA sent the first unmanned spacecraft, or probes, to explore the Moon, Venus, and Mars. Since then, probes have visited the Sun, all the other planets in our solar system, and many moons, asteroids, and comets.

The far side of the Moon

In January 1959, the Soviet probe Luna 1 became the first spacecraft to fly past the Moon. This was followed in October 1959 by Luna 3, which sent back the very first images of the far side of the Moon. Luna 3 was launched into an elliptical (oval-shaped) Earth orbit that enabled it to swing behind the Moon, just 6,200 km (3,850 miles) above its surface. The onboard camera took photographs of the far side, which revealed that it has very few "seas".

TRACKING PROBES

Probes transmit images and other data back to Earth in the form of radio waves in the extremely high-frequency bands. This information is picked up by tracking antennas on ground stations.

▲ THE MILKY WAY *in the night sky over a spacecraft-tracking antenna.*

Mars

Phobos, one of Mars's two moons.

FIRST PLANET ORBITER

The US probe Mariner 9 was launched in May 1971, on a mission to orbit the planet Mars. It sent back remarkable images of huge volcanoes, a vast canyon system, dry river beds, and close-up pictures of its two moons.

of 34,838 km (21,648 miles) on 14 December 1962. The probe scanned the planet for 42 minutes as it passed, revealing that Venus has cool clouds and a very hot surface, with temperatures of at least 425°C (800°F).

▲ MARINER 2 *The spacecraft had a conical frame of magnesium and aluminium, with two solar panels and a dish antenna.*

Journey to Jupiter

Pioneer 10 was launched in March 1972, and became the first spacecraft to travel through the asteroid belt (between July 1972 and February 1973) and the first to reach the planet Jupiter. The probe sent back close-up images of Jupiter, then continued on its journey out of the solar system, crossing Neptune's orbit in May 1983. The last signal was received from the probe in 2003. Pioneer 10 is heading for the star Aldebaran, in the constellation Taurus, but it will take more than 2 million years to get there!

▶ MISSING AREA *Mariner 10 was unable to see this part of the planet's surface.*

Mission to Mercury

In 1974, Mariner 10 became the first spacecraft to visit the planet Mercury. It was also the first to use another planet's gravity to alter its course when it flew past Venus on 5 February 1974. The first Mercury flyby took place on 29 March 1974, with two more over the following months. The probe sent back 12,000 pictures of Mercury, which showed a heavily cratered world, much like our Moon.

First planetary balloons

The two Soviet probes Vega 1 and 2 were launched in December 1984 on a mission to fly past Venus. They released two landers and two instrument packs, attached to Teflon-coated balloons, into the planet's atmosphere. Both balloons survived for about 46 hours and sent back data on the clouds and winds, while the landers explored the lower atmosphere and surface rocks.

FACT FILE

■ When it was launched, Pioneer 10 was the fastest spacecraft ever to fly. It left Earth at a record-breaking 51,670 km/h (32,107 mph).

■ For many years, Pioneer 10 was the most remote man-made object in the solar system, but on 17 February 1998 it was overtaken by the probe Voyager 1.

■ Vega 1 and 2 flew on from Venus to fly past Halley's Comet in March 1986.

Vega probes were powered by solar panels and carried an antenna dish, cameras, and an infrared sounder.

Space *debris*

There are about 900 satellites in operation, most of them in orbit around Earth. However, these satellites are flying through an ever-increasing sea of space debris. This debris field includes objects ranging from the size of a car to tiny specks of dust and paint.

▼ OUTER RING *This consists mainly of debris from telecommunications satellites.*

▶ LOW EARTH ORBIT
About 70 per cent of the debris is in low Earth orbit, which extends to 2,000 km (1,242 miles) above Earth's surface. The objects are most closely spaced at high latitudes above the polar regions.

WHERE IS THE DEBRIS?

At present, there are around 19,000 pieces of debris more than 10 cm (4 in) across and millions of smaller pieces orbiting our planet. The majority of them are in low Earth orbit, but there is a second ring of debris at an altitude of about 36,000 km (22,000 miles), an orbit used mainly by communications satellites. This ring is rapidly filling up, so most elderly satellites are now boosted into a higher "graveyard" orbit before they are shut down.

Falling to Earth
Pieces of debris that fall into Earth's atmosphere normally burn up, like man-made shooting stars. But occasionally an object reaches the ground almost intact. This propellant tank from a Delta 2 rocket landed in Texas in 1997.

EXPLOSIONS

So far, there have been more than 200 explosions in space, and more are very likely. Explosions are usually caused by uncontrolled events, such as pressure build-up in a rocket's fuel tanks, battery explosions, or the fuel igniting. Each explosion creates thousands of small fragments of debris.

Collisions

The first recorded collision between two large objects took place in 1996, when the French Cerise satellite was hit by a fragment from an Ariane rocket. In 2009 two satellites, Cosmos 2251 and Iridium 33, actually collided (above). The resulting explosion created a massive cloud of debris – perhaps 100,000 pieces of junk.

The Cerise satellite collided with a piece of debris from an Ariane rocket, which tore off a piece from the boom, leaving the satellite severely damaged.

FAST FACTS

■ Even tiny pieces of debris can cause a lot of damage, because they are travelling at speeds around 27,000 km/h (17,000 mph). The high speed turns a fleck of paint into the equivalent of a rifle bullet.

■ The International Space Station is fitted with special shields to protect its skin from debris impacts. It can also be moved out of harm's way if a particularly large piece of debris poses a threat.

■ Optical telescopes and radars are used to track large pieces of debris from the ground.

■ The amount of man-made debris in space is expected to grow in the future, even if there are no more explosions. This is because collisions between pieces of debris will create dozens, or even hundreds, of smaller fragments.

▲ PIECE OF DEBRIS
This fragment measures about 5 cm (2 in) – big enough to cause major damage to a spacecraft.

Damage to the space shuttle

Crewed spacecraft, such as the space shuttle, fly in low Earth orbit, where debris is most common. The US military tracks big pieces of debris and issues a warning if a close encounter is likely. The shuttle then moves away from the danger. However, hits from small debris are unavoidable. During the 54 shuttle missions up to 2005, space junk and small meteorites hit the windows 1,634 times.

◄ WINDOW DAMAGE
Shuttle windows often have to be replaced because of chips in the glass caused by debris.

▶ DEBRIS HOLE
This is a hole in a panel on SolarMax, a satellite monitoring solar flares.

Space *nations*

For many years space exploration was dominated by two countries – Russia and the United States. However, over time, Europe and Japan built their own satellites and launch rockets. Today, a new generation of space powers, including China, India, Brazil, South Korea, and Israel is prepared to spend large sums on developing its space industry.

> ## ▶▶ FAST FACTS ▶▶
>
> ■ It only takes about 10–30 minutes for a rocket to put a satellite in orbit.
>
> ■ Chinese-Brazilian satellites can get very detailed photographs of cities from 700 km (435 miles) away.
>
> ■ The US Space Surveillance Network tracks objects in space; at present, there are 900 satellites operating above Earth.
>
> ■ Satellites that do not appear to move through the sky are in fact orbiting at the same speed as Earth.

ROCKET FLEETS

To get their satellites into orbit many smaller countries book a ride on a European, Russian, or Japanese rocket, but India and China now have launch sites and reliable rocket fleets that can be used instead. India's Polar Satellite Launch Vehicle (PSLV) has launched more than 40 satellites so far, including 10 in one go in 2008. Israel has a small launcher, while Brazil, Iran, and North and South Korea are developing their own rockets and launch sites.

🔍 TAKE A LOOK: OVER THE MOON

In 2009, the Indian lunar orbiter Chandrayaan-1, with NASA equipment on board, sent back data that indicated that water was present in the Moon rock. The discovery was backed up by previous data collected by two US spacecraft, Cassini and Deep Impact.

▲ THIS INFRARED *image of a crater on the far side of the Moon looks quite dry and dusty.*

▲ HOWEVER *when the crater is seen in false colour, there is widespread evidence of water in the rocks and soil.*

MANNED MISSIONS

So far, the only new country to put a man in space is China. In 2003 they sent a single astronaut (or "taikonaut" in Chinese), Yang Liwei, into orbit. The second mission in 2005 carried two astronauts. On the third mission in 2008, Zhai Zhigang became the first Chinese person to space walk. He spent 20 minutes in space retrieving an experiment from the outside of the module.

▲ THE THREE-MAN CREW *on China's third manned space mission Shenzhou-7 were treated like celebrities both before and after their trip into space.*

China's Chang'e-1

China's first lunar mission was launched in October 2007. The unmanned probe Chang'e-1, named after the Chinese Moon goddess, took 15 days to reach the Moon. It then spent 16 months mapping the lunar surface before it made a deliberate crash landing.

Satellites are used for many different things. Countries such as India, Brazil, China, and South Korea have been sending up rockets carrying survey satellites that can help them monitor the weather and pollution, look for minerals and resources, or check on farming or urban areas. Others carry telecommunications or global positioning equipment.

▲ ENVIRONMENTAL *monitoring by the joint China-Brazil Earth Resources Satellite (CERBS-1) has located areas of deforestation (shown here in pink) in the Amazon rainforest.*

LIFT-OFF!

▼ THE JAPANESE *Aerospace Exploration Agency (JAXA) is a major player in space exploration today. It uses its own rockets to launch its satellites and spacecraft. SELENE was launched by its H-IIA rocket.*

HIGH DEFINITION MOON

In September 2007, Japan launched its SELENE orbiter, nicknamed Kaguya after a legendary princess. It was the biggest lunar mission since Apollo. The aim of the mission was to investigate the Moon's origin and evolution, but Kaguya also carried a high-definition video camera that filmed a sensational movie of Earth rising over the lunar horizon.

WATCH THIS SPACE

The JAXA spacecraft also mapped the Moon's rugged terrain in 3D and studied its magnetic field. The mission was a great success and in 2009, after a year and eight months, the orbiter had a planned crash-landing onto the Moon.

◄ THE *amazing video of Earth rising was loaded onto YouTube and has been viewed by over a million people.*

Super spacecraft

Travelling through space can take a very long time. Robotic spacecraft have flown huge distances to explore most of the solar system, but the difficulties of people travelling to Mars and beyond have yet to be solved. However, many ideas are being tested to speed up space travel and save on fuel. Could these lead to crews exploring distant worlds in the not-too-distant future?

POWERED BY ELECTRICITY

Traditional rocket engines burn large amounts of fuel. This makes the vehicles very large and heavy, and very expensive to fly. Electric propulsion – also known as an ion drive – is much lighter and more efficient. It works by firing a stream of electrically charged particles (ions) into space. The ions pass through an electrically charged grid, which makes them move very fast. The thrust is weak, but over time it can propel the spacecraft to very high speeds.

The European Space Agency's SMART-1 lunar probe is powered by an ion drive.

SMART-1 probe

Moon

Earth

This is where SMART-1 escaped Earth's gravity and was pulled into orbiting the Moon.

SMART MOVES

Launched in 2003, SMART-1 was the first European spacecraft to use the Moon's gravity to pull it into orbit. First it spiralled around Earth on an ever-enlarging orbit, firing its ion drive to turn the natural circular path into an ellipse (oval). When it was far enough away to escape Earth's gravity, it was pulled into a new orbit by the Moon.

Project Orion was designed to explore Saturn, and even reach the nearest stars, but it didn't take off.

There was a huge risk of radiation from the nuclear explosions.

IT GOES LIKE A BOMB!

Another alternative to heavy chemical fuel was suggested by NASA's Project Orion in the 1950s and 1960s: bomb power. Every second, a nuclear bomb would be exploded at the rear of the rocket. The explosions would push against a giant steel shield 1 m (3 ft) thick, propelling the rocket up and into space.

LIFT-OFF!

AEROBRAKING

Spacecraft use a lot of fuel as they brake into orbit around the Moon and planets. However, if the planet has an atmosphere, it is possible to slow down without using a rocket engine. This is done by dipping in and out of the upper atmosphere – a process known as aerobraking. Each time the spacecraft enters the atmosphere it is slowed a little by friction. This technique can also be used to change its orbit.

Mars Reconnaissance Orbiter aerobraking.

PROJECT DAEDALUS

In the 1970s, the British Interplanetary Society's Project Daedalus described a two-stage, unmanned craft that would be built in Earth's orbit. Its engines would use nuclear fusion – the same power source as the Sun – to fire high-speed jets of gas into space. Nearly all of its 54,000 tonne (60,000 ton) weight would be fuel. While it would be fast enough to reach Barnard's Star (almost 6 light years away) within 50 years, it would need as much fuel to slow down as to accelerate, so it would just speed past the star and keep on going.

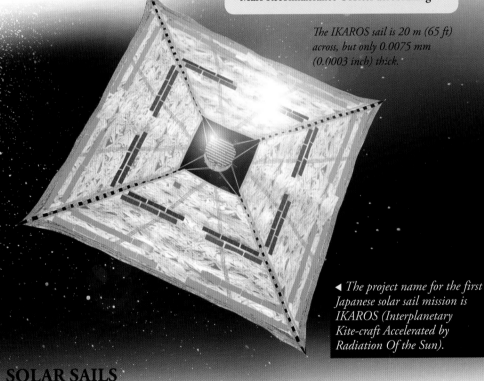

The IKAROS sail is 20 m (65 ft) across, but only 0.0075 mm (0.0003 inch) thick.

◄ *The project name for the first Japanese solar sail mission is IKAROS (Interplanetary Kite-craft Accelerated by Radiation Of the Sun).*

SOLAR SAILS

Sailing ships have been used on Earth for thousands of years, but soon there may be sails in space. The idea behind solar sails is that sunlight pushes down on solid surfaces. So if enough light was bounced off a large, lightweight sail, it could push a spacecraft through space. The thrust would be small, but continuous, and over time, the spacecraft could reach high speeds.

HUMANS IN SPACE

Living in space is not easy. From preflight training to building a space station in orbit, there is a lot of work for astronauts to do – in zero gravity, a long way from home.

and indeed animals, have taken part in mankind's efforts to develop spacecraft and explore outer space. Here are a select few whose contributions changed the course of history.

Space animals
Animals were sent into space in the 1940s and 1950s to see how weightlessness affected them. Two monkeys, Able and Miss Baker, were launched 483 km (300 miles) above the Earth in 1959 and experienced weightlessness for nine minutes before returning safely to Earth.

Konstantin Tsiolkovsky

"The Earth is the cradle of mankind – one cannot remain in the cradle forever." So said Konstantin Tsiolkovsky, a Russian rocket scientist and pioneer of human space travel. He first became interested in space flight in 1874, when he was only 17. He went on to write about his ideas for multi-stage rockets, liquid gas propulsion, pressurized spacesuits, and orbital space stations. These theories were used to develop space exploration after his death in 1935.

Verne's spacecraft was fired from a huge cannon called Columbiad. NASA used the name Columbia for the command module that took man to the Moon in 1969.

Jules Verne
Jules Verne was a science-fiction writer in the 19th century. His story *From the Earth to the Moon* and its sequel inspired many space pioneers, including Konstantin Tsiolkovsky, Robert Goddard, and Wernher von Braun.

Goddard worked on his own, conducting many practical experiments with his rockets in the 1920s.

Robert Goddard
People thought the American physicist Robert Goddard was mad when he first began developing his ideas on rocket propulsion and space flight. His first liquid-fuelled rocket was successfully launched at his aunt Effie's farm in 1926. His 3 m (10 ft) rocket went 12.5 m (41 ft) high, travelled 56 m (184 ft) and flew for only 2.4 seconds. Now, Goddard is recognized as one of the fathers of modern rocketry.

> I could have gone on flying through space forever.

Gagarin had to parachute from the capsule before it landed – although this was kept a closely guarded secret for many years.

▼ ONLY A DOZEN *men have set foot on the Moon with Neil Armstrong leading the way on 20 July 1969.*

Yuri Gagarin – first person in space

A keen jet-fighter pilot, Yuri Gagarin became a cosmonaut candidate in 1959. On 12 April 1961, his Vostok spacecraft was launched into orbit 327 km (203 miles) above Earth. Travelling at 28,000 kilometres an hour (17,500 mph), his single orbit around the Earth only lasted 108 minutes, but it caused a sensation and made him world famous.

Dr von Braun standing by the engines of the Saturn V rocket.

Neil Armstrong – first person on the Moon

Another keen flyer, Armstrong went on his first plane ride aged six and built hundreds of model aeroplanes as a child. He even gained his pilot's licence before passing his driving test. Selected as a NASA astronaut in 1962, he flew on Gemini 8 in 1966, then commanded Apollo 11, the first manned mission to the Moon, in 1969.

Wernher von Braun

Originally, von Braun lived in Germany, where he developed the V-2 rockets used as weapons during World War II. After the war he worked in the US on the Saturn V rockets, which helped the Americans win the race to the Moon. The Saturn V was famous for being the only rocket that worked every time without blowing up!

Sergei Korolev

An enthusiastic experimenter with rockets, Sergei Korolev attracted the attention of the Russian military in the 1930s and became the mastermind behind the development of the Russian space programme, including the world's first artificial satellite, Sputnik. The Russians however, kept his identity a secret and he was only known as "Chief Designer" until after his death in 1966.

Becoming an *astronaut*

Becoming an astronaut is far from easy. Thousands of people apply, but only a few are chosen. Those selected have to undergo months of study and training before they can fly in space. Some astronauts say that the training is harder than the actual mission.

ASTRONAUT NEEDED!

Do you have the necessary qualifications to pilot a spacecraft?
- **Military pilot:** high-performance jets
- **University degree:** engineering, science, or mathematics
- **Physically fit and healthy**
- **Good people skills**
- **Able to work in a team**

To be a mission specialist, you also need:
- **An advanced degree**
- **Professional experience:** engineering, or space-related occupation

THE CHOSEN FEW

In the early years of the Space Age, the only people chosen as astronauts were young military pilots with the highest levels of physical and mental toughness. Today, astronauts experience much lower stresses during lift-off and re-entry, but they still have to pass an intensive physical examination.

WHAT A STAR!

US senator John Glenn has broken two space records: in 1962 on the Friendship 7 mission, he became the first American to orbit Earth, and in 1998 aged 77, he became the oldest person to go into space when he went up on the space shuttle.

Have you got what it takes?

Each country has its own training schedule, but they usually follow the same guidelines. Training lasts for approximately two years and typically covers about 230 subjects, including scuba diving, space engineering, language skills (English and Russian), space-walk training, and how to live and work in a zero-gravity environment – some 1,600 hours of instruction in all. It's hard work and you have to be extremely dedicated, but what a reward at the end!

HUMANS IN SPACE

ASTRONAUT TRAINING **LOG BOOK:**

**5, 4, 3, 2, 1…
lift-off!**

FEBRUARY

We get to learn how to fly a spacecraft in flight simulators: from lift-off, to landing, to re-entering Earth's atmosphere… again and again and again. Practice makes perfect!

MARCH

Have to train in the gym regularly to keep fit – being an astronaut is a very physical job.

APRIL

I love learning how to fly T-38 high-performance jets. Had to practise escaping from one sinking underwater last week. Learning how to use the ejector seat and a parachute, too.

Went swimming in a tank with a full-size replica of a spacecraft! Underwater, the normal pull of gravity isn't as strong and we got to know every inch of the craft, inside and out. We also rehearsed space walks.

Today went swimmingly!

JULY

To get us used to weightlessness, we had to travel in a special padded plane. The pilot gave us a rollercoaster ride – hard not to feel sick, but fun playing at being superman!

This plane is known as the "vomit comet".

Survival training in the jungle.

OCTOBER

We had to learn survival techniques in case we crash-landed in the jungle or somewhere cold after re-entry. We are given medical training too. We need to work as a team.

NOVEMBER

Winter training! Cold and hungry.

DECEMBER

We've been given our missions and are busy studying in the classroom now.

WHAT A CHORE!

Michael Lopez-Alegria, astronaut at Johnson Space Center, USA, said that while training, learning how to brush his teeth in zero gravity was harder than surviving at sea. Arranging facilities, finding water, and getting rid of the rubbish all became complex parts of the mission.

Space walking

One of the most dangerous things astronauts can do is leave the safety of a spacecraft. Out in space they are exposed to all kinds of hazards: lack of air, radiation, extreme temperatures, and fast-moving space debris. However, space walking is essential – it enables astronauts to repair equipment, install new hardware, and even to walk on the Moon.

▲ AIRLOCK *Astronauts enter space through a special room called an airlock. This room is sealed off from the rest of the spacecraft.*

FANCY A WALK?

During the early days of space exploration, Russia and the US were fierce rivals. When NASA announced that Ed White would soon make the first space walk, Russia decided to beat them to it, sending cosmonaut Alexei Leonov out on a space walk in 1965. The mission almost ended in disaster when Leonov's suit ballooned outwards and he couldn't fit back through the door of the spacecraft. Only by reducing the pressure in the suit – a very dangerous thing to do – was he able to squeeze back into the airlock.

▲ ED WHITE *was the first astronaut to use jet propulsion during a space walk.*

▲ SPACE WALK
Astronauts Carl J. Meade and Mark C. Lee testing a SAFER jet pack 240 km (150 miles) above Earth in 1994.

▲ ROBOTICS
Mark C. Lee is shown anchored to the Remote Manipulator System (RMS) robotic arm on space shuttle Discovery.

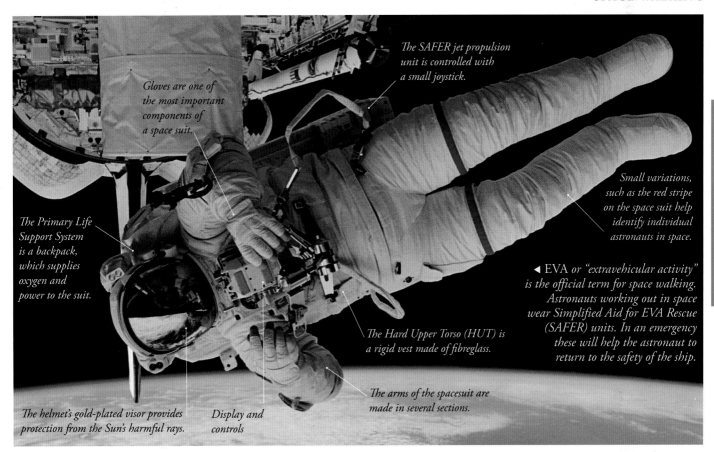

Gloves are one of the most important components of a space suit.

The SAFER jet propulsion unit is controlled with a small joystick.

The Primary Life Support System is a backpack, which supplies oxygen and power to the suit.

Small variations, such as the red stripe on the space suit help identify individual astronauts in space.

◀ EVA or "extravehicular activity" is the official term for space walking. Astronauts working out in space wear Simplified Aid for EVA Rescue (SAFER) units. In an emergency these will help the astronaut to return to the safety of the ship.

The Hard Upper Torso (HUT) is a rigid vest made of fibreglass.

The arms of the spacesuit are made in several sections.

The helmet's gold-plated visor provides protection from the Sun's harmful rays.

Display and controls

Flying free

One of the greatest threats to space walkers is the possibility that they will accidentally drift away from the spacecraft, unable to return. The result would be a long, slow death in the emptiness of space. Nearly all space walkers are carefully tethered to the spacecraft, although special "flying armchairs" or jet packs are sometimes used, which allow astronauts to fly freely.

▶ SPACE ARMCHAIR
The Manned Manoeuvring Unit (MMU), was used on three NASA missions in 1984.

Repair and construction

Crews working in space rely on handholds fitted on the outside of the spacecraft to move around. They may also be lifted to worksites by a robotic crane operated by another astronaut from inside the shuttle or space station. Lights on the spacesuit helmets allow astronauts to work in the dark.

▶ HUBBLE TROUBLE
Astronaut Kathryn C. Thornton making essential repairs to the faulty Hubble Space Telescope in 1993 (👁 p28–29).

Satellite recovery

In 1984 Manned Manoeuvring Units (MMUs) were used to retrieve two faulty satellites that had become stuck in the wrong orbits. Astronauts Joe Allen and Dale Gardner performed an EVA, using the MMUs to reach the satellites and drag them back to the shuttle. The satellites were then returned to Earth for repairs. This was the last mission to use the MMU, which was retired by NASA soon after due to fears over its safety.

▲ ON APPROACH *Dale Gardner moving towards satellite Westar VI.*

▲ MANOEUVERS *Gardner and Allen guiding Westar to the shuttle.*

Living in space

Sending people into space means providing the right conditions for them to live in. Between three and six people live on the International Space Station (ISS) at a time, usually staying for up to six months. The ISS is fitted with everything that the crew needs to make their mission comfortable and successful.

▲ WINDOW WATCHING *One of the most popular pastimes on the ISS is looking out of the window at Earth speeding past.*

LEISURE TIME

When they are not busy working, astronauts on the ISS have many ways of relaxing. This includes spending time communicating with Earth, by video-link, radio, or email. As well as chatting to friends and family, the crew speak with amateur radio enthusiasts and schools as they fly overhead.

▶ PLAY TIME *Many astronauts like to read, listen to music, watch DVDs, or play board games. Some play musical instruments – a keyboard, guitar, and even a trumpet have been played in orbit.*

Keeping clean

The ISS crew cannot wash their hands under a tap, like on Earth. Water does not flow in zero gravity, so there are no sinks or showers inside the station. When the astronauts want to get clean, they wipe themselves with alcohol or a wet towel containing liquid soap. Astronauts take sponge baths daily, using two cloths – one for washing and one for rinsing. They use rinseless shampoo, and usually swallow their toothpaste after brushing their teeth.

▲ SITTING COMFORTABLY *Astronauts strap themselves onto toilets that use suction to remove waste. On early missions, astronauts collected their waste in hoses and plastic bags.*

TAKE A LOOK: DOWN AT THE GYM

The human body loses muscle and bone in weightlessness, so to keep their muscles in shape, astronauts on board the ISS go to the gym twice a day for an hour-long session of exercise. This ensures the astronauts do not collapse when they return to normal gravity. There are different exercise machines on the ISS, including a floating treadmill, exercise bikes, and an apparatus for "lifting" weights. The astronauts have to strap themselves onto the machines so they don't float away. The latest equipment enables the crew to perform resistance exercises (such as bench presses, sit-ups, and squats) despite the station's zero-gravity environment.

▶ SPACE SNUFFLES
In space the human body's circulatory (blood) system turns upside down. Without gravity tugging the body's fluids downwards, blood pressure is equal all over the body, so blood builds up in the head and causes swelling. Exercise helps relieve these "space snuffles".

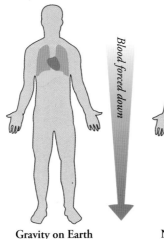

Blood forced down

Blood spreads around body

Gravity on Earth   **No gravity in space**

Sleep sweet sleep
Astronauts are happy sleeping almost anywhere – floor, wall, or ceiling – but they need to be near a ventilator fan. Without airflow, the carbon dioxide they breathe out will build up around them, leaving them gasping for oxygen.

Is it bedtime yet?
With 16 sunrises and sunsets a day on the ISS and the space shuttle, it's not easy to work out when it is time to sleep. Work schedules and sleep periods are based on the time at the mission control centre, in Houston, Texas.

FOOD AND DRINK

■ The first astronauts had to eat bite-sized cubes, freeze-dried powders, and pastes that were squeezed straight from a tube into the mouth!

■ Today, the ISS menu includes more than 100 different meals, plus snacks, and hot and cold drinks. A lot of the food is freeze-dried and water must be added before it can be eaten. All food is processed so that it does not have to be stored in a fridge.

▲ FOOD TUBE *The first space meals were soft, gloopy foods a lot like baby food.*

◀ A SOLID MEAL
Solid food can be eaten with a knife and fork, which are held down by magnets to stop them floating away from the table.

1 *Cheese spread*
2 *Shortbread cookies*
3 *Creamed spinach*
4 *Sugar-coated peanuts*
5 *Crackers*
6 *Beef steak*

Animals *in space*

Long before the first person set foot in space, scientists sent animals into orbit to see how they would cope with effects such as zero gravity. If animals could survive the journey into space, then maybe people could too.

SPACE DOGS TAKE THE LEAD

Can canine success pave the way for manned flight?

▲ DOG DAYS *In 1960, Strelka and Belka (left) became the first animals in orbit to return to Earth alive. In 1966, Veterok and Ugolyok (above) spent 22 days in space. Their record stood until 1973.*

Laika the cosmonaut

Laika was the first animal ever to be sent into orbit. Scientists believed that dogs would be good candidates for space flight because they can sit for long periods of time. Unfortunately, Laika did not survive, dying about 5 hours into the trip.

▲ LAIKA *A stray off the streets of Moscow, Laika was quickly trained and sent into orbit in Sputnik II in November 1957. It was a major achievement for the Russians in the space race against the USA.*

Champion chimps

Chimpanzees are our nearest animal relatives, so it made sense to send some into space as a trial run ahead of humans. Many were trained and, in 1961, Ham was chosen as the first chimp to go into space. Although the capsule lost some air pressure during the flight, Ham's space suit protected him. The only thing he suffered from the 16-minute flight was a bruised nose.

TIMELINE OF SPACE ANIMALS

1940s

1947
Fruit flies were sent on a suborbital flight on a US V-2 rocket.

1948–1950
Five US suborbital flights carried three monkeys and two mice to altitudes of 130 km (80 miles). The mice survived.

1950s

1951
On 20 September, Yorick the monkey and 11 mice were sent to an altitude of 72 km (44 miles) on a US Aerobee rocket. Yorick was the first monkey to survive a flight to the edge of space.

1957
Laika the dog became the first animal to be sent into orbit.

1959
Able, a rhesus monkey, and Miss Baker, a squirrel monkey, become the first living beings to successfully return to Earth after travelling in space on a suborbital flight.

Monkey business

There are obvious problems when sending animals into space. How do they feed themselves? How can their behaviour be controlled? Monkeys on the Cosmos missions were strapped into seats for their own protection. They had been trained to bite on tubes to release food and drink, and also to press levers when a light shone, which kept them mentally alert.

◀ ANIMAL CARRIER
In 1983, the Cosmos 1514 mission took two monkeys and 10 pregnant rats into orbit. The trip lasted five days.

TAKE A LOOK: EGGS

There have been a number of experiments on eggs in space. Quail eggs fertilized on Earth and incubated on the Mir Space Station in 1990 did hatch, although there were not as many as would have hatched on Earth.

▶ SPACE CHICKS *Unfortunately, the quails that hatched on Mir did not survive very long.*

Mission TARDIS

These creatures are tardigrades, tough invertebrates that seem almost indestructible on Earth. But how would they fare in space? Mission TARDIS, a European Space Agency experiment, showed them to be the first animals to survive the weightlessness and coldness of space. They not only survived being frozen, but could also cope with UV light 1,000 times stronger than on Earth.

Weightless webs

On Earth, a spider uses wind and gravity to construct its web. So how would a spider spin a web in space, where there is neither of these? Two spiders, called Anita and Arabella, were sent into space on board the 1973 Skylab 3 mission to find out. Once they got used to being weightless, they were soon spinning near-perfect webs.

Spiders use their weight to work out the thickness of the web silk.

The experiment was designed by an American schoolgirl called Judith Miles.

Scientists used the information from this experiment to find out more about how a spider's central nervous system works.

1960s		1970s	1990s	2000s	
1960 Dogs Strelka and Belka's day trip into space ended with a safe return to Earth by parachute.	**1961** Ham became the first chimp in space.	**1973** Arabella and Anita, common cross spiders, taken up by Skylab 3.	**1990** Journalist Toyohiro Akiyama took some Japanese tree frogs to the Mir Space Station.	**2008** ESA's Mission TARDIS sends tardigrades 270 km (167 miles) into space.	**2009** 4,000 roundworms blasted off on space shuttle Atlantis in 2009. They were in space for 11 days.

101

EXTENDING THE HOUSE

Imagine having to make building repairs to your home – while hovering in low Earth orbit 340 km (210 miles) above New Zealand! Tethered by the thinnest of wires, two astronauts go out on a space walk to attach a new truss segment to the International Space Station.

The first space *stations*

If astronauts want to live and work in orbit for months, or even years, a spacecraft such as the shuttle is not practical. They need a much larger structure, known as a space station.

◄ SALYUT 1 *was powered by solar panels and completed 2,800 orbits of Earth.*

SALYUT 1

The world's first space station was the Soviet Union's Salyut 1, launched in 1971. The largest of its three sections was the service module, which housed the fuel, oxygen, and water tanks with the main engine at the rear. The central section was the work and living area. At the front was the docking section. A three-man crew lived in the station for 22 days, but after that Salyut 1 remained unoccupied and was lowered from orbit later that year.

►► FAST FACTS ►►

■ The name Salyut (salute) was a tribute to Yuri Gagarin, the first man in space, who had died in 1968.
■ Two Salyut stations (3 and 5) were used to spy on Western rivals. An onboard camera took detailed pictures of Earth's surface and the film was returned to Earth in a special capsule.
■ Salyut 3 carried a machine gun, in case of attack by other spacecraft. It was modified to work in the vacuum of space.

SCI-FI STATIONS

The first story about a space station, called "Brick Moon", was published in a magazine in 1869. By the early 20th century, wheel-shaped space stations were in fashion in science fiction. In reality, all the space stations so far built have been made of modules that are launched separately, then joined together when they are in orbit. The size and weight limitations of rockets have meant that stations have to be built like giant building blocks, one piece at a time.

▲ IN THE STORY, *the brick moon was accidentally launched with people on board.*

▲ THE WHEEL-SHAPED STATION *was made famous when it appeared in the 1968 film* 2001: A Space Odyssey. *Space scientists did seriously consider wheel-shaped stations in the 1950s.*

Skylab crashed to Earth in 1979

Skylab

Skylab was the USA's first space station and the largest spacecraft ever placed in Earth orbit. It was in use from 1973 to 1974. Skylab lost one of its two main solar panels when it was damaged during launch. But three crews were able to visit, with missions lasting 28, 59, and 84 days. They performed astronomy experiments, X-ray studies of the Sun, remote sensing of Earth, and medical studies.

MIR

This was the successor to the Russian Salyut series of space stations. The first module was launched in 1986 and was soon occupied by two crew members. Six more modules were added over the next 10 years, including a docking module for use by the space shuttle.

Experiments operation area

Kitchen and eating area

Waste management area

Sleep compartment

▲ SKYLAB WORKSHOP *This was the largest section of the space station. It contained the crew quarters, including a toilet, shower, and galley (kitchen), along with the laboratory facilities and a large waste disposal tank.*

► MIR IN ORBIT *The crew's quarters were in the base module. A service section contained the main engine and thrusters, while a third section housed five docking ports. In all, 31 crewed spacecraft and 64 cargo ships docked with Mir.*

Mir

Near disaster
In 1997, Mir suffered a serious fire. Four months later, an incoming Progress ship collided with the station, damaging the Spektr module and allowing air to leak into space. Luckily, the crew managed to close Spektr's hatch before they were forced to abandon the station and head for home.

The International *Space Station*

The International Space Station (ISS) is the largest and most expensive spacecraft ever built. Sixteen countries have worked together to construct and operate the station and, for at least the next five to ten years, it will be a permanent home to six astronauts.

ISS final layout

- **Width (truss):** 109 m (356 ft)
- **Length (modules):** 88 m (290 ft)
- **Weight:** 419,600 kg (925,000 lbs)
- **Operating altitude:** 385 km (240 miles) above Earth's surface
- **Orbiting speed:** 8 km (5 miles) per second
- **Atmospheric pressure inside:** 1013 millibars (14.7 psi) – the same as on Earth.
- **Pressurized area:** 935 m³ (33,000 cubic ft). This is about the same as a five bedroom house.
- **Crew size:** Three to six people

First launches

At the core of the ISS are the Russian-built Zvezda and Zarya modules. Zarya was the first module to be launched into orbit, in 1998. It is now used mainly for storage and propulsion. The main living quarters were added in July 2000. America's Destiny, the first science lab, arrived in February 2001.

SOLAR POWER

The largest feature of the ISS is its eight pairs of solar panels. Each panel measures 73 m (240 ft) – longer than the wingspan of a Boeing 777 aircraft. The panels produce electricity from sunlight and can be turned so that they receive as much light as possible. They contain more than 262,000 solar cells, producing a maximum 110 kW of power.

Working in the laboratory

Every day, ISS crews carry out science experiments in the labs. Hundreds of scientists on the ground also take part. These experiments cover many fields, including human biology, medical research, physical sciences, and Earth observation. Research topics range from growing protein crystals to making new metal alloys.

Robotic arms

The ISS has two robotic arms that are used to lift astronauts and pieces of equipment outside in space. The arms are controlled by astronauts inside the station. The main arm is called Canadarm 2, because it was built in Canada. It is 16.7 m (55 ft) long and can handle objects weighing up to 116 tonnes (128 tons) – the weight of the shuttle. The arm has seven joints and four hand-like grapple fixtures.

Zvezda

Zarya

Canadarm 2

Solar panels

Canadarm 2

Kibo

Truss

Kibo

The Japanese Experiment Module, or Kibo (right), is a laboratory that was delivered in sections on three shuttle flights during 2009. The main Kibo lab is used by astronauts for zero-gravity experiments. An additional, unpressurized room is used for storage and Kibo has its own robotic arm. Experiments can also take place on a platform outside Kibo. Astronauts reach this by exiting through an airlock and space walking to the platform.

Fresh supplies

Supplies of food, water, and equipment are brought to the ISS by various spacecraft. In addition to the shuttle, crews look forward to regular visits from Russian Progress craft. Other types of unmanned supply ships have also been introduced in recent years. The first European Automated Transfer Vehicle (ATV) docked with the ISS in April 2008, while Japan's H-II Transfer Vehicle (HTV, right) approaches the station and is then docked using one of the robotic arms. All of the supply craft except the shuttle burn up during re-entry.

Science in *space*

The zero-gravity conditions of space offer a special environment for scientific research. Short periods of weightlessness can be created inside very tall drop towers or on aircraft flying high above Earth. However, the only way to experience weeks or months of weightlessness is on board a space station.

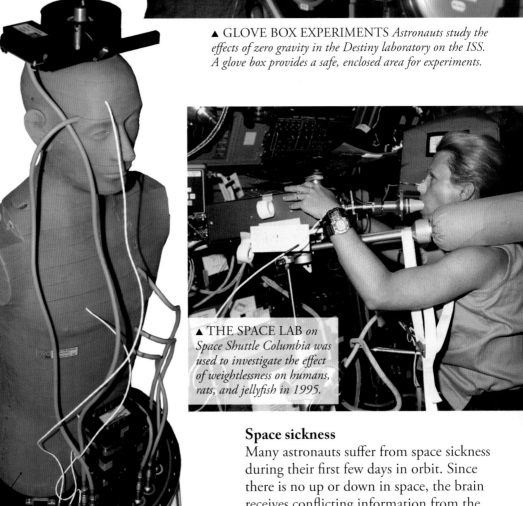

▲ GLOVE BOX EXPERIMENTS *Astronauts study the effects of zero gravity in the Destiny laboratory on the ISS. A glove box provides a safe, enclosed area for experiments.*

▶ MATROSHKA *is a dummy used by the European Space Agency to study the effects of radiation upon humans in space. Matroshka contains radiation sensors, samples of bone and blood, and man-made materials very like human tissues and organs.*

IMPROVING HEALTH

Without any gravity to push against, human muscles and bones become very weak. Astronauts on the International Space Station test ways of preventing damage to muscles and bones. This includes use of exercise machines, drugs, and small electric shocks.

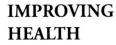

Matroshka is named after the famous Matryoshka Russian dolls because it is made of so many layers.

▲ THE SPACE LAB *on Space Shuttle Columbia was used to investigate the effect of weightlessness on humans, rats, and jellyfish in 1995.*

Space sickness

Many astronauts suffer from space sickness during their first few days in orbit. Since there is no up or down in space, the brain receives conflicting information from the eyes, muscles, skin, and balance organs. Numerous experiments have been done to study how the human brain deals with these signals and how it adapts to weightless conditions.

LIFE IN SPACE

Experiments with many different forms of life have been conducted in space, ranging from spiders and fruit flies to tomatoes, fish, and quail. Harmful bacteria seem to thrive in zero gravity, while the human ability to fight infections becomes weaker. It is impossible to sterilize spacecraft completely, so the spread of bacteria could be very dangerous for astronauts on long missions.

Crystals

Crystals grown in space are much bigger and have fewer flaws than those on Earth. Scientists are especially interested in studying protein crystals in space. There are more than 300,000 proteins in the human body and yet very little is known about most of them. Producing protein crystals of high quality can help us to work out their shape and structure – and learn about how they work in the body.

Studying protein crystals can help us develop medicines to treat diseases such as HIV and cancer.

These protein crystals were grown in space.

PLANTS IN SPACE

Plants were first sent into space on board the Sputnik 4 satellite in 1960. Since then, scientists have been investigating how plants grow in space and looking at ways of growing lots of high-quality plants in a small area. This is important research for future space missions, on which astronauts might have to grow their own food, and also for growing crops on Earth.

▶ PLANTS IN SPACE *are grown aeroponically – in air instead of soil.*

Flames, liquids, and metals in space

Convection is the process by which hot liquids and gases on Earth rise, and cool liquids and gases sink. Because convection can't operate in zero gravity, flames in space burn with a rounded shape rather than in the upwards-pointing tapers seen on Earth. Liquids that would separate into layers of different densities on Earth also behave differently in zero gravity and mix very easily. Metals in liquid form can be mixed in space to form super-strong alloys that are much stronger than those made on Earth.

▲ EARTH FLAME
Flames on Earth point upwards because heated air, which is less dense than the surrounding cooler air, rises up.

◀ SPACE FLAME
In zero gravity, convection has no effect so flames burn with a rounded flame.

TAKE A LOOK: SPIN-OFFS

The transfer of technology from space use to everyday use is called a "spin-off". A lot of the science from space has found a use here on Earth.

■ **Golf-ball aerodynamics**
NASA technology was used to design a golf ball that would fly faster and farther when struck.

■ **Shock-absorbing helmet**
Protective helmets use a shock-absorbing padding first developed by NASA for use in aircraft seats.

■ **Fogless ski goggles**
A NASA-developed coating is applied to goggles, deep-sea diving masks, and fire-protection helmets to prevent them fogging up.

■ **Quartz crystal**
NASA developed highly accurate clocks and watches using quartz crystal.

Space *tourism*

Nowadays, not everyone who goes into space is a professional astronaut. Scientists, various politicians, a Japanese journalist, two US teachers, and several businessmen have all flown. As space tourism becomes a reality, companies are springing up, offering to fly people on suborbital hops from new spaceports.

SPACESHIPONE

The race to build new types of spacecraft for tourists was boosted by a $10 million prize in 2004 from the X Prize Foundation. It was offered to the first company to build a spaceship that flew above 100 km (62 miles) twice within two weeks.

White Knight launcher

SpaceShipOne

▲ THE PRIZE *was won by SpaceShipOne, a three-seat research rocket built like an aircraft.*

Holiday of a lifetime

Got a spare $20–35 million? Fancy a trip to space? That's the price that the Russian Space Agency is asking for a flight aboard a Soyuz spacecraft and a week-long stay on the International Space Station (ISS).

▲ THE COCKPIT *of SpaceShipOne.*

▲ ONCE RELEASED *from the White Knight launcher, SpaceShipOne flew for 24 minutes.*

SpaceShipTwo

A much larger, more advanced version of SpaceShipOne is being developed for suborbital tourist flights. Known as SpaceShipTwo, it will be flown to a height of 15 km (9½ miles) by White Knight Two, a strange-looking launch aircraft with a wingspan of 43 m (140 ft). SpaceShipTwo will then be released and use its own rocket motor to reach a height of 110 km (68 miles). SpaceShipTwo will then glide back to the runway.

SpaceShipTwo release

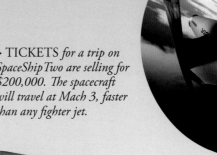

▶ TICKETS *for a trip on SpaceShipTwo are selling for $200,000. The spacecraft will travel at Mach 3, faster than any fighter jet.*

◀ THE CABIN *is 18 m (60 ft) long and 2.3 m (7½ ft) in diameter. It will carry six passengers and two pilots. Each passenger will sit by a large window and will be able to float freely for about four minutes before returning to Earth.*

FIRST TOURIST

- The first person to pay for a flight into space was 60-year-old American Dennis Tito. The millionaire businessman went through a training programme at Russia's Star City.
- He flew on a Soyuz spacecraft to the ISS, arriving on 30 April 2001. He spent six days on the station, before returning to Earth in another Soyuz.
- While in space, Dennis Tito listened to opera, shot video and photos through the porthole, helped to prepare the meals, and spent time admiring the view as the space station swept around the planet once every 90 minutes.

Space hotels

Once cheaper ways of flying to space have been developed, space hotels are likely to be the next step. Ordinary people will then be able to orbit Earth and experience the wonders of weightlessness. Detailed plans have already been put forward for large inflatable modules in which people can stay. Once the first of these is launched, it can be joined by a propulsion unit and a docking module, enabling more inflatable sections to be added.

▲ THIS SPACE HOTEL *may seem revolutionary, but the rotating design was suggested over 40 years ago by science-fiction writer Arthur C. Clarke.*

▲ AN ARTIST'S *impression of a plan by US company Bigelow Aerospace for inflatable modules that connect to create a space station.*

Future *flyers*

Launchers have changed very little since the beginning of the space age, more than 50 years ago – they still involve rockets and large amounts of heavy fuel. Space agencies are now trying to develop cheaper, reusable vehicles, but these would require new technologies, such as air-breathing engines.

One day, spacecraft may be able to reach orbit on a space elevator. Various designs have been proposed, usually involving a cable structure. This would stretch from the surface to geostationary orbit, with a counterweight at the upper end. Earth's rotation would keep the cable taut, so that a car or cabin could climb up the cable. Making this type of cable would require new materials that are light but strong.

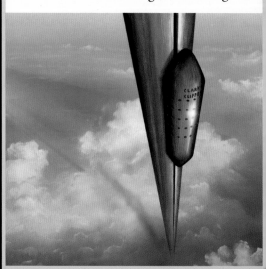

▼ SKYLON *This unpiloted, reusable spaceplane is being developed in the UK. It will carry engines that breathe air in Earth's atmosphere and then switch to more normal rocket engines in space.*

SPACEPLANES

This type of reusable vehicle is already being developed. A spaceplane has its own rocket engines and could one day carry people or cargo into orbit. It would take off from a runway, or be carried to high altitude by an aircraft before being released. At the end of the mission, it would land on a runway, like an aircraft.

Private enterprise

Until now, almost all spacecraft that deliver cargo or crews to space have been developed by space agencies. However, this may soon change. NASA is supporting private companies to build spacecraft that could carry supplies to the International Space Station. These will be launched on rockets also provided by private companies. The Dragon spacecraft (seen here) will initially be used to deliver 6 tonnes (6.6 tons) of cargo. It may later be able to carry crew, or be a free-flying laboratory.

Space station

The Dragon will deliver supplies and other cargo

Space tether

Space tethers

A space tether is a long cable that is used to connect a spacecraft to something else. This could be another spacecraft, a spent booster rocket, or a space station. Tethers are made of thin strands of high-strength fibres or wires and can be used to move objects through space without consuming fuel. This is done by the transfer of energy and motion from one object to the other.

Air-breathing launchers

Several countries are studying air-breathing engines, which would reduce the amount of liquid oxygen fuel that has to be carried. This type of launcher would be boosted to high speed by a normal jet engine or booster rocket. The engine, which has no moving parts, compresses air as it passes through, mixes it with fuel, and then ignites it.

TAKE A LOOK: POWER FROM SPACE

We are using more and more energy. With the threat of global warming, caused by the build-up of greenhouse gases, clean, renewable power will become increasingly important. One idea that is being studied is to get power from space, using large solar panels flying in Earth orbit. The energy they generate could be beamed to the ground using lasers or microwaves, and collected by gigantic dish antennas, likely to be located in restricted areas at sea. The first Japanese test of space power could take place by 2030.

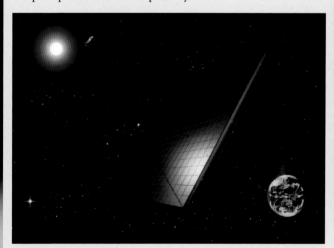

▲ GIANT SOLAR PANELS *orbiting above the equator could capture sunlight 24 hours a day and beam the energy to Earth.*

NASA

X-43

NASA's experimental Hyper-X air-breathing vehicle

Reaching *for the stars*

So far in the history of human space travel, 12 people have walked on the Moon and many more have lived aboard the International Space Station. One day we may set foot on Mars, and perhaps even settle on a planet in orbit around another star. But to do this, we have to overcome many challenges, including surviving the journey there.

A LONG JOURNEY

One of the main challenges of a manned mission to Mars is the six months it will take to reach the planet, followed by a long stay, then the return trip. The crew of up to six people will be shut in a confined space, far from home. Messages will take up to 20 minutes to reach Earth, with the same delay for replies. They will have to learn to live together and deal with problems with little help from Earth.

ALONE WITH ALGAE

In the 1970s, the Russian BIOS 3 buildings in Siberia were used to test how people would cope with isolated living. Chlorella algae were grown indoors to recycle the air and make sure that the people living in the buildings didn't suffocate.

Chlorella algae

Living in isolation

A number of experiments have been carried out to see how people cope with isolation and cramped space. In the early 1990s, eight people were shut inside an artificial Earth during the Biosphere 2 project. The project lasted two years, and the biggest issues they faced were problems with the air system, and arguments in the group.

📷 WATCH THIS SPACE

Biosphere 2 was built in Arizona, USA. Different areas inside were built to mimic different environments on Earth. The view above is the ocean biome. Other biomes included grassland, rainforest, and desert.

*Another possibility
is that the crew is
put into hibernation
and sleeps through
the journey.*

The generation game
Voyages to the stars will probably take
many thousands of years. Unless some way can be
found to shorten the journey, the people who leave
Earth will never live long enough to arrive at another star
system. If whole families travelled, perhaps future generations
could reach the goal, but with nowhere to stop off along the
way, they would have to take all their supplies with them.

*Often used in science-fiction
films, human hibernation has
yet to be achieved in real life.*

SPACE FARMING

'Yecora Rojo'
83 days old

Every three months, a cargo ship
delivers a supply of food to the crew
on the space station. These supplies
are bulky, heavy, very expensive to
deliver – and impossible to provide
for a crew heading to Mars. A crew of
six people would need 33,000 tonnes
(37,000 tons) of food, water, and
oxygen for a three-year return trip.
The answer is for astronauts to grow
their own food. Experiments to grow
plants from seed have already taken
place in small space greenhouses.

FICTION AND REALITY

Unlike real life, it's quick and easy to cross
our galaxy in science-fiction stories and
films. The USS Enterprise in Star Trek dives
down "wormholes" – tunnels in space that
cut out huge chunks of travel time. It also
has warp drive to travel faster than light.
Unfortunately, wormholes have yet to be
proved to exist, and the laws of physics
state that it's impossible to travel faster
than the speed of light.

*The USS Enterprise takes shortcuts through
wormholes, but there's no proof they really exist.*

RECYCLING
Scientists try to find ways to recycle as much waste as
possible on spacecraft. There are already
machines that purify urine for
drinking and washing.
Oxygen for breathing can
be made by splitting
water atoms. Systems
are also being
developed that use
bacteria to recycle
human waste for use
in growing food and
producing water.

SOLAR
SYSTEM

Our solar system is the region of space that falls under the influence of the Sun's gravity. It extends two light years into space, and contains planets, moons, asteroids, and comets.

Birth of the *solar system*

Everything in the solar system – the Sun, planets, moons, and smaller objects – was born inside a vast, spinning cloud. The story began about five billion years ago, with a giant cloud made of dust and hydrogen gas. The cloud began to shrink and contract. Eventually our Sun formed in the centre of the cloud, where it was denser and hotter. The rest of the cloud formed a swirling disc called the solar nebula.

◄ SHOCK REACTION
No one knows why the cloud began to shrink, but it may have been triggered by a shock wave from a star that exploded as a supernova.

THE SOLAR NEBULA

Within the solar nebula, dust and ice particles were colliding and merging. Through this process the tiny particles grew into larger bodies a few kilometres across. In the inner, hotter part of the solar nebula, these building blocks (called planetesimals) were mostly made of rock and metals. Further from the centre, where the nebula was much colder, they were mainly made of water ice.

COLLISIONS AND MERGERS

As the planetesimals grew bigger, their gravity pulled more material towards them, which led to more collisions. Eventually, regions of the nebula were dominated by a few large bodies. In the outer solar system, these objects attracted huge amounts of gas. This led to the formation of the planets known as gas giants – Jupiter, Saturn, Uranus, and Neptune.

TAKE A LOOK: THE BIRTH OF THE MOON

Most scientists think that the Moon was born during a collision between a Mars-sized object and the young Earth. It may have taken only a few hundred years from the time of collision until the formation of the Moon. At first the Moon was much closer to Earth than it is now, orbiting once every few days. Now it takes just over 27 days to complete one orbit.

▲ COLLISION COURSE *A large object, the same size as the planet Mars, collided with Earth.*

▲ CRACKING UP *The impact vaporized and melted parts of Earth and the object, throwing debris into space.*

▲ ALL IN ORDER *The debris from the collision formed a ring around Earth.*

▲ NEW MOON *Material within the ring eventually combined to form our Moon.*

OTHER PLANETARY SYSTEMS

Planetary systems are now thought to be very common. Most young stars in our galaxy are surrounded by discs of dust and hydrogen gas – just like the young Sun. By studying these stellar discs, scientists can learn a lot about the early history of the solar system. Well over 400 planets have been found in orbit around distant stars. At present, nearly all of the discoveries have been large, Jupiter-type planets. However, as instruments become more powerful, millions of planets the size of Earth are expected to be found (p226–227).

This artist's impression shows a possible moon orbiting a planet outside of our solar system.

The planet has about the same mass as Jupiter, and orbits the star Tau1 Gruis.

▲ HEAVY BOMBARDMENT *After the planets had formed, there was still a lot of material left over. Most of the fine material was blown away by a strong solar wind. Larger rocks continued to collide with Earth and the other planets until about four billion years ago.*

The Sun's *family*

The Sun rules over a vast area of space. Its gravity, radiation, and magnetic influence extend outwards for billions of kilometres. Within this solar system are eight planets, five dwarf planets, about 170 moons, millions of asteroids, and billions of comets.

MERCURY *The closest planet to the Sun has changed little in billions of years. It is a small, heavily cratered world with no atmosphere and no moons. Its year lasts 88 Earth days.*

PLUTO *Discovered by Clyde Tombaugh in 1930, Pluto was once known as the ninth planet from the Sun, but it is now classified as a dwarf planet.*

MARS *The fourth planet from the Sun has many craters as well as volcanoes, rift valleys, and winding canyons. It also has two moons. Its year lasts 687 Earth days.*

URANUS *Discovered by William Herschel in 1781. The seventh planet from the Sun has a dark ring system and 27 moons. Its year lasts 84 Earth years.*

JUPITER *The fifth planet from the Sun is also the largest. It has thin rings, 63 moons, and a cloud feature called the Great Red Spot. Its year lasts almost 12 Earth years.*

Sun · Mercury · Venus · Earth · Mars · *Asteroid belt* · Jupiter · Saturn · Uranus

0 · *Distance from the Sun, in millions of km* · 250 · 1,000 · 1,500 · 2,000 · 2,500

Inner planets
The four inner planets (Mercury, Venus, Earth, and Mars), asteroids, and many of the moons are made of rock. The rocky planets are much smaller than the gassy, outer planets. They also have fewer moons (some have none at all), and no rings.

ORBITAL PATHS
Most of the planets, moons, and asteroids travel in almost circular orbits in the same direction (west to east) around the Sun. Most orbits also lie close to the plane of Earth's orbit, called the ecliptic. So if you looked at the solar system side-on, you would see most of the orbits are roughly on the same level. Mercury's and Pluto's orbits are not – they orbit at an angle.

Orbits and rotations

An orbital period is the time it takes one object to travel around another in a complete circuit. The orbital period of a planet around the Sun is also the length of its year. The rotational period of a planet is how long it takes to make a complete turn on its axis. This is its day.

ASTEROID BELT *Lying between Mars and Jupiter, the belt is around 180 million km (112 million miles) wide and contains thousands of asteroids.*

NEPTUNE *Discovered by Johann Galle in 1846. The eighth planet from the Sun has a thin ring system and 13 moons. Its year lasts almost 165 Earth years.*

VENUS *The second planet from the Sun is similar in size to Earth, but the air pressure is 90 times greater than on Earth. It has no moon. Its year lasts 224 Earth days.*

SATURN *The sixth planet from the Sun is the second largest, after Jupiter, but is light enough to float. It has 62 moons, and its year lasts 29.5 Earth years.*

EARTH *The third planet from the Sun is the largest of the four rocky planets and the only planet with liquid water. Its year lasts 365 days.*

COMET HALLEY

The order of the planets

If you find it tricky to remember the order of the eight planets of the solar system, try using this sentence to help you: **My Very Educated Mother Just Served Us Noodles.** (**M**ercury, **V**enus, **E**arth, **M**ars, **J**upiter, **S**aturn, **U**ranus, **N**eptune.)

Neptune

3,000   3,500   4,000   4,500

Outer planets

The four large outer planets (Jupiter, Saturn, Uranus, and Neptune) are known as gas giants. This is because they are made of gases, with a solid core of rock and ice. The furthest objects from the Sun, such as Pluto and the comets, are mostly made of ice.

DWARF PLANETS

A dwarf planet is like other planets – it revolves around the Sun and reflects the Sun's light. However, a planet clears all other objects from its orbit, whereas there are still lots of objects in a dwarf planet's orbit. There are five known dwarf planets – Pluto, Eris (the largest), Ceres (also the largest asteroid), Haumea, and Makemake. They are icy debris left over from the formation of the planets 4.5 billion years ago.

◄ PLUTO *The best-known of the dwarf planets, Pluto is a dark, icy world with three moons and no atmosphere. It is smaller than Mercury, and its year lasts 248 Earth years.*

Mercury

Mercury is the smallest planet. It is also the closest planet to the Sun, so we always see it near the Sun in the sky. This makes it very hard to see, except at sunrise or sunset, because it is hidden by the Sun's glare. Mercury has no moons and is too small to hold on to any atmosphere.

▲ WHAT A GAS *Mercury has no atmosphere, but tiny amounts of sodium and helium gas have been found floating above the surface.*

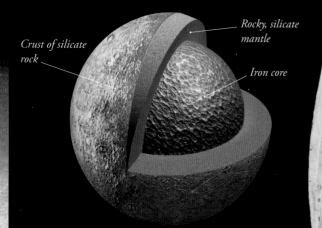

Crust of silicate rock

Rocky, silicate mantle

Iron core

TELL ME MORE...

Astronauts would find it easy to move around on Mercury as its surface gravity is quite low. A 50 kg (110 lb) astronaut would weigh 19 kg (42 lb).

A SMALL WORLD

Mercury is very small – about 18 Mercurys would fit inside Earth. But it is denser than any planet except Earth. This is because it seems to have a very large core of iron and nickel, covered by a rocky mantle and crust. Mercury's iron core produces a magnetic field that is 100 times weaker than Earth's. This may be because Mercury spins more slowly on its axis.

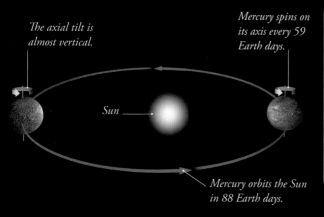

The axial tilt is almost vertical.

Mercury spins on its axis every 59 Earth days.

Sun

Mercury orbits the Sun in 88 Earth days.

PLANET PROFILE

- **Average distance from the Sun** 58 million km (36 million miles)
- **Surface temperature** –180°C to 430°C (–290°F to 800°F)
- **Diameter** 4,875 km (3,030 miles)
- **Length of day** 59 Earth days
- **Length of year** 88 Earth days
- **Number of moons** 0
- **Gravity at the surface (Earth = 1)** 0.38
- **Size comparison**

Meteors are constantly striking the Caloris Basin forming huge craters.

Shock waves travel through the core...

... and spread over the surface.

Shock waves meet and shatter the surface opposite the impact site.

Giant impact basins

Like the Moon, Mercury is covered with craters. These show that it has been battered by millions of impacts with asteroids and meteors since it formed. Some of these impacts blasted out huge hollows in the surface. The most famous of these is the circular Caloris Basin, which is about 1,300 km (800 miles) across. Its floor shows ridges and fractures, with mountains around the edge. The explosion that formed the Caloris Basin seems to have sent shock waves through the planet. These produced a large area of jumbled hills on the opposite side of Mercury.

◀ CHAOTIC TERRAIN *Land opposite the Caloris Basin shows the impact of shock waves, which have caused faultlines, small lines, and depressions.*

TAKE A LOOK: TRANSIT ACROSS THE SUN

Mercury is the closest planet to the Sun, although its orbit is more oval-shaped (elliptical) than circular, so it varies from 46 million km (28 million miles, or less than one-third Earth's distance) to 70 million km (44 million miles, or almost half Earth's distance). Sometimes Mercury passes exactly between the Earth and the Sun. We see the planet as a tiny dot moving slowly across the face of the huge Sun. This is known as a transit, and it can only happen in May or November. The next transit of Mercury will be on 9 May 2016.

▶ MERCURY'S JOURNEY *On the evening of 8 November 2006, Mercury moved across the Sun. It finished its journey just after midnight. The three tiny black dots show how small Mercury is compared to the Sun.*

The last contact was at 12:10 am.

The first contact was at 7:12 pm.

High-gain antenna

Mariner 10

Magnetometer

Charged-particle telescope

Television cameras

Solar panel

Spacecraft visitors

Until recently, only one spacecraft had visited Mercury. Between 1974 and 1975, Mariner 10 flew past the planet three times and sent back 12,000 pictures – but during each flyby it saw the same face of Mercury. Now a US spacecraft called Messenger has imaged almost all of the surface and will enter Mercury's orbit in March 2011.

The equatorial region nearest the Sun is the hottest area.

An astronaut would fry in the heat of the day.

There is no air to spread heat, so Mercury's night side is very cold.

Hot and cold spots

The sunlit side of Mercury gets very hot, especially close to the equator where the Sun is overhead and sunlight is most intense. The Caloris Basin lies in one of these hot spots – Caloris is Latin for "heat". Temperatures here can reach 430°C (800°F) – hot enough to melt lead. Despite the intense heat, there is evidence that water ice may exist at the bottom of deep craters near the planet's poles.

Venus

Venus is the most similar planet in the solar system to Earth. Although it is closer to the Sun, making it hotter than Earth, both planets are similar in size, mass, and composition. However, Venus has no water or life, and is covered with a very thick, suffocating atmosphere.

TELL ME MORE..

It's not just astronauts that wouldn't survive on Venus. The few spacecraft to land on the surface of the planet have only operated for an hour or two before being destroyed by the hostile conditions.

Silicate crust

Rocky mantle

Molten iron and nickel outer core

Solid iron and nickel inner core

▶ ROCKY TERRAIN
The highest mountains on Venus are the Maxwell Montes. They rise almost 12 km (7.5 miles) above the ground, and are taller than Mount Everest.

DON'T GO THERE!

Venus may be closer to Earth than any other planet, but you wouldn't want to go there. Thick clouds of sulphuric acid and a suffocating blanket of carbon dioxide gas trap the Sun's heat, turning it into a scorching oven. Astronauts visiting Venus would die from a combination of acid burns, roasting, crushing, and suffocation.

About 80 per cent of sunlight reflects away.

Thick clouds of sulphuric acid stop most of the sunlight reaching the surface.

Reflected light makes the cloud surface bright and easy to see.

Carbon dioxide in the atmosphere absorbs heat so it cannot escape.

Just 20 per cent of sunlight reaches the surface.

Cloud cover

The surface of Venus is hidden by a dense layer of pale yellow clouds. These are made of sulphur and sulphuric acid. Winds move the clouds around the planet from east to west at about 350 km/h (220 mph). This wind sweeps the clouds right around Venus in only four days.

PLANET PROFILE

- **Average distance from the Sun** 108 million km (67 million miles)
- **Cloud-top temperature** 460°C (865°F)
- **Diameter** 12,100 km (7,520 miles)
- **Length of day** 243 Earth days
- **Length of year** 224.7 Earth days
- **Number of moons** 0
- **Gravity at the surface (Earth = 1)** 0.91
- **Size comparison**

Spinning around

Venus spins very slowly clockwise, the opposite of most other planets. If you were standing on Venus, you would see the Sun go backwards across the sky, rising in the west and setting in the east. It takes 243 Earth days to rotate once, so its day is longer than its year (224.7 Earth days).

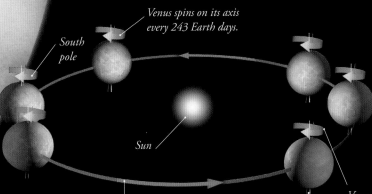

Venus spins on its axis every 243 Earth days.

South pole

Sun

It takes 224.7 Earth days to orbit the Sun.

The planet tilts by 177.4 degrees so the north pole is at the bottom of the globe.

Venus rotates clockwise.

📷 WATCH THIS SPACE

There are more than 1,600 volcanoes on Venus. Among the more unusual features are the pancake lava domes, each about 25 km (15 miles) across and 750 m (2,460 feet) high. They are probably small eruptions of very thick, sticky lava that flowed onto a flat plain and then cooled before it could flow very far.

🔍 TAKE A LOOK: THE SWIRLING SOUTH

The first ever image of Venus's south pole was taken by the European Space Agency's Venus Express in 2006. Taken from more than 200,000 km (124,000 miles) away from the planet, this shows the "night side" of Venus (the hemisphere that is away from the Sun). It was taken by a VIRTIS spectrometer, which uses heat as well as light to make images. False colour added to the picture shows clouds swirling around the south pole.

The darker the red, the thicker the clouds.

Brighter red shows thinner cloud, where heat has escaped and been picked up by VIRTIS.

There is a double vortex over the south pole. This is the centre of the spinning clouds.

▶ VENERA ON VENUS *Venera 13 and 14 carried soil samplers to test the surface of Venus.*

Touchdown

In March 1982, the Venera 13 and 14 landers sent back the only colour pictures we have from the surface. They showed an orange sky and a desert covered in rocks of different sizes. Many of these were flat, suggesting thin layers of lava. At least 85 per cent of the surface of Venus is covered in volcanic rock.

Views of Venus

As our closest neighbour, Venus is an obvious place to send space probes. The first successful landing was in 1970 – all the earlier probes were destroyed by the extreme heat and pressure. Since 1978, orbiters have used radar to peer through the thick cloud and reveal the surface.

VENUSIAN VOLCANOES

The most noticeable features on the surface of Venus are its volcanoes, of which there are at least 1,600. The tallest is Maat Mons (the peak at the back of the landscape below), about 5 km (3 miles) high. Its lava flows stretch for hundreds of kilometres across the surrounding plains.

▲ COMPUTER DESIGN *This computer-created image of Maat Mons is based on radar data from the Magellan orbiter. Colours are based on images returned by the Venera 13 and 14 landers.*

It's thought that Maat Mons is not currently active, but no one knows for sure.

▲ DOUBLE SUMMIT *The Magellan spacecraft used radar to get this image looking straight down on Sapas Mons. The two dark spots are its mesas (flat tops).*

Sapas Mons

This landscape is the Atla Regio, a region in the northern hemisphere of Venus that was probably formed by large amounts of molten rock rising up from inside the planet. The bright area to the front is Sapas Mons, a shield-shaped volcano 217 km (135 miles) across that gently rises to a height of 1.6 km (1 mile) above the surrounding terrain.

▶ LINE UP *The Ovda Regio area of Aphrodite Terra is crossed by long, narrow ridges. The dark patches may be lava or wind-blown dust.*

Aphrodite Terra

Just as there are mountains and plains on Earth, Venus has highlands and lowlands too. The largest highland region is Aphrodite Terra, in the equatorial area of Venus. The size of a continent on Earth, it runs two-thirds of the way around Venus, and is divided into two main regions: the western Ovda Regio, and the eastern Thetis Regio.

Pioneer Venus

NASA's Pioneer Venus mission was made up of two different spacecraft. The orbiter, launched in 1978, was the first spacecraft to use radar to map the surface. It burned up after 14 years. Pioneer Venus 2 carried four probes to collect atmospheric data.

Magellan

Launched in May 1989, NASA's Magellan spacecraft arrived at Venus in August 1990. It spent more than four years in orbit and produced the most detailed radar map of the planet's surface. It was deliberately burned up in Venus's atmosphere in 1994.

▼ THREE CRATERS *Magellan found this trio of craters in the Lavinia Planitia region of Venus. The distance between them is no more than 500 km (340 miles).*

▲ CRATER CREATOR *Combining radar data from Magellan and colour images from Venera 13 and 14, we can see how Howe Crater appears on Venus. It is 37 km (23 miles) wide.*

Impact craters

Compared with other planets, Venus doesn't appear to have many impact craters. This might be because many meteorites burn up in the thick atmosphere before they reach the surface and create an impact crater. Another idea is that the surface of Venus is too young to have had many collisions with large meteorites. Most of the craters on the planet are less than 500 million years old.

📷 WATCH THIS SPACE

Maxwell Montes are the highest mountains on Venus, rising over 10 km (6 miles). The colour suggests that the rock is rich in iron.

Venus Express

Europe's first mission to Venus was launched in November 2005, arriving at Venus in April 2006. As it flies over the polar regions, it is able to study the cloud layers and atmosphere in great detail. A special camera has made the first infrared map of the surface.

127

Mars

After Earth, Mars is the most suitable planet for humans to live on. Its day is only a little over 24 hours long, and it has Earth-like seasons. Mars was named after the Roman god of war because of its blood-red colour, which is caused by rusty iron-rich rocks.

Red sky at night
The Martian sky is full of fine dust, which makes it appear orange-red. It means that sunsets on Mars are always orange-red, and there's so much dust the sky stays bright for an hour after sunset. The daytime temperature can reach a pleasant 25°C (77°F) in summer, but it plummets as soon as the Sun sets and can drop to a bitter –125°C (–195°F) on winter nights.

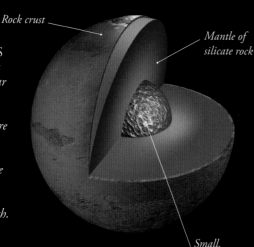

► MINI MARS
The surface area of Mars is similar to that of all the continents on Earth. Details are hard to see from ground-based telescopes because Mars is so small – about half the diameter of Earth.

Rock crust

Mantle of silicate rock

Small, probably solid iron core

MARTIAN MOONS

Mars has two small, black, potato-shaped moons called Phobos and Deimos. They may be asteroids that were captured by Mars long ago. Phobos is slightly larger than Deimos and has a large impact crater called Stickney. Both are heavily cratered and seem to be covered in a layer of dust at least 1 m (3 ft) thick.

POLAR ICE CAPS

There are permanent ice caps at both Martian poles, but they are quite different. The northern ice sheet is 3 km (1.8 miles) thick and mainly made of water ice. The southern polar cap is thicker and colder (–110°C/–166°F even in summer), and mostly made of carbon dioxide ice.

◄ ORBITER REPORT *NASA's Mars Reconnaissance Orbiter was launched in August 2005. Its instruments can take detailed photographs of the surface, look for water, analyse minerals, check for dust and water in the air, and observe weather.*

▲ MOUNTAIN FROST *Much of the Martian surface is thought to be in deep freeze – known as permafrost – such as the frost shown here in the Charitum Montes mountains.*

Deimos completes one orbit of Mars every 30 hours.

Phobos is much closer to Mars, completing one orbit every 7 hours 40 minutes.

TAKE A LOOK: DUST STORMS

Mars is a dry planet, although there is lots of evidence that there used to be water on its surface. Today the temperature is too cold and the air too thin for liquid water to exist on the surface. But the planet does have lots of wind. High-level winds reach speeds of up to 400 km/h (250 mph), kicking up huge clouds of dust 1,000 m (3,000 ft) high. The dust storms can cover vast areas of the planet, and may last for months.

▲ BREWING A STORM
The beginning of a storm takes shape on 30 June 1999.

▲ SHAPE SHIFTER
A cloud of orange-brown dust is raised by high winds.

▲ GETTING LARGER
Dust blows over the northern polar ice-cap (the white area in the top middle of the image).

▲ ... AND LARGER STILL
This photo was taken six hours after the first one, and the storm is still building.

The heights of Olympus

Mars has the largest volcanoes in the solar system. The most impressive is called Olympus Mons, or Mount Olympus. At 600 km (373 miles) across, it would cover most of England, and at 26 km (16 miles), high it is three times taller than Mount Everest. In the centre is a huge, sunken crater that is 90 km (56 miles) across.

Viking 1 Lander and Pathfinder landed near the Chryse Planitia.

Olympus Mons is the largest volcano in the solar system.

In places, the Kasei Vallis valley is more than 3 km (2 miles) deep. It was the result of a devastating flood.

The volcanoes Ascraeus Mons, Pavonis Mons, and Arsia Mons make up the Tharsis Montes range.

Valles Marineris runs like a scar just below the Martian equator. This system of canyons is 4,000 km (2,485 miles) long.

The Lowell Crater is 4 billion years old.

PLANET PROFILE

- **Average distance from the Sun** 228 million km (142 million miles)
- **Surface temperature** –125 to 25°C (–195 to 77°F)
- **Diameter** 6,800 km (4,200 miles)
- **Length of day** 24.5 hours (1 Earth day)
- **Length of year** 687 Earth days
- **Number of moons** 2
- **Gravity at the surface (Earth = 1)** 0.38
- **Size comparison**

Mars missions

We know more about Mars than any other planet (except Earth). More than 20 spacecraft have been sent to study it since 1965, and the number of missions is increasing every couple of years as more robots are sent up. Eventually, these missions may pave the way for human colonization of the planet.

WATCH THIS SPACE

These gullies, or channels, run down from cliffs (top left) into a crater. They look like those on Earth that have been carved out by flowing water.

WHY EXPLORE MARS?

Mars is the most Earth-like planet in the solar system and one of the closest planets to Earth. As missions landed on the surface, we learned more about Mars, including finding lots of evidence that there was once liquid water on Mars. Now the search is on for signs of life.

Geography and geology

The valleys, volcanoes, and other surface features on Mars were formed in one of three ways: by tectonics (movement of the planet's crust); by water, ice, or wind; or by meteorite impacts. The largest tectonic feature is Valles Marineris, running like a huge gash across the planet. This series of canyons was created billions of years ago, when the surface of the young planet was stretched and split by internal movement.

▶ THE LONG RUN
Valles Marineris extends about a quarter of the way around Mars. It is 10 times longer and five times deeper than Earth's Grand Canyon.

▲ LOTS OF LAYERS *The above image shows the floor of one of the chasmata, or canyons, in the Valles Marineris. The floor is made up of about 100 layers of built-up rock.*

SUCCESSFUL MISSIONS TO MARS

1960s

1964
Mariner 4 (USA) made the first successful flyby, taking 21 images.

1969
Mariner 7 (USA) returned 126 images from its flyby.

1970s

1971
Mariner 9 (USA) became the first successful Mars orbiter.

1973
Mars 5 (Russian) Orbiter recorded 22 days of data.

1976
Viking 1 (USA) made the first successful landing on Mars.

Endurance Crater

When large meteorites crash-land, they leave impact craters (👁 p160–161). Endurance Crater is quite small – about 130 m (420 ft) wide and no more than 30 m (100 ft) deep. Around the crater are small, dark grey pebbles that scientists nicknamed "blueberries". They contain an iron-rich mineral called haematite. On Earth, haematite forms in lakes and springs, so the pebbles could be a sign of water on Mars.

▲ DUSTY DUNES *The middle of the crater's floor looks like a desert. Red dust has piled up into small sand dunes that are up to 1 m (3 ft) tall.*

► A GOOD OPPORTUNITY
In 2004, the Opportunity rover spent six months taking images and examining rocks and soil in Endurance Crater. The rover is still on Mars, exploring other craters.

Polar ice cap

Like Earth, Mars has ice caps at its northern and southern poles. The caps can be seen from Earth, but missions to Mars allow scientists to study them closely. In winter, the ice is covered in frozen carbon dioxide. In summer, this evaporates and just the caps of water ice remain.

▼ ICE ROCKS *Viking 2 landed on the Utopia Planitia plain in 1979. During winter, its volcanic rocks were covered in a layer of water ice.*

Twin Peaks

In 1997, Pathfinder landed on Mars in an area that was covered with rocks. One of its first views included the Twin Peaks, two small mountains around 35 m (100 ft) tall. Images taken by Viking in orbit 20 years earlier showed the same peaks.

1990s

2000s

1997
Mars Pathfinder (USA) delivered the first successful rover to Mars.

1997
Mars Global Surveyor (USA) mapped entire planet, providing more evidence that water had flowed on Mars in the past.

2003
Europe's Mars Express orbiter began taking detailed pictures of Mars.

2008
Phoenix (USA) landed in Martian Arctic and operated for over five months (before its batteries went flat).

MARTIAN SAND ART

This close-up image from the Mars Reconnaissance Orbiter looks like an elaborate tattoo, but it's actually sand on the surface of the planet. The patterns have been created by dust devils – spinning columns of rising air up to 8 km (5 miles) high. As they whirl across the surface of Mars, they pick up loose red dust, uncovering darker, heavier sand underneath.

Asteroids

For thousands of years there were six recognized planets (including Earth) in the solar system. No one dreamt that there were any worlds beyond Saturn, but there were suggestions that something existed between Mars and Jupiter. Rather than a single planet, many thousands of rocky objects have since been discovered. These are asteroids.

📷 WHAT A STAR!

In 1772, Johann Bode proposed a formula to work out the distances of the planets from the Sun. Bode's Law seemed proven by the discovery of Uranus, and of Ceres in Bode's "gap" between Mars and Jupiter, but it failed when Neptune and Pluto were discovered.

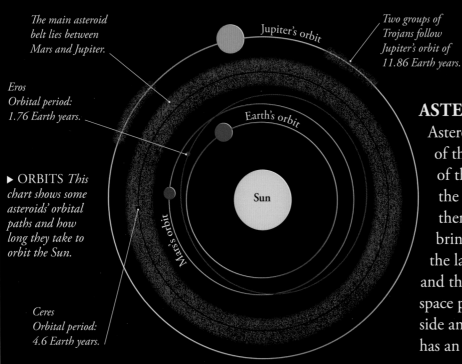

The main asteroid belt lies between Mars and Jupiter.

Jupiter's orbit

Two groups of Trojans follow Jupiter's orbit of 11.86 Earth years.

Eros
Orbital period: 1.76 Earth years.

Earth's orbit

Sun

Mars's orbit

▶ ORBITS *This chart shows some asteroids' orbital paths and how long they take to orbit the Sun.*

Ceres
Orbital period: 4.6 Earth years.

ASTEROIDS IN ORBIT

Asteroids are leftovers from the formation of the planets 4.5 billion years ago. Most of them travel around the Sun between the orbits of Mars and Jupiter, although there are some groups whose orbits bring them close to Earth. Eros is one of the largest of these near-Earth asteroids, and the first asteroid to be orbited by a space probe. With a large crater on one side and a depression on the other, Eros has an uneven shape, like a cosmic potato.

Ceres

On 1 January 1801, Giuseppe Piazzi, director of the Palermo Observatory in Sicily, found a mysterious object in the constellation of Taurus. It was found to follow a nearly circular, planet-like path between Mars and Jupiter – but it was too small to be a planet. Today, the object Piazzi named Ceres is classified as a dwarf planet. It is the largest of the asteroids, and may have an ocean beneath its icy surface.

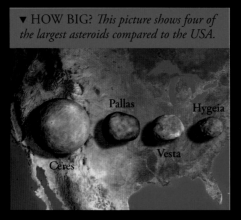

▼ HOW BIG? *This picture shows four of the largest asteroids compared to the USA.*

Pallas

Hygeia

Ceres

Vesta

Vesta

Vesta is the brightest of the main belt asteroids and is occasionally visible to the naked eye. The asteroid has a giant impact crater 460 km (285 miles) across – nearly as wide as Vesta itself. Vesta was strong enough to survive the huge impact, but some of the debris still falls to Earth as meteorites.

ASTEROIDS UP CLOSE

Only a handful of asteroids have been seen at close quarters. Ida is a main belt asteroid that was imaged by the Galileo spacecraft in 1993. Ida is 52 km (32 miles) long and rotates once every 4 hours 38 minutes. Galileo also found the first asteroid moon to be discovered. The tiny moon, called Dactyl, orbits less than 100 km (62 miles) from Ida.

▼ CREATED ON IMPACT? *Dactyl is only 1.6 km (1 mile) across, and may be a piece of Ida that broke off during an impact.*

Dactyl

Ida

TOO CLOSE FOR COMFORT!

There are far more small asteroids than large ones. Nearly every week, a small asteroid passes close to Earth. There are thought to be 1,100 near-Earth asteroids bigger than 1 km (0.6 miles) across, and more than a million longer than 40 m (131 ft). Some have collided with Earth in the past.

CHICXULUB *is a crater in Mexico left by an asteroid that collided with Earth 65 million years ago.*

What's in a name?

The astronomer who discovers a new asteroid has the right to name it. Asteroids are usually named after people, but among the more unusual names are Dizzy, Dodo, Brontosaurus, Humptydumpty, and Wombat.

Crater, fracture, or shatter?

Collisions are common among asteroids, but what happens when they collide depends how large the asteroid is. If a small asteroid hits a larger one it will leave a crater. Slightly bigger asteroids may fracture the large asteroid, but the fragments clump back together to form a ball of rubble. If an asteroid is big enough or travelling fast enough it could shatter a large asteroid, leaving a trail of mini asteroids orbiting in its wake.

▶ TWO WORLDS COLLIDE
When the solar system first formed, asteroids continually collided and grew in size until only one large rocky body was left in an orbit. This became a planet. (◉ p120–121)

Jupiter

Jupiter is the king of the planets. This huge world has more than two-and-a-half times the mass of all the other planets combined. Around 1,300 Earths would fit inside this giant world, but because it is mainly made up of light gases Jupiter weighs only 318 times as much as Earth.

▼ POLAR GLOW *The auroras at Jupiter's poles are hundreds of times more powerful than those on Earth.*

Awesome auroras

Like Earth, Jupiter has a magnetic field, as if there were a giant magnet buried deep inside the planet. It causes auroras (also known as the northern and southern lights). When solar wind particles collide with atmospheric gases, the gases glow and "curtains" of auroral light spread out several hundred kilometres (miles) above Jupiter's clouds.

▶ WHAT'S INSIDE? *Jupiter has a relatively small solid core. Most of the planet is made up of hydrogen and helium. Near the surface, the gases are cold, but closer to the core, they get hotter and act more like liquid metal.*

Hydrogen and helium gas

Outer layer of liquid hydrogen and helium

Inner layer of metallic hydrogen

Core of rock, metal, and hydrogen compounds

TAKE A LOOK: RED SPOTS

The most famous feature on Jupiter is the Great Red Spot. This is a giant atmospheric storm, which was first recorded in 1664 and has been blowing non-stop ever since. The storm turns clockwise once every six days. The chemicals that give the Spot its orange-red colour are still not known, but the Spot is colder than nearby clouds. In recent years, two more red spots appeared on Jupiter, in the same band of clouds.

▲ THE HUBBLE *telescope took this image in May 2008. It shows a new red spot to the left of the Great Red Spot and Red Spot Junior.*

CLOUDS OF MANY COLOURS

Ninety per cent of Jupiter's atmosphere is hydrogen gas. Most of the rest is helium, with some hydrogen compounds such as methane, ammonia, water, and ethane. The compounds condense (turn to liquid) at different temperatures, making different types and colours of cloud at different altitudes.

Rising air forms a zone of white ammonia clouds.

Air flowing east, pushed by the Coriolis effect.

Falling cooler air

Air flowing west

Clouds of water vapour at lower altitude

Red-brown cloud belt

◀ CLOUD MOVEMENT *As air from the equator gets warmed by the Sun, it rises and flows towards the poles. The cooler air at the poles flows back to take its place. A force called the Coriolis effect turns it all round so the air flows from north–south to east–west.*

28,000 mph), and causes the equatorial region to bulge outwards.

Storm system

North Temperate Zone

North Temperate Belt

North Tropical Zone

North Equatorial Belt

Equatorial Zone

South Equatorial Belt

South Tropical Zone

South Temperate Belt

Great Red Spot

South polar region

WATCH THIS SPACE

Jupiter is orbited by thin, dark rings of dust. The rings were discovered by Voyager 1 when it flew past the planet in 1979. The main rings are about 125,000 km (77,670 miles) across. The particles in each ring range from microscopic dust to chunks several metres (feet) across.

TELL ME MORE...

This picture is made from a set of images taken by the Cassini spacecraft as it travelled 10 million km (6 million miles) away from the planet.

A warm interior

Jupiter's cloud tops are very cold, about −143°C (−234°F). However, despite its distance from the Sun, Jupiter is very warm inside.

▲ In this infrared image, cold areas appear dark – such as the cold orange-red and white clouds high up in Jupiter's atmosphere.

▲ In this visible light image, paler colours show warmer, bright clouds that have risen from deep inside the planet.

PLANET PROFILE

- **Average distance from the Sun** 780 million km (484 million miles)
- **Cloud-top temperature** −143°C (−234°F)
- **Diameter** 143,000 km (89,000 miles)
- **Length of day** 9.93 hours
- **Length of year** 11.86 Earth years
- **Number of moons** 63
- **Gravity at cloud tops (Earth = 1)** 2.53
- **Size comparison**

Jupiter's moons

Jupiter has 63 known moons: four "Galilean moons", four inner moons, and the rest are small outer moons. The Galilean moons (Io, Europa, Callisto, and Ganymede) were first discovered in 1610, but very little was known about them until the two Voyager spacecraft imaged them in 1979.

WHAT A STAR!

On 7 January 1610, Italian scientist Galileo Galilei looked through his small telescope and found three small, bright "stars" in a straight line near Jupiter. After weeks of observation he concluded that there were actually four stars – each a large satellite orbiting the planet. We now call these the Galilean moons.

Io with cheese on top

Io is about the same size as Earth's moon, but it looks like a giant pizza. This is because it's covered by sulphur, which is usually yellow. When sulphur is heated, it changes colour, first to red and then to black. The temperature of some of these hot spots can reach 1,500°C (2,730°F). Io is the most volcanically active object in the solar system. There are often a dozen or more volcanoes blasting umbrella-shaped clouds of gas and sulphur compounds into space.

Sulphur dioxide from a volcano settles as a ring of "snow" on the surface.

The black areas scattered over the surface are all active volcanoes.

Plume of gas from the Pele volcano

Pele's plume

Pele is one of Io's largest volcanoes. When Voyager 1 passed it, a plume of gas and dust was rising 300 km (190 miles) above the surface and covered an area the size of Alaska. It can rise high above the moon before falling back to the surface because the gravity on Io is very low. The volcano is surrounded by a blanket of material thrown out during repeated eruptions that has fallen back down to the surface.

The craters of Callisto

Callisto is the most distant of the large Galilean moons. Its surface is billions of years old and is one of the most heavily cratered objects in the solar system. Only a little smaller than Mercury, Callisto is a mixture of ice and rock, and has a very weak magnetic field. It also seems to have a salty ocean deep beneath the surface – even though Callisto is not tidally heated like Io, Europa, and Ganymede. Tidal heating happens when the moon is warmed up from the inside, pulled by the gravity of Jupiter and the other Galilean moons.

▲ CLOSE-UP CRATERS *These views of Jupiter's second-largest moon reveal that what appear to be lights are actually craters.*

TAKE A LOOK: EUROPA

Europa is a similar size to Io (and Earth's Moon). It has a smooth surface covered in ice – there are no deep valleys or high mountains, and very few impact craters. This shows that its surface is very young. The ice is continually being renewed from below. In fact, parts of the surface look like broken ice floating in the Arctic on Earth. It is thought that Europa has an ocean of water under the outer shell of ice, no more than 10–20 km (6–12 miles) below the airless surface. This is made possible by tidal heating.

◀ ◉ FIND OUT MORE *about the inside of Europa p163.*

▲ ICY SURFACE *The white and blue areas in this picture show a layer of ice particles covering Europa's crust. It's thought that the dust came from the creation of a large crater about 1,000 km (620 miles) south of the area.*

Giant Ganymede

With a diameter of 5,260 km (3,270 miles), Ganymede is the largest satellite in the solar system. It is bigger than Mercury, but has only about half its mass because Ganymede is a mixture of rock and ice. The interior is thought to be separated into three layers: a small, iron-rich core surrounded by a rocky mantle with an icy shell on top. The surface is divided into two different types of landscape: very old, dark, highly cratered regions; and younger, lighter regions with grooves, ridges, and craters. Ganymede has a weak magnetic field and may have a salty ocean buried 200 km (125 miles) beneath the icy surface.

Did you know
that you can see Jupiter from Earth? When it comes close to Earth, it is very bright and visible for most of the night. Jupiter is one of the brightest planets – only the Moon and Venus outshine it. You can also see the four Galilean moons with just a small telescope, good pair of binoculars, or sometimes simply with the naked eye.

Arbela Sulcus is a light region of furrows and ridges 24 km (15 miles) wide surrounded by dark regions.

Ganymede's dark regions are old and full of craters.

The lighter regions are younger and have lots of unusual groove patterns.

Voyager 1 & 2

On 20 August 1977, Voyager 2 lifted off from Cape Canaveral, Florida, USA. Voyager 1 followed on 5 September. They are two of only four spacecraft to have ever been sent out beyond the solar system. The other two craft, Pioneer 10 and 11, are no longer in touch with Earth, but we still receive regular data transmissions from the Voyagers – even though they are nearly in interstellar space.

▶ VOYAGER 1 *was launched into space aboard a Titan III/Centaur rocket.*

Earth

Sun

Jupiter

Saturn

Uranus

To boldly go
Voyager 1 is the furthest human-made object in space. In December 2009 it was 112 AU (astronomical units) from the Sun. 1 AU is 150 million km (93 million miles). It takes 15 hours, 37 minutes for a signal from Voyager to reach Earth.

SPACE HOPPING

When the Voyagers were launched, Jupiter, Saturn, Uranus, and Neptune were in a rare alignment that only occurs every 175 years. The Voyagers were able to use the powerful gravity of the planets to boost their speed and change direction so they could fly on to the next planet. Voyager 1 arrived at Jupiter in March 1979; Voyager 2 followed in July. Voyager 1 was sent off course by Saturn, but Voyager 2 went on to Uranus and Neptune.

Voyager 1's encounter with Saturn bent the spacecraft's flightpath on a course towards interstellar space, preventing it from continuing on to the outer planets.

We've got the power – just!

Each Voyager carried 10 instruments to investigate the planets and their moons. They get their electricity from nuclear power packs. Over time the power levels have dropped, and the output is now about equal to two 150 watt light bulbs. Their computer power is also tiny by modern standards – they both have three computers with 8,000 words of memory each.

Star trek

The Voyagers are leaving the solar system and heading into the Milky Way galaxy in different directions. Scientists estimate that in about 40,000 years, each spacecraft will be in the neighbourhood of other stars and about two light years from the Sun. So far the Voyagers have reached the solar system's outer boundary, a region called the heliosheath, where the solar wind collides with interstellar space. Both spacecraft have enough electrical power and attitude-control propellant to continue operating until about 2025.

IRIS (infrared radiometer and spectrometer) measures radiation

UV spectrometer detects ultraviolet light

Plasma detector studies hot gases

Cosmic ray detector picks up high-energy particles

The electronics are stored here

Antenna for sending signals to Earth

High-field magnetometer measures the effects of solar wind

These two antennae pick up radio signals sent out from planets

Voyager's power source

Magnetometer measures changes in the Sun's magnetic field

Neptune

HELIOSHEATH
This is the outer edge of the heliosphere (a huge bubble containing the solar system, solar wind, and the solar magnetic field). Voyager 1 entered the heliosphere about 14 billion km (8.7 billion miles) from the Sun.

BOW SHOCK
As the heliosphere travels through interstellar space, it forms a bow shock, just like waves form around a rock in a stream.

Voyager 1

Cassini

Voyager 2

TERMINATION SHOCK *Solar wind (a thin stream of electrically charged gas) blows outwards from the Sun until it reaches the termination shock. Then it drops abruptly as it meets oncoming interstellar wind.*

HELIOPAUSE
The heliosphere boundary is where the pressures of the solar wind and the interstellar wind balance. When Voyager passes through this boundary, it will be in interstellar space.

📷 WATCH THIS SPACE

Taken from a distance of more than 6 billion km (4 billion miles) from Earth, this picture shows Earth as a tiny dot in a beam of light. The image was taken by Voyager 1 and is part of the first "portrait" of the solar system, which shows six planets (Mercury and Mars weren't visible).

The Voyager record

Both Voyagers carry a message that will tell any alien life they encounter about where they have come from. The message is carried on a phonograph record – a 30 cm (12 in) gold-plated copper disc containing sounds and images selected to show the variety of life and culture on Earth. The cover shows Earth's location and has instructions on how to play the record. The contents include images, a variety of natural sounds, music from different cultures and ages, and greetings in 55 languages.

THE SOUNDS OF EARTH

UNITED STATES OF AMERICA PLANET EARTH

Saturn

The second-largest planet and sixth planet from the Sun, Saturn is the most distant planet we can see without a telescope. It's visible for about ten months of the year, and is surrounded by an amazing series of rings (but you will need a telescope to see them).

▲ RING CYCLES *Sometimes we see the north side of Saturn's rings, and sometimes the south. This is because the orbits of Earth and Saturn are not on the same level, so sometimes Earth is above the rings, and sometimes below them.*

Thin, gaseous atmosphere

▶ LARGE BUT LIGHT *More than 750 Earths could fit inside Saturn, but it is only 95 times heavier than Earth. This is because it is mainly made of hydrogen and helium gas. It is the only planet light enough to float on water – if you can find an ocean big enough!*

Outer layer of liquid hydrogen and helium

Inner layer of liquid metallic hydrogen and helium

Core of rock and ice

TELL ME MORE...

Saturn's rings were first seen by Galileo in 1610, but through his simple telescope they looked like ears sticking out from the planet!

RINGS GALORE

Saturn's rings are so spectacular, it is often known as the ringed planet (even though Jupiter, Uranus, and Neptune also have rings). There are three main rings, which are so large and bright they can be seen in a small telescope. Going outwards from the planet, they are known as C, B, and A. Outside these are the F, G, and E rings, which are very faint.

▲ SATURN ROCKS *Saturn's rings are made up of dust, rocks, and chunks of water ice. They cover a distance of 280,000 km (175,000 miles), but are only about 1 km (0.6 miles) thick.*

▲ C RING *Inside the C ring is a thin ring called D. There is no gap between these two rings.*

▲ B RING *The widest main ring at 25,500 km (15,850 miles) across. It is 5–15 m (15–50 ft) thick and is also the brightest of the main rings.*

▲ A RING *The first ring to be discovered. The rings are named in order of discovery, not their position.*

◀ MIND THE GAP *Some parts of the rings have been swept clear by the gravity from Saturn's moons, leaving gaps between the rings. The largest gap is the Cassini Division, between the A and B rings.*

The dark spots on this ultra-violet photo are thousands of storms.

The grey bands are layers of high cloud.

The Dragon Storm is said to be like a thunderstorm.

Stormy Saturn

Through a telescope, Saturn looks pale yellow, streaked with faint bands of cloud. But from time to time, large white spots appear. They are giant storms, and they can be seen from Earth. High-speed winds spread the storm clouds around the planet's equator. Wind speed at the equator can be 1,800 km/h (1,100 mph), six times faster than the strongest winds on Earth. Huge storms also occur at the poles. These have an "eye" like a hurricane. Similar polar storms are found on Venus and Jupiter.

▲ SPOT THE STORM *Huge, hurricane-like storms lie above Saturn's poles. Small storm clouds (shown here as dark spots) move around these huge "whirlpools" in Saturn's atmosphere.*

▲ WATCH THE DRAGON *In Saturn's southern hemisphere is a band of cloud called "storm alley" because so many storms have occurred there – including the large, bright, electrical storm called the Dragon Storm.*

TAKE A LOOK: POLAR LIGHTS

Saturn's strong magnetic field forms an invisible bubble around the planet. This protects it from most of the electrically charged particles that flow past the planet in the solar wind. However, some of these particles become trapped and flow down the magnetic field lines towards Saturn's magnetic poles. When they strike the upper atmosphere, they form rings of light called auroras.

▶ SOUTHERN LIGHTS *This aurora formed at Saturn's south pole in January 2005.*

PLANET PROFILE

- **Average distance from the Sun** 1,400 million km (870 million miles)
- **Cloud-top temperature** –180°C (–290°F)
- **Diameter** 120,540 km (74,900 miles)
- **Length of day** 10.6 hours
- **Length of year** 29.4 Earth years

- **Number of moons** 62
- **Gravity at cloud tops** (Earth = 1) 1.07
- **Size comparison**

Saturn's moons

Saturn has 62 known moons. There are the large round major moons, smaller irregular inner moons, and tiny irregular outer moons that lie way beyond Saturn's rings. Some of the small moons lie within or very near to Saturn's rings. The outer moons may be comets that were captured by Saturn's powerful gravity. There are also seven "medium-sized" moons that orbit quite close to Saturn.

WHAT A STAR!

Dutch astronomer Christiaan Huygens discovered the first of Saturn's moons, Titan, in 1655. The European Space Agency's Saturn probe is named for him.

TELL ME MORE...

Saturn's moons are so cold, their icy surfaces are as hard as rock. They all have impact craters where comets have thumped into them.

Prometheus
Janus
Enceladus
Pan Atlas
Pandora Mimas
Tethys Dione
Epimetheus
Rhea

▲ MANY MOONS *The moons within or close to Saturn's main rings are (from left to right): Pan, Atlas, Prometheus (above), Pandora (below), Janus (above), and Epimetheus (below). Mimas, Enceladus, Tethys, Dione, and Rhea all lie well outside the main rings but within or near to the thin E ring.*

▶ PHOEBE *Like most of Saturn's moons, the outer moon called Phoebe travels in an elliptical (oval-shaped) orbit. It has created its own ring of ice and dust, known as Phoebe's Ring, 6–12 million km (3.7–7.4 million miles) outside Saturn.*

▲ HYPERION *Most of Saturn's moons keep the same face towards the planet. However, Hyperion tumbles over as it orbits Saturn. This may be due to one or more collisions with comets.*

◀ IAPETUS *The 22nd moon from the planet, Iapetus is Saturn's most distant major moon. Its forward-facing side is covered in dust that has been knocked off Phoebe by comet collisions. Unlike nearly all the other moons, it travels in the same direction as Saturn.*

▲ TITAN *The second-largest moon in the solar system (Jupiter's Ganymede is the first), Titan is bigger than the planet Mercury. Its orbit is 1.2 million km (758,000 miles) from Saturn.*

TERRIFIC TITAN

Saturn's largest moon is unique – it is the only moon to have an atmosphere. Titan's atmosphere is nitrogen-rich and dense like Earth's, but it is far too cold to support life. Radar and infrared instruments have been used to study Titan's surface, which is hidden beneath a thick orange haze. The surface was found to be covered in ice, with mountains, huge dunes, and rivers and lakes of liquid methane.

▲ HUYGENS -CASSINI *The Huygens probe was designed to explore Titan's atmosphere and surface. The Cassini orbiter is spending many years studying Saturn and its main moons.*

▶ TITAN'S *surface has channels that were probably carved out by flowing methane. On Earth methane is a gas, but Titan is so cold, (–179°C/–290°F), methane is a liquid and falls as rain from the clouds.*

◀ POLES APART *Taken two months later, in December 2005, this view is of Titan's opposite hemisphere (the "back" of the first image). You can clearly see the north and south polar regions.*

▲ BRIGHT LIGHTS *This false-colour image was taken by the Cassini spacecraft. The very bright area is called Tui Reggio and is thought to be frozen water or carbon dioxide that has come from a volcano.*

🔍 TAKE A LOOK: ENCELADUS

Perhaps the most surprising of Saturn's moons is Enceladus. Only about 500 km (300 miles) across, Enceladus was expected to be a cold, dead world. However, the Cassini spacecraft discovered powerful geysers near the moon's south pole. Tidal movement inside the moon creates heat that turns ice into water vapour. This escapes through cracks, or fault lines, in Enceladus's icy shell, and is blasted into space.

Water ice particles in the geysers feed the E ring that circles Saturn.

The water becomes much warmer near the surface.

▲ IT'S YOUR FAULT *The plumes of gas and icy particles blast into space through large fault lines in the surface known as "tiger stripe" fractures.*

Touchdown on Titan

After a 4 billion km (2.5 billion mile) piggyback ride lasting almost seven years, the European Space Agency's Huygens probe separated from the Cassini orbiter on 25 December 2004. It landed on Titan on 14 January 2005, making it the first (and, so far, only) time that a spacecraft had touched down on a world in the outer solar system. The probe's instruments swung into action, sampling the atmosphere and taking pictures.

(1) The top image shows the area where Huygens landed. (2) View as Huygens parachutes to Titan, taken from 6 km (4 miles) above. (3) Titan's tallest mountains are thought to be just a few hundred metres (yards) tall. (4) Artist's impression of Huygens.

SATURN BY SUNLIGHT

This amazing view of Saturn directly in line
with the Sun is made up of 165 images taken
by the Cassini orbiter. Lit from behind, the
planet is in shadow, but the glow reveals
previously unseen, unknown rings – and,
billions of kilometres in the distance, Earth.

Earth

Uranus

Uranus is the third largest planet, and the seventh planet from the Sun. At this distance it receives little heat or light from the Sun, so the cloud tops are extremely cold. Each orbit around the Sun takes 84 Earth years, so birthdays on Uranus are extremely rare!

GAS AND ICE

Around 67 Earths would fit inside Uranus, but since it is mostly made of gas it is only 14 times heavier than Earth. Uranus and Neptune are sometimes called ice giants because a large part of their interiors is thought to be composed of ices made from water, methane, and ammonia.

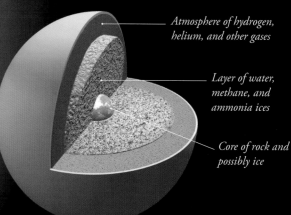

Atmosphere of hydrogen, helium, and other gases

Layer of water, methane, and ammonia ices

Core of rock and possibly ice

📷 WHAT A STAR!

William Herschel discovered Uranus in 1781. Looking through his home-made telescope, he noticed a greenish star in the constellation of Gemini that was not shown on his sky charts. Herschel thought it was a comet, but a year later it was confirmed as a new planet.

🔍 TAKE A LOOK: BLACK RINGS

Uranus has a system of 13 dark, thin rings around the planet. They are very black, extremely narrow – less than 10 km (6 miles) across – and mostly made of dust and boulders up to a metre (3 ft) across. The rings are too faint to be seen from Earth and were only discovered in 1977 when the planet passed in front of a star. The light from the star was dimmed as it passed through the rings.

Clouds on Uranus

Through most of Earth's largest telescopes Uranus appears as an almost featureless disc. When Voyager 2 flew past the planet in 1986, it sent back images of a pale blue ball with a few clouds or storm features. The Hubble Space Telescope has since found that some large clouds travel around the planet more than twice as fast as hurricane winds on Earth.

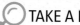

▲ KECK'S CLOUDS *This false colour image was taken by the Keck Telescope in Hawaii. The rings appear red and storm clouds are white.*

▲ LINE UP *The outermost ring, Epsilon, is shown as a white line in this false-colour image.*

Uranus's moons

Uranus has a family of 27 known moons, many of them named after characters from Shakespeare's plays. Most of these are small objects less than 200 km (125 miles) across, which orbit the planet close to the rings. They include Cordelia and Ophelia, which are "shepherd moons" – they keep the particles of the thin Epsilon ring in place.

PLANET PROFILE

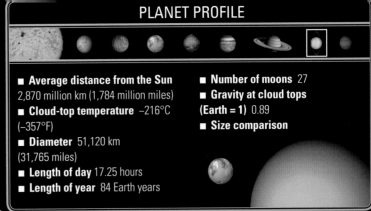

- **Average distance from the Sun**
  2,870 million km (1,784 million miles)
- **Cloud-top temperature** –216°C (–357°F)
- **Diameter** 51,120 km (31,765 miles)
- **Length of day** 17.25 hours
- **Length of year** 84 Earth years
- **Number of moons** 27
- **Gravity at cloud tops (Earth = 1)** 0.89
- **Size comparison**

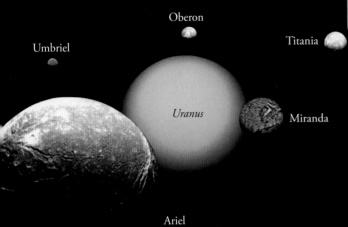

Oberon

Umbriel

Titania

Uranus

Miranda

Ariel

Major moons

The five major moons of Uranus are cold, icy worlds. Miranda is the smallest. Ariel is the brightest, and was discovered in 1851 at the same time as the heavily cratered Umbriel. Titania and Oberon, the two largest moons, show some signs of internal warming in the past.

▲ OBERON *was the first moon to be discovered, by William Herschel in 1787.*

▲ ARIEL *has deep grooves and some small craters. It also shows signs that its surface has changed over time.*

Miranda

Miranda has unique surface features, including deep canyons, terraced layers, and much younger, smoother layers. These point to a turbulent history. Some suggest that Miranda suffered a catastrophic collision in the distant past, and then reassembled in the chaotic way that we see today. Alternatively, it may have started to evolve, with heavier material sinking towards the centre and lighter material rising to the surface, but this process stopped before it was completed.

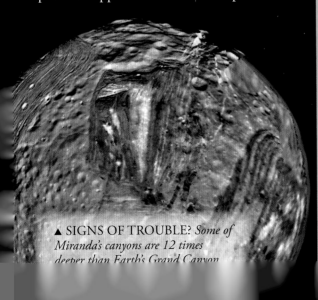

▲ SIGNS OF TROUBLE? *Some of Miranda's canyons are 12 times deeper than Earth's Grand Canyon.*

The toppled planet

Uranus is unusual because it is tipped over on its side so that the equator is almost at right angles to the orbit and its poles take turns in pointing towards the Sun. Each pole has 21 years of permanent sunlight during its summer and 21 years of permanent darkness in its winter. It is believed that Uranus may have been knocked over by a huge collision with a planet-sized body early in its history.

▶ UPRIGHT ORBIT *This Hubble Space Telescope view shows how Uranus's moons follow the tilt of the planet and orbit it top to bottom.*

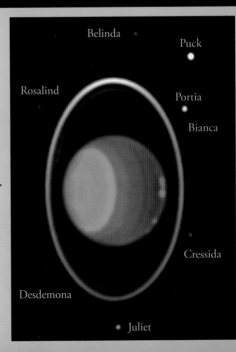

Belinda

Puck

Rosalind

Portia

Bianca

Cressida

Desdemona

Juliet

Neptune

The eighth planet from the Sun, Neptune is an icy gas giant 54 times the size of Earth, but only 17 times heavier. It is an extremely cold, dark world – 30 times further from the Sun than Earth, it receives 900 times less light and heat than Earth.

size of Earth, Neptune is mainly made of gas, water, and ices, which makes it relatively light.

Atmosphere of hydrogen, helium, and methane gases

Icy layer of frozen water, methane, and ammonia

Solid core of rock and possibly ice

A BLUE PLANET

Like Uranus, Neptune appears blue – not because it is covered with oceans, but because it has methane gas in its atmosphere. This gas absorbs red light from the Sun, and when red light is taken away from visible light, it leaves behind blue light.

Active atmosphere

Heat rising from inside Neptune makes the planet's atmosphere very active – it feeds some large storms and drives the fastest winds in the solar system. Cloud features on Neptune have been seen to sweep around the planet at around 2,000 km/h (1,240 mph), 10 times the speed of hurricane force winds on Earth. Sometimes these winds are revealed by long banks of high-level cloud.

◄ SHADOWS *Methane ice clouds cast shadows on the main deck of blue cloud 50 km (30 miles) below. The cloud streaks are 50–200 km (30–125 miles) wide but stretch for thousands of kilometres around the planet.*

THE GREAT DARK SPOT

Neptune's atmosphere changes quite quickly as large storms and cloud features rush around the planet in the opposite direction to its rotation. A white cloud feature called Scooter took just 16.8 days to zip around the planet. The largest feature seen so far was the Great Dark Spot, a storm about the same size as Earth. It disappeared within a few years.

TELL ME MORE...

Almost everything we know about Neptune comes from the Voyager 2 spacecraft, which flew past the planet in 1989. Neptune was the fourth and last planet visited by Voyager 2 as it headed out of the solar system towards interstellar space.

NEPTUNE'S MOONS

■ **Neptune has 13 known moons.** The largest of these is Triton, which is smaller than Earth's moon but larger than the dwarf planet Pluto. It travels the opposite way around the planet compared with most other moons, and is gradually being pulled towards Neptune. Triton is one of the coldest worlds we know, with a surface temperature of –235°C (–391°F). It is covered by frozen nitrogen gas. Despite the extreme cold, Triton seems to be warm inside.

◄ SMALL BUT SPEEDY *Proteus is the largest of the six inner moons. It takes 27 hours to travel around Neptune.*

◄ TRITON'S TRAILS *Dark trails across Triton's surface show where ice "geysers" throw black dust into the thin atmosphere. This is blown away from the polar region and coats the surface.*

■ **Most of Neptune's outer moons** are small – Nereid is 340 km (210 miles) across, and the others are less than 200 km (125 miles) across. Six of them orbit close to the planet, within 120,000 km (74,500 miles). Five follow distant orbits more than 15 million km (9 million miles) away and are probably captured comets.

Neptune's rings

Neptune has a system of six very narrow, dark rings. Four small moons lie inside the ring system. Two of these – Galatea and Despina – act as shepherds for the ring particles, keeping two of the rings in shape. Galatea is probably also the cause of the Adams ring being unusually clumpy. This ring has arcs, meaning it is thicker in some places than others.

Orbit oddity

Neptune is normally the eighth planet from the Sun, but it has such an elliptical (oval-shaped) orbit that for about 20 years of its 164-year-long trip around the Sun it is actually further away than Pluto. This was the case from 1979 to 1999.

Johann Galle

📷 WHAT A STAR!

The search for Neptune began when astronomers noticed that something seemed to pull on Uranus so that it sometimes travelled faster than expected and sometimes slower. The new planet was found by Johann Galle in 1846, after its position was worked out by John Couch Adams and Urbain Le Verrier.

◄ RINGS *These photos from Voyager 2 show four rings. The two bright rings are Adams ring (outer) and Le Verrier (inner).*

PLANET PROFILE

■ **Average distance from the Sun** 4,500 million km (2,800 million miles)
■ **Cloud-top temperature** –220°C (–364°F)
■ **Diameter** 49,500 km (30,760 miles)
■ **Length of day** 16 hours
■ **Length of year** 165 Earth years

■ **Number of moons** 13
■ **Gravity at cloud tops (Earth = 1)** 1.13
■ **Size comparison**

Pluto and beyond

Pluto used to be known as the smallest and the furthest of the planets. In 2006, it was reclassified as a dwarf planet because of its small size and weak gravity. Everything we know about Pluto has been detected by observatories on or near Earth. Many mysteries remain.

▲ A NEW VIEW *This is the clearest view of Pluto ever seen, made up of images taken by the Hubble Space Telescope.*

▼ MAIN MOON *Charon is the largest of Pluto's three moons, orbiting 18,400 km (11,400 miles) from the planet. It is also the solar system's largest moon in relation to the size of its planet.*

Pluto

Charon

▶ PLUTO'S LONG JOURNEY *Pluto's eccentric orbit overlaps both the Kuiper Belt and Neptune's orbit. Pluto is sometimes nearer to the Sun than Neptune.*

AN ECCENTRIC ORBIT

Pluto's orbit is very different to those of other planets. Rather than following an orbital path that is nearly circular, its path is a very stretched circle, which is known as eccentric. Sometimes the path brings Pluto closer to the Sun than Neptune's orbit. At its closest it is 30 times Earth's distance from the Sun, but at the furthest point of its orbit it is 50 times. Since its discovery in 1930, Pluto has only completed about one-third of an orbit around the Sun.

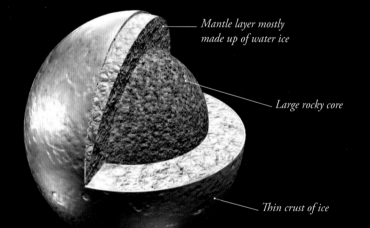

Mantle layer mostly made up of water ice

Large rocky core

Thin crust of ice

Frozen Pluto

Pluto is a world in deep freeze, with a surface temperature of around –230°C (–382°F), even in the summer! The most common gas in its thin atmosphere is nitrogen. As the planet moves away from the Sun into its 200-year-long winter, most of the atmosphere will freeze, covering the surface in frosts of methane and nitrogen.

PLANET PROFILE

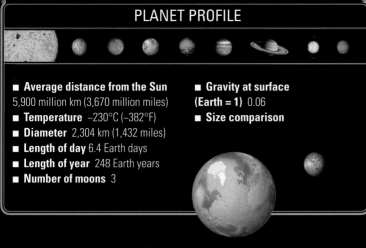

- **Average distance from the Sun** 5,900 million km (3,670 million miles)
- **Temperature** –230°C (–382°F)
- **Diameter** 2,304 km (1,432 miles)
- **Length of day** 6.4 Earth days
- **Length of year** 248 Earth years
- **Number of moons** 3
- **Gravity at surface (Earth = 1)** 0.06
- **Size comparison**

Pluto is now known to be the largest of many millions of objects that orbit the Sun in a region known as the Kuiper Belt, beyond Neptune. Kuiper Belt objects are icy debris left over from the formation of the planets 4.5 billion years ago. When these objects are nudged closer to the Sun they are thought to become short-period comets, which make regular journeys to the inner solar system.

Kuiper Belt

Uranus

Orbit of Mars

Jupiter

Pluto

Saturn

Neptune

Pluto's moons

Pluto's two tiny moons, Nix and Hydra, were only discovered in 2005. It is thought they may be rocky debris left over from the formation of the solar system that have been captured into orbit around Pluto. Charon, the largest moon, is more likely to be a piece of Pluto broken off by a collision at the time of formation.

Pluto

Nix

Hydra

Charon

Daytime darkness

If people lived on Pluto, they would need to carry torches – even in the daytime, light levels are between 900 and 2,500 times lower than on Earth.

A BELT OF PLANETS

Three more of the five dwarf planets are found in the Kuiper Belt. Eris, which is slightly larger than Pluto, was discovered in 2005. Eris is probably made of ice and rock, and so is very similar in composition to Pluto. It has one known moon and follows a very elliptical orbit that takes 560 years. Makemake is slightly smaller and dimmer than Pluto, with a reddish colour. Haumea is shaped like an airship and rotates very fast – once every four hours.

Comets

Every now and then, a strange object with a wispy tail appears in the night sky. This is a comet, a large lump of dust and ice a few kilometres long hurtling towards the Sun. There are billions of comets circling the Sun, far beyond the orbit of Pluto.

DIRTY SNOWBALLS

The nucleus (solid centre) of a comet is made of dirty water ice. The "dirt" is rock dust. When a comet warms up, the nucleus releases gas and dust. They form a cloud called a coma. Sometimes, long tails develop and extend millions of kilometres into space. There are two main tails: a bluish gas tail and a white dust tail. The tails always point away from the Sun.

Collision course
Sometimes a comet can be nudged out of its orbit so that it travels into the inner solar system. If it hits Earth, it may result in widespread destruction. But don't worry, the chance of this happening is very small!

Dust tail is curved

Gas tail

Perihelion

Sun

Tails are longest close to the Sun

Tail grows as comet moves towards the Sun

Naked nucleus

Aphelion (furthest point from Sun)

Jets of gas and dust

LIFE CYCLES

A comet spends most of its life in a frozen state, until it moves near the Sun, when it warms up and gets active. The coma is largest at the perihelion (the point nearest the Sun) when the icy nucleus is releasing most gas and dust. Each time a comet passes near the Sun it gets slightly smaller. If a comet stayed on the same orbit for thousands of years, it could eventually evaporate to nothing.

Nucleus made of water ice and silicate rock dust

Black crust made of carbon

Bright side faces the Sun

Comet Hale-Bopp
Many new comets are found each year, but few of them can be seen without large telescopes. Sometimes a very bright comet appears in our skies. The great comet of 1997 was comet Hale-Bopp, named after its discoverers, Alan Hale and Tom Bopp. Hundreds of millions of people were able to see the comet after dark with the naked eye.

Halley's comet

Halley is the most famous of all the comets. It is named after Edmund Halley, who first realized that the comets seen in 1531, 1607, and 1682 were actually the same object. Halley worked out that it reappeared every 76 years after travelling out beyond the orbit of Neptune. He predicted that it would return in 1758–59 and it did, although he did not live to see it. Like many comets, it orbits the Sun in the opposite direction to the planets.

► BAD OMEN
Halley features in the Bayeux Tapestry. It appeared just before the Battle of Hastings in 1066.

Fan-tastic tails

Some comets produce spectacular tails that spread out like fans. Comet McNaught, which was the brightest comet for more than 40 years, provided a great example of this in the skies above the southern hemisphere in early 2007. Outbursts of dust created a broad, fan-shaped tail that was visible even in daylight. It was mistaken for a brush fire, an explosion, and a mysterious cloud.

BREAKING UP IS EASY TO DO

A comet's nucleus is not very strong, and sometimes it breaks into small pieces. Comet Shoemaker-Levy 9 was broken into 21 pieces by Jupiter's gravity in 1994. Fragments crashed into the planet, leaving craters on its surface. Other comets have broken up on their orbit near the Sun. In 1995, comet Schwassmann-Wachmann 3 broke into five large pieces. It continues to split into smaller and smaller pieces and is likely to soon disintegrate completely.

Jupiter's surface is scarred by comet pieces.

► MANY PIECES *form as Shoemaker-Levy breaks up.*

Oort Cloud

Billions of comets are thought to exist in the Oort Cloud, named after scientist Jan Oort. This vast, ball-shaped cloud exists far beyond Pluto, more than one light year from the Sun. The comets spend most of their lives here in deep freeze. Occasionally, when one is disturbed by a passing star, it begins to travel inwards towards the Sun. We only know of its existence when it starts to evaporate and grows tails during the approach. Comet Hyakutake, one of the brightest comets of the late 20th century, came from the Oort Cloud. It won't return to Earth's skies for 14,000 years.

Professor Jan H. Oort

► STAR STRUCK
A star passes close to the Oort Cloud and knocks a comet into a new orbit.

Sun

Comet

Comet missions

Comets were once mysterious visitors to the solar system. Since 1986 we have discovered more about them by sending spacecraft to have a closer look. Probes have not only flown past comets, but have also collected samples of comet dust and even crashed into a comet's nucleus.

Giotto

The first close-up views of a comet's nucleus came from the European Space Agency's Giotto spacecraft. In 1986, it flew past the nucleus of comet Halley at a distance of less than 600 km (373 miles). Images showed a black, potato-shaped object with jets of gas and dust spewing into space from the Sun-facing side. Giotto was damaged by a high-speed impact with a large dust grain, but recovered to become the first spacecraft to visit two comets – in 1992, it passed within 200 km (124 miles) of comet Grigg-Skjellerup.

Back-up antenna

Dish-shaped main antenna

▲ HALLEY'S NUCLEUS *ESA's Giotto space probe returned 2,333 images of comet Halley from its close flyby on 14 March 1986.*

Model of Giotto spacecraft

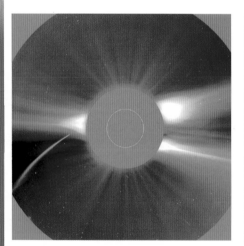

SOHO and its sungrazers

Designed to observe the Sun, the ESA–NASA SOHO spacecraft is able to block out the Sun's glare. This has revealed many "sungrazers" – comets that pass close to the Sun (and usually fall into it). SOHO has discovered nearly 1,700 comets since 1996.

STARDUST

■ NASA's Stardust spacecraft was launched towards comet Wild 2 in February 1999. Stardust was designed to collect dust samples from the comet. The particles were captured in aerogel and brought back to Earth for analysis.

■ In January 2004 Stardust swept past Wild 2 at a distance of 236 km (147 miles). Images taken by the spacecraft revealed the comet to be surprisingly different to comets Borrelly and Halley. Although its hamburger-shaped nucleus was only 5 km (3 miles) across, its surface was strong enough to support cliffs and pinnacles over 100 m (328 ft) high. Most noticeable of all were large circular craters up to 1.6 km (1 mile) wide, and 150 m (500 ft) deep.

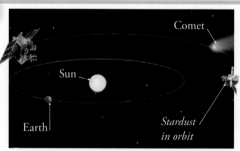

Comet

Sun

Earth

Stardust in orbit

▲ IN SPACE *This artist's impression shows Stardust on its mission to comet Wild 2. It is now on a mission to fly by comet Tempel 1.*

◄ LIGHT AS AIR *Made of 99.8% air, the ghostly looking aerogel is the only substance that can collect high-speed comet particles without damaging them.*

Deep Space 1

NASA's Deep Space 1 was launched in October 1998. It passed within 2,200 km (1,400 miles) of comet Borrelly in September 2001, and sent back the best pictures of a nucleus ever seen before. The nucleus measured about 8 km (5 miles) long and 4 km (2.5 miles) wide. It was found to be the blackest object in the solar system, reflecting less than 3 per cent of the sunlight that it receives.

WATCH THIS SPACE

Images taken by Deep Space 1 have been combined to show the coma, dust jets, and nucleus (shown in black) of comet Borrelly.

NEAR and far

NEAR (Near Earth Asteroid Rendezvous) Shoemaker made history when it became the first spacecraft not only to orbit but also land on an asteroid. It touched down on Eros on 12 February 2001 and sent data and images back to Earth. NEAR stopped working on 28 February and remains on Eros.

NEAR-Shoemaker is 2.8 m (9 ft 2 in) tall to the top of its antenna.

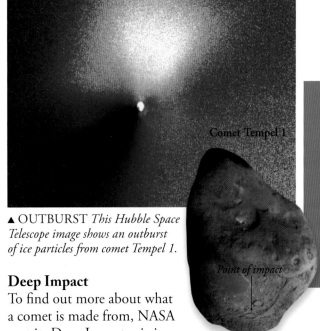

Comet Tempel 1

▲ OUTBURST *This Hubble Space Telescope image shows an outburst of ice particles from comet Tempel 1.*

Point of impact

Deep Impact

To find out more about what a comet is made from, NASA sent its Deep Impact mission to collide with comet Tempel 1. The probe released by the spaceship collided with the nucleus at 36,000 km/h (22,370 mph) and exploded on arrival, throwing out a huge cloud of ice and dust and creating a stadium-sized crater. The nucleus was revealed to be 5 km (3.1 miles) long and 7 km (4.3 miles) wide, with ridges and curved slopes.

▲ PHILAE *This computer image shows the Philae probe on the surface of comet Churyumov-Gerasimenko.*

Rosetta

Rosetta is the most ambitious comet mission ever launched. Developed by the European Space Agency, Rosetta is made up of an orbiter and a small lander named Philae. Altogether, the spacecraft carries more than 20 experiments designed to survey comet Churyumov-Gerasimenko in great detail. Launched on 2 March 2004, it will take 10 years to reach its target. Then, orbiting a few kilometres above the nucleus, it will release the lander for a controlled descent to the surface in 2014.

Meteors

Look up into the night sky and you might just see a brief trail of light left by a meteor. Also called shooting stars, meteors appear without warning and usually last less than a second. They are particles of dust that burn up as they hit the upper atmosphere at high speed – around 54,000 km/h (33,500 mph).

METEOR MENU

Many meteor showers occur at the same time each year. Here are some of the best, and the constellations they appear to come from.

- **Quadrantids**, early January, Boötes
- **Lyrids**, mid-April, Lyra
- **Aquarids**, late June, Aquarius
- **Capricornids**, late June, Capricorn
- **Perseids**, mid-August, Perseus
- **Orionids**, late October, Orion
- **Leonids**, mid-November, Leo
- **Geminids**, mid-December, Gemini

A METEOR SHOWER

The best time to look out for meteors is during an annual shower. They appear around the same dates each year, when Earth passes through a stream of dust left behind by a passing comet. It may be particularly impressive if the comet has entered the inner solar system quite recently.

TAKE A LOOK: LUNAR METEORS

Meteors also occur on other worlds, such as the Moon and Mars. Mars has a thin atmosphere, and meteors can appear as shooting stars. However, there is no air on the Moon, so lunar meteors are not destroyed in the sky. Instead, they hit the ground and explode, causing a flash of heat and light that can be seen on Earth 400,000 km (250,000 miles) away. Each explosion is equivalent to 45 kg (100 lb) of dynamite. When the Moon passes through dense streams of comet dust the rate of lunar flashes can go as high as one per hour.

▲ COPERNICUS CRATER
Meteorites hit the Moon's surface at such high speeds, they create craters 15 times their size. The Copernicus Crater is 91 km (57 miles) wide and 3.7 km (2.3 miles) deep.

▲ NAME GAME *Meteor showers are named after the constellation (area of sky) they appear to come from. The Perseids are named after the constellation Perseus.*

The Leonids

First reported by Chinese astronomers in 902 CE, the Leonids appear to come from the constellation Leo. This shower can be seen every year in mid-November, when 10 to 15 meteors per hour are usually visible around peak times. Every 33 years or so, the Leonids go through a period of great activity in which thousands of meteors an hour hurtle across the sky. Although most meteoroids are no larger than a grain of sand, the shower can be so active that it looks like falling snow.

— Star trail

— Meteor

▲ LOTS OF LEONIDS
This Leonid shower occurred over Korea in November 2001.

Fireballs

Extremely bright meteors are known as fireballs. They occur when a small piece of rock becomes very hot and bright as it enters Earth's atmosphere. Some fireballs are so bright that they are visible in daylight, and some can create a very loud sonic boom (like an aircraft breaking the sound barrier) that can shake houses. Sometimes the chunks of rock explode, scattering small meteorites on the ground.

▲ FAST FLIGHT *This Leonid fireball moved at a speed of 70 km (43 miles) per second.*

Meteorites

MAKING AN IMPACT

When an meteorite or asteroid lands, it can make a crater.

▲ A METEORITE *hits the ground at speed, creating heat that vaporizes it.*

▲ ENERGY *from the impact throws rocks up and out from the ground.*

▲ LARGE IMPACTS *cause the crust to rebound, creating a central peak.*

Every year, around 200,000 tonnes (220,000 tons) of cosmic dust and rock enter Earth's atmosphere as meteors. Those that are large enough to survive the fiery entry and reach the ground are called meteorites. Most meteorites that fall to Earth are pieces that have broken off asteroids during collisions in space.

▲ WHO IS HOBA? *Most meteorites are named after the place they fell. Hoba is named for Hoba Farm near Grootfontein, Namibia.*

HEFTY HOBA

The Hoba meteorite is the largest on Earth. The iron meteorite is thought to have landed less than 80,000 years ago and still lies at Hoba Farm where it was found in 1920. Surprisingly, the 60,000 kg (132,280 lb) meteorite did not dig out a crater when it hit the ground, perhaps because it entered the atmosphere at a shallow angle and was slowed down by atmospheric drag.

What's what?
- *Meteoroid* A small piece from an asteroid or comet orbiting the Sun.
- *Meteor* A meteoroid that has entered Earth's atmosphere and burns brightly.
- *Meteorite* A meteoroid that lands on the Earth's surface.

Meteor Crater
More than 100 impact craters have been found on Earth. One of the youngest is in Arizona, USA. Meteor Crater (also called Barringer Crater) was probably excavated about 50,000 years ago by a 270,000 tonne (300,000 ton) iron meteorite. The crater is 1,200 m (3,940 ft) wide, 183 m (600 ft) deep, and surrounded by a wall of loose rock up to 45 m (148 ft) high.

TAKE A LOOK: METEORITE TYPES

Meteorites help us to understand conditions in the early solar system 4.5 billion years ago. There are three main types. Stony meteorites are common, but tend to break up as they fall to Earth. Iron meteorites are less common in space, but they are very strong and usually land in one piece. "Stony-irons" are a mixture of the two types. Meteorites are usually coated with a black crust that forms when they are heated during passage through the atmosphere.

Iron meteorite

Stony-iron meteorite

Stony meteorite

Tagish Lake meteorite

This rare meteorite fell to Earth on the frozen surface of Tagish Lake, Canada, in 2000. The fragile, charcoal-like meteorite is rich in carbon and contains some of the oldest solar system material yet studied.

Meteorites *on* Mars...

Meteorites fall on other worlds, as well as Earth. NASA's Opportunity rover has come across several meteorites on the surface of Mars. The largest of these rocks was found in the Meridani Planum region in July 2009. Named Block Island, it is made of iron and nickel and may have been lying on Mars for millions of years.

▶ BIG BLOCK
Block Island is 60 cm (2 ft) long and 30 cm (1 ft) wide.

... and meteorites *from* Mars

Of the 24,000 or so meteorites that have been found on Earth, 34 have been identified as coming from Mars. These rocks were blasted into space long ago by large impacts, and travelled through space for many thousands or even millions of years until they fell to Earth. Although no one saw them land, we know that they come from Mars because they contain gases that are exactly the same as those found there. There are also more than 130 named meteorites that have been identified as lunar (they come from the Moon).

NWA 2626 meteorite

▲ CLOSE-UP CRYSTALS *Found in Algeria in November 2004, the NWA 2626 meteorite comes from Mars. It contains large crystals and glassy veins.*

ANYONE FOR TENNIS? *More than 2,000 tennis courts can fit inside Meteor Crater!*

Trail left by fireball

WATCH THIS SPACE

Meteoroid 2008 TC3 became the first to be seen BEFORE it hit Earth. Spotted out in space, astronomers correctly predicted when and where it would enter Earth's atmosphere: 7 October 2008, in Sudan.

Life on other worlds

Life is found in some surprising places on Earth, from inside solid rock to volcanic vents and the frozen Antarctic. Some experts think that simple organisms may exist in other parts of the solar system – if the ingredients for life can be found.

◄ INGREDIENTS FOR LIFE *Life seems to be able to survive where water and a source of energy are present. This slime mould lives on, and eats, rock.*

LIFE FROM MARS

■ **Today Mars is a freezing desert,** but long ago it may have been warm and wet enough to harbour life. Space probes have found water ice on Mars but so far no evidence of life. Scientists have discovered possible hints of life in a Martian meteorite that was found in Antarctica in 1984. This rock was blasted off the surface of Mars 16 million years ago.

Lowell's map of Mars

Criss-crossing canals

◄ MICROLIFE *Inside the Martian meteorite were tiny wormlike structures and magnetite crystals, which are associated with some kinds of bacteria.*

■ **In the 19th century,** astronomers thought they could see vegetation (plants) on Mars. Some even thought they could see canals crossing the surface. One, Percival Lowell, drew maps of Mars showing a network of canals that he claimed were built by Martians to bring water to the desert. Spacecraft pictures have since shown that no such canals exist.

■ **In 1976,** a picture from the Viking probe showed what appeared to be a mysterious human face on Mars. Some people claimed it was evidence of a long-lost Martian civilization. When the Mars Reconnaissance Orbiter visited 20 years later and took better photos, its showed the face was just an illusion created by the viewing angle.

The face in 1976... ... is gone in 2007.

Life in the clouds

The gas giant Jupiter has no solid surface or oceans of water, but scientists have suggested that life-forms could exist floating in the clouds. Such life could only survive in the upper atmosphere, as the pressure and temperature are too high in the lower atmosphere. However, probes have found no evidence of life at all.

▲ SWIMMING IN THE SKY
Could alien life-forms on gas giants behave like jellyfish or rays floating in Earth's oceans?

EUROPA

Scientists think that Jupiter's ice-covered moon Europa is the most likely location for extraterrestrial life in the solar system. Europa's surface is covered with fractured ice, but below the surface may be a hidden ocean where life might flourish. There might even be hot, hydrothermal vents on the sea floor. On Earth, such vents are surrounded by strange life forms and are considered a likely site for the origin of life on our planet.

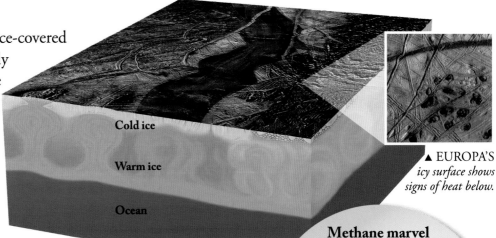

Cold ice

Warm ice

Ocean

▲ WHAT LIES BENEATH?
Although the surface is a freezing −170°C (−274°F), heat generated deep in the moon by Jupiter's gravity could have created a hidden ocean where life might flourish.

▲ EUROPA'S *icy surface shows signs of heat below.*

Methane marvel

In 1997, scientists discovered a new species of centipede-like worm. It was found living on and within piles of methane ice on the seabed of the Gulf of Mexico. If the animal could survive in methane on Earth, could others survive in methane in space?

1 mm

What an atmosphere

Saturn's largest moon, Titan, has a dense atmosphere – thought to be like the one on early Earth when life began. Titan has the right chemical ingredients for life, including water in the form of ice, and carbon compounds, which form lakes on the surface. Titan's surface temperature is far too cold for life to survive there, but alien life forms might exist deep underground in hidden lakes of liquid water or ammonia.

▶ WATER OF LIFE? *This false-colour radar map shows lakes of liquid methane (a carbon compound) on Titan.*

TERRAFORMING PLANETS

Some NASA scientists think it may be possible to transform lifeless planets into Earth-like planets suitable for humans. This is called terraforming – "forming an Earth". Mars could be terraformed if it were heated up...

▶ BEFORE
Enough warmth would melt the frozen water and carbon dioxide on Mars, forming oceans and lakes.

▶ AFTER *With enough water, micro-organisms and plant life could be brought from Earth to release oxygen into the air and make it breathable.*

Space colonies

None of the solar system's worlds are habitable except Earth, but space scientists believe it may be possible in the future to set up colonies on other worlds. The Moon would be first, and could provide a stepping stone to further exploration.

▲ BEST FOR BASE *The Moon's south-polar region, where there are water deposits, is being considered for a base. Using solar power, the water could be split into oxygen for breathing and hydrogen for rocket fuel.*

EARTH

Our home planet is unique. "The third rock from the Sun" is the only world known to have the right conditions for life to flourish – and what an amazing planet it has turned out to be.

The unique Earth

Earth is a unique planet – the only world known to support any life. It has liquid water on its surface and lots of oxygen. The thick atmosphere protects the surface from radiation and meteorites and the strong magnetic field shields us from harmful particles streaming out from the Sun.

Earth's rocky crust is only about 6.5 km (4 miles) thick under the oceans, and about 35 km (22 miles) thick on land.

PLANET PROFILE

- **Average distance from the Sun** 150 million km (93 million miles)
- **Average surface temperature** 15°C (59°F)
- **Diameter** 12,760 km (7,930 miles)
- **Length of day** 24 hours
- **Length of year** 365.26 days
- **Number of moons** 1
- **Gravity at the surface** 1

Crust

Mantle

Inner core

Outer core

The atmosphere is a blanket of gas that surrounds Earth. It is mainly made up of nitrogen (78 per cent), oxygen (21 per cent), and argon (1 per cent).

INSIDE EARTH

Earth has the highest density of any planet in the solar system because its core is mainly made of iron. The very high pressures at the centre mean that the inner core remains solid, even at 6,000°C (10,832°F). The outer core is made of molten metal and the surrounding mantle is a thick layer of partly molten rock. Floating on top of this is a thin, rocky skin called the crust.

Antarctica contains 90 per cent of the world's ice and 70 per cent of its fresh water. If all of Antarctica's ice melted away, sea levels would rise by more than 60 m (200 ft).

The habitable zone

Earth is at just the right distance from the Sun for liquid water to exist. Any closer and the oceans would boil away: any further out and the planet would freeze. The availability of liquid water is very important. Life on Earth can exist wherever there is water – without it life would die. The part of the solar system where conditions are suitable for life is known as the habitable zone. Earth is the only planet found here.

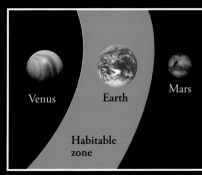

Venus   Earth   Mars

Habitable zone

▲ HOME, SWEET HOME
Earth sits in the narrow region of space where water can exist in liquid form. Our neighbouring planets fall outside this zone – hot Venus is too close to the Sun and cold Mars is too far away.

Water covers more than two-thirds of Earth's surface. About 97 per cent of this is salt water found in the seas and oceans.

MAGNETIC FIELD

Earth has a strong magnetic field, which creates a magnetic bubble around the planet. Shaped like a tadpole, it extends about 64,000 km (40,000 miles) from Earth's surface in the sunward direction and more in other directions. The magnetic field usually protects satellites and astronauts that are inside the bubble from blasts of particles from the Sun. However, massive solar explosions can weaken it and severe space weather can cause widespread power cuts and communication blackouts.

Solar explosion

Sun

Earth's magnetic field

TAKE A LOOK: AURORAS

The red and green curtains of light that appear in the night sky at the north and south poles are known as the northern lights (aurora borealis) and southern lights (aurora australis). The auroras are caused when high-energy particles from the Sun pour through weak spots in Earth's magnetic field, colliding with atoms in the upper atmosphere and giving off light.

THE PERFECT PLANET

We live on the most amazing rock in the Universe.
Despite all our efforts to find new, habitable
worlds, ours is the only planet so far that has the
right conditions for life. Situated at just the right
distance from our Sun, it is not too hot nor too
cold. The key to life is liquid water, which Earth
has in abundance. It drives our weather and makes
plants grow, forming the basis of the food chain for
animals. Earth is also the only planet we know of
that has enough oxygen to keep us alive.

Earth's seasons

We live our lives according to Earth's timetable. With a few exceptions, we get up and work in the day and go to sleep at night. The Sun shining on Earth produces day and night. It also plays a role in creating the seasons – spring, summer, autumn, and winter.

▲ AN ALIEN'S VIEW *Earth and the Moon appear here in first-quarter phase – half in daylight, half in night.*

EARTH AND MOON

An alien flying past would see the Earth and Moon appearing to change shape. Sometimes the alien would see Earth fully lit, as a bright blue and green disc, sometimes half-illuminated, and sometimes fully in shadow – with various stages in between. The different shapes are called phases. We can see the Moon's phases from Earth.

Vertical

Axis of spin leans at a 23.5° angle to the vertical

Solar radiation

Direction of Earth's spin

▲ SUNLIGHT INTENSITY *The amount of sunlight received by Earth is affected by the tilt of the axis, towards or away from the Sun.*

Day and night

Because Earth is tilted as it spins, the period of daylight changes throughout the year, unless you live on the equator. The polar regions experience this to the extreme, with very long days in summer and very long nights in winter. North of the Arctic Circle and south of the Antarctic Circle, the Sun does not rise in midwinter or set in midsummer. Because of this, areas such as northern Norway and Alaska are known as the "land of the midnight Sun".

▲ MIDNIGHT SUN *This multiple exposure image shows how the Sun dips towards the horizon but never sets below it in a polar summer.*

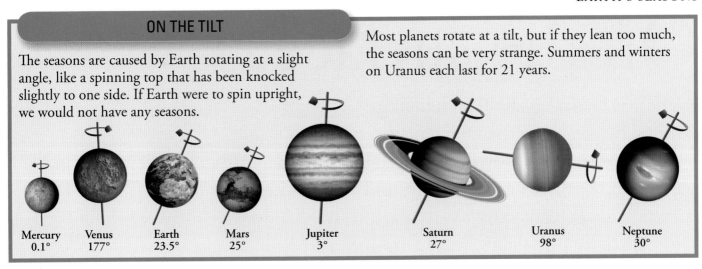

ON THE TILT

The seasons are caused by Earth rotating at a slight angle, like a spinning top that has been knocked slightly to one side. If Earth were to spin upright, we would not have any seasons.

Most planets rotate at a tilt, but if they lean too much, the seasons can be very strange. Summers and winters on Uranus each last for 21 years.

| Mercury 0.1° | Venus 177° | Earth 23.5° | Mars 25° | Jupiter 3° | Saturn 27° | Uranus 98° | Neptune 30° |

SEASONS

Unless you live near the equator or the poles, you will experience four seasons – spring, summer, autumn, and winter. At the equator the period of daylight hardly changes and the Sun is high in the sky, so it is always warm. Our spinning Earth is tilted at 23.5 degrees to the plane of its orbit. When the north pole is tilted towards the Sun it is summer in the northern hemisphere and winter in the southern hemisphere. When the north pole is tilted away from the Sun it is winter in the northern hemisphere and summer in the southern hemisphere.

Southern summer occurs when the north pole tilts away from the Sun.

Sun

Earth

Day   Night

Northern summer occurs when the north pole tilts towards the Sun.

▲ EARTH'S ORBIT *Earth moves around the Sun in an oval-shaped orbit, which varies Earth's distance from the Sun but is not responsible for the seasons.*

▼ VEGETATION *patterns (green) change according to how much light is received in each season.*

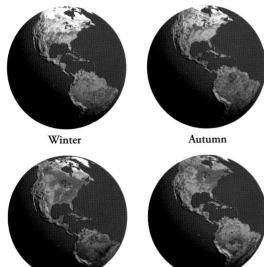

Winter   Autumn

Spring   Summer

The seasonal Sun

Earth's temperature is influenced by the length of the day and by the seasons. In summer, the Sun is above the horizon for longer, and higher in the sky. Less heat is absorbed by the atmosphere and more heat is absorbed by the ground and oceans. In winter, the Sun is above the horizon for a shorter length of time. During the long nights, more heat escapes to space than is provided by the Sun during the day.

▶ IN HOT WATER
This map shows how sunlight affects sea temperatures around the world, with warm waters in red around the equator, cooling through orange, yellow, and green. Cold waters are shown in blue.

On the surface

Earth's surface is constantly changing. Although covered by a rocky crust, it is far from stiff and static. The crust is divided into huge slabs, called plates, which move very slowly around Earth. The surface is also changed by rivers, glaciers, wind, and rain, which help shape the world around us.

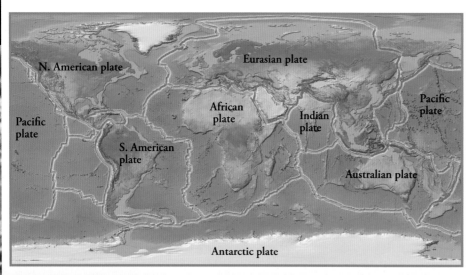

N. American plate
Eurasian plate
African plate
Indian plate
Pacific plate
Pacific plate
S. American plate
Australian plate
Antarctic plate

EARTH'S PLATES

The rocky plates that make up the crust float on Earth's dense mantle. They move between 3 and 15 cm (1 and 6 in) a year, changing the positions of the continents over time. Some plates move apart, others slide towards or past each other. Their movements build mountain ranges, and cause earthquakes, tidal waves, and volcanic eruptions.

Earthquakes and volcanoes
The edges of plates are dangerous places to live. Major earthquakes occur where plates collide and cities such as San Francisco and Tokyo, which lie near active plate boundaries, suffer from frequent, large earthquakes. Many volcanoes occur at plate boundaries where one plate slides under another, allowing molten rock to escape to the surface.

Mountain ranges
Most continents have mountain ranges. These occur where two plates collide, pushing the crust up to form high peaks. Standing at 8,848 m (29,029 ft), Mount Everest is the highest mountain in the world. It is part of the Himalayan mountain range that formed when the Indian plate crashed into the Eurasian plate. There are also volcanic mountains that rise from the seabed. The tallest of these is Mauna Kea, an inactive volcano in Hawaii. Measured from the ocean floor, Mauna Kea is even taller than Everest.

EARTH

WIND

WATER

Waterworld

As streams and rivers flow down from high ground, they pick up sediment and small rock fragments. These abrasive particles grind away at the landscape. Over time, this process wears away mountainsides and carves out deep canyons. Rivers can also build up and create new landscape features by depositing mud and silt as they approach the sea. The sea itself is a massive force of change – the waves grind away at cliffs and shorelines, changing coastlines and forming spectacular shapes in the rocks.

▼ WILD, ROCKY LANDSCAPE *of wind-eroded red sandstone in Colorado, USA.*

Windswept In dry places with little water or plant life, wind is the major source of erosion. The wind blasts rocks at high speed, carrying away loose particles, and grinding these against existing landscape features. Over years, this wears down rocks and can produce some amazing shapes – arches, towers, and strange, wind-blown sculptures.

ICE

Rivers of ice

Glaciers are large, moving sheets of ice that occur at the poles and high in mountain ranges. Some barely move while others surge forward, travelling as fast as 20–30 m (66–100 ft) a day. These rivers of ice dramatically alter the landscape, eroding rock, sculpting mountains, and carving out deep glacial valleys. Glaciers pick up rocks and debris, dragging them along and leaving holes in the valley floor. As glaciers melt, they produce lakes and leave boulders and mounds of gravel strewn across the landscape.

◄ SAN ANDREAS FAULT
San Andreas in California is a fault, or crack, in Earth's crust where two plates, the Pacific and the North American, are sliding past each other. On average, they move only a few centimetres each year. This motion is not consistent – the plates remain locked together until enough stress builds up and a slip occurs. The sudden movement of the plates releases energy and causes earthquakes.

Up in the air

Life could not survive on Earth without the thick blanket of gases known as the atmosphere. The atmosphere protects us from harmful radiation and small incoming meteorites. It also provides us with our weather and helps keep Earth warm.

ATMOSPHERIC ZONES

EXOSPHERE

Satellite

Space shuttle

600 km (375 miles)

THERMOSPHERE

Northern lights

80 km (50 miles)

MESOSPHERE

Shooting stars

50 km (30 miles)

STRATOSPHERE

Aeroplanes

8–16 km (5–10 miles)

TROPOSPHERE

Clouds

Other gases

Oxygen

Nitrogen

The sky appears blue because blue light is scattered more than other colours by the gases in the atmosphere.

IT'S ALL A GAS

The atmosphere extends about 1,000 km (600 miles) into space. It is thickest near the ground and quickly becomes thinner as you move upward. The most common gases in the atmosphere are nitrogen (78 per cent) and oxygen (21 per cent). Other gases include argon, carbon dioxide, and water vapour.

◄ ZONES *Earth's atmosphere consists of five layers. The layer closest to the ground is the troposphere. All our weather occurs in this layer. The stratosphere is more stable, and also contains the ozone layer. Although the air is much thinner in the mesosphere, there is enough to cause meteors to burn up on entry. Auroras occur in the thermosphere. The exosphere marks the upper limit of the atmosphere, where most spacecraft orbit.*

WATER CYCLE

The water cycle is a continuous movement of water between Earth's surface and its atmosphere. It is powered by heat from the Sun and provides us with a constant source of fresh water.

High above the ground, the water vapour cools. It turns back into droplets of water and clouds are formed.

When the droplets get too heavy they fall back to the surface as rain or snow.

Water in the rivers and oceans is heated by the Sun and evaporates, turning into a gas called water vapour.

Some water soaks into the ground to form groundwater.

The rest of the water runs off the land, flowing into streams and rivers.

About 90 per cent of the evaporated water that enters the water cycle comes from the oceans.

Streams and rivers channel water back into lakes or towards the ocean.

TAKE A LOOK: CLOUDS AND WEATHER

Stratus clouds

Cumulus clouds

Thunder clouds

Earth's weather takes place in the troposphere, where water vapour cools to form clouds. There are many types of cloud. Stratus clouds form wide layers in still air. Cumulus clouds bubble up where warm air rises. Rapidly rising air carries clouds to great heights and large, tall clouds called cumulonimbus often produce rain and sometimes hailstones. Cirrus clouds at the very top of the troposphere are made of tiny crystals of ice.

◀ SUPER STORM *The rarest type of thunderstorm is the supercell. It produces the most violent weather, including deadly lightning, giant hail, flash floods, and tornadoes.*

Storm forces

Hurricanes are the most powerful storms on Earth. Storms over tropical waters become hurricanes when wind speeds reach more than 120 km/h (74 mph). Hurricanes in the southern hemisphere spin in a clockwise direction, while those in the northern hemisphere spin anticlockwise.

▲ EYE OF THE STORM *The air at the centre of a hurricane (the eye) remains still while powerful winds rage around it.*

▼ DUST STORMS *are caused by strong winds passing across deserts or dry, dusty areas. They can pick up thousands of tonnes of sand or dust. An approaching storm can appear as a solid wall, reaching up to 1.6 km (1 mile) from the ground.*

Life on Earth

Earth is the only place we know where life exists. Life is found almost everywhere on the planet – from the highest mountains to the deepest ocean trenches. It is even found in boiling hot springs and inside solid rock.

THE ORIGINS OF LIFE

The first simple life forms probably appeared on Earth about 3.8 billion years ago. No one knows how life began but scientists think it may have started in the oceans, since the land was very hot and the atmosphere was poisonous. Others think comets or meteors brought complex chemicals from outer space. However it began, simple molecules formed and began to copy themselves, eventually growing into cells, and then colonies. Over time, these evolved into more complicated organisms that began to colonize the land.

Life begins

The first life forms were simple, single cells that probably lived in the oceans and hot springs. Over billions of years, single-celled organisms became a lot more complex and multicellular life evolved.

Early cell

TIMELINE OF LIFE ON EARTH

EARLY EARTH

4.5 billion years: Earth forms

3.6 billion years: Blue-green algae release oxygen into atmosphere

3.8 billion years: Simple bacteria appear in the oceans

1.8 billion years: First complex organisms, the ancestors of animals, plants, and fungi

FIRST LIFE

630 million years: First complex animals appear in sea

490 million years: Fish evolve

430 million years: First plants colonize land

360 million years: Winged insects take to the skies and reptiles evolve from amphibians

415 million years: Tetrapods take first steps onto dry land

From prehistoric elephant…

… to Asian elephant

Evolution

Earth supports many forms of life, including plants, animals, and tiny bacteria. All living things have adapted to their surroundings through a process called evolution. This takes place over many generations and is often called "survival of the fittest". Life that is too slow to adapt to competition or changes in its environment will die out.

Extinctions

At various times during Earth's history, many life forms have been wiped out. Some mass extinctions were probably caused by huge volcanic eruptions belching out clouds of gas and ash. These would have blocked out the Sun, causing the temperature to drop and killing many of the plants that animals needed for food. The extinction of the dinosaurs 65 million years ago has been blamed on volcanic eruptions triggered by an asteroid impact.

▲ TIKTAALIK
This extinct lobe-finned fish lived during the Late Devonian period, 375 million years ago.

Hydrothermal mussels and shrimps

Black smoker

Giant tube worm

Black smokers

Most plants and animals rely on sunlight to survive but some deep-sea creatures live in total darkness. Thousands of metres below the surface, water escapes from the super-hot mantle through cracks in the rock. These hot volcanic vents, or "black smokers", are home to dense communities of giant tube worms, mussels, shrimps, and crabs. They live on bacteria that are able to harness energy from chemicals dissolved in the hot water. Some bacteria also live inside solid rock or on cold parts of the ocean floor and get their energy by eating the minerals in the rock.

TAKE A LOOK: OCEAN BLOOMS

The oceans are not only home to large creatures, such as fish and whales. Among the most important forms of ocean life are microscopic plants called phytoplankton. These tiny organisms float in the surface waters where there is plenty of sunlight. They provide an important source of food for a range of animals, from small shrimps to huge whales. When a great number of phytoplankton are concentrated in one area, they change the colour of the ocean's surface. Sometimes these "blooms" are so big, they can be seen from space.

▲ PLENTIFUL PLANKTON *A turquoise-coloured phytoplankton bloom appeared off the coast of Ireland in June 2006.*

MORE COMPLEX LIFE FORMS

300 million years: Seed plants appear

250 million years: Reptiles begin to fly (pterosaurs) and plants start producing flowers

200 million years: Dinosaurs and birds evolve from reptiles

150 million years: First mammals emerge

65 million years: Mass extinction wipes out dinosaurs and many other life forms

MODERN TIMES

60 million years: Mammals take over the world and modern forms of fish, reptiles, plants, and insects appear

5 million years: Apes descend from the trees and start walking upright

250,000 years: Modern man (*Homo sapiens*) evolves

THE
MOON

A full Moon is the second-brightest object in the sky, after the Sun. Our Moon was humankind's first destination in space, but only 12 people have ever walked on its surface.

Earth's companion

Earth and the Moon have been close partners for about 4.5 billion years. Although the Moon is much smaller than Earth, it influences our planet in many ways and has fascinated humans for thousands of years.

TIDAL ATTRACTION

Lunar tides

Tides are created by the Moon's gravity pulling on Earth's water. At any one time, there is a place on Earth that is nearest to the Moon and one that is furthest away. Here the seas "bulge" out, creating high tides. The bulges move around Earth as it rotates.

▲ LOW TIDES *occur twice a day when a place is at right angles to the Moon's gravity pull.*

▲ HIGH TIDES *happen twice daily too when a place is aligned with the Moon.*

Solar tides

The Sun also has a weak effect on tides. When the Moon, Earth, and Sun align, their combined gravity causes very low and very high spring tides. When the Moon and Sun are at right angles, you have a neap tide.

Solar tide

Lunar tide

Moon (full or new)

Moon (quarter phase)

Solar tide

Lunar tide

▲ SPRING TIDES *occur when solar and lunar tides join forces to create an extremely strong gravitational pull.*

▲ DURING A NEAP *tide the high tide is slightly lower than usual and the low tide is slightly higher than usual.*

Rocky mantle, possibly molten nearer the centre

Possible small metal core

Thin crust of granite-like rock

MOON PROFILE

- **Average distance from Earth** 384,400 km (238,900 miles)
- **Diameter** 3,476 km (2,160 miles)
- **Length of lunar day** 27.3 Earth days
- **Length of lunar month (new Moon to new Moon)** 29.5 days
- **Surface temperature** –150°C to 120°C (–240°F to 240°F)
- **Surface gravity (Earth = 1)** 0.17 (one-sixth of Earth's gravity)

INSIDE THE MOON

The Moon has a crust of brittle rock about 50 km (31 miles) thick that is riddled with cracks. Beneath the crust is a deep mantle that is thought to be rich in minerals, similar to those found in Earth rock. The mantle may extend all the way to the centre, or the Moon may have a small metal core.

Slowing down

Tidal forces between the Earth and Moon are gradually slowing down Earth's rotation, making the day longer. When Earth was formed, a day lasted only six hours. By 620 million years ago, a day had lengthened to 22 hours. Eventually, tidal forces will increase our day length to 27.3 Earth days, matching the lunar day exactly.

In a spin

The Moon takes 27.3 days to orbit Earth once, but also 27.3 days to spin once on its axis. As a result, it keeps the same side facing Earth – the "near side". Even so, variations in the Moon's orbit allow parts of its far side to come into view now and then. Tidal forces between the Earth and Moon are causing the Moon to move slowly away from Earth by 3.8 cm (1.5 in) a year.

New Moon

Crescent Moon waning

Crescent Moon waxing

Last quarter

AS THE MOON moves from new Moon to full Moon it is said to be "waxing". As it moves from a full Moon through to the next new Moon it is said to be "waning". When more than half of the Moon's face is visible it is described as "gibbous".

First quarter

Gibbous Moon waning

Gibbous Moon waxing

Full Moon

▼ VIEW OF *the Earth and the Moon looking down onto their north poles.*

Same face always points to Earth.

Direction of Moon's orbit

Moon rotates anticlockwise.

PHASES OF THE MOON

For centuries, people have been fascinated by the way the Moon goes through a cycle of "phases" that repeats every 29.5 days. These phases occur because we see different amounts of the Moon's sunlit side as the Moon orbits Earth.

Eclipses

Eclipses are among the most spectacular astronomical events you can see. They occur when the Earth, Moon, and Sun all line up so that Earth casts a shadow on the Moon or the Moon casts a shadow on Earth. The Sun or Moon appear to go dark to people standing inside these shadows.

not to scale

Sun   **Moon** **Earth**

▲ MOON BLOCK *A total solar eclipse occurs when the Moon completely blocks the light from the Sun. All that can be seen is the corona (the Sun's atmosphere) as a shimmering halo of light around it.*

▶ MASKED BY THE MOON *As the Moon passes in front of the Sun, we see less and less of the Sun's disc.*

▶ DIAMOND RING
At the start and end of a total eclipse, sunlight shining through lunar mountains can create the stunning "diamond ring" effect.

Shadow play
A total solar eclipse can be seen only from the centre of the Moon's shadow – the umbra. The umbra sweeps across Earth during an eclipse, tracing a path thousands of kilometres long but no more than 100 km (60 miles) wide. Outside the umbra, the Moon casts a partial shadow causing a partial solar eclipse.

SOLAR ECLIPSES

The Moon passes between the Sun and Earth every month at "new moon", but because its orbit is slightly tilted it usually does not pass directly in front of the Sun. Occasionally, however, it does move directly in front of the Sun and causes a solar eclipse. Although the Sun is 400 times wider than the Moon, by a curious coincidence it is also 400 times further away. As a result, when viewed from Earth the Moon's disc fits exactly over the Sun's disc during a total solar eclipse.

WATCH THIS SPACE

... Carefully! When viewing a solar eclipse, you shouldn't look directly at the Sun without proper eye protection. Although most of the Sun is masked, the corona is still bright enough to damage your eyes.

Predicted paths of solar eclipses until 2024

LUNAR ECLIPSES

Two or three times a year, the Moon passes through Earth's enormous shadow and a lunar eclipse occurs. Surprisingly, the Moon does not become completely black. Some sunlight is refracted (bent) by Earth's atmosphere and makes the Moon turn orange-red, like a red sunset. Lunar eclipses are easier and much safer to see than solar eclipses as anybody with a view of the Moon can see them.

When day becomes night

A total solar eclipse occurs about every 18 months. If you are in the right place to see one, it is an amazing experience. As the last rays of sunlight are eclipsed, darkness falls, stars appear, and day turns to twilight. All that can be seen of the Sun is its hazy outer atmosphere.

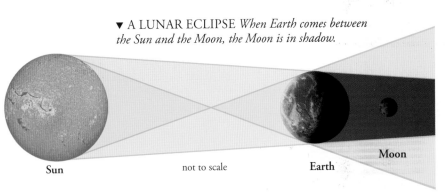

▼ A LUNAR ECLIPSE *When Earth comes between the Sun and the Moon, the Moon is in shadow.*

Sun   not to scale   Earth   Moon

WHEN AND WHERE TO SEE A TOTAL LUNAR ECLIPSE

21 December 2010	*East Asia, Australia, Americas, Europe*
15 June 2011	*Europe, South America, Africa, Asia, Australia*
10 December 2011	*Europe, East Africa, Asia, Australia*
15 April 2014	*Australia, Americas*
8 October 2014	*Asia, Australia, Americas*
4 April 2015	*Asia, Australia, Americas*
28 September 2015	*Americas, Europe, Africa, West Asia*
31 January 2018	*Europe, Africa, Asia, Australia*
27 July 2018	*Asia, Australia, western North America*
21 January 2019	*South America, Europe, Africa, Asia, Australia*
26 May 2021	*Asia, Australia, Americas*

▲ RED MOON *This time-delay photograph shows the stages of a single lunar eclipse. Earth's shadow can take four hours to move across the Moon, but "totality", when the Moon is fully inside the shadow, lasts only around one hour.*

The *lunar surface*

Even with the naked eye we can see surface features on the Moon. The dark areas are called "maria", the Latin word for seas, because early astronomers mistook them for oceans. The Italian scientist Galileo was the first person to view the Moon with a telescope and was amazed to see mountains, plains, and valleys.

Maria

Highlands

Thousands of craters pepper the Moon's face like scars, evidence of violent clashes with asteroids and comets.

▲ MOON CRATERS *vary in size from a few millimetres to about 300 km (186 miles) in diameter. The larger craters often have central mountains where the crust rebounded after impact, as in the 58 km (36 mile) wide Eratosthenes Crater. It is surrounded by rays of material thrown out from the nearby Copernicus Crater.*

LUNAR HIGHLANDS

The cratered areas outside the maria are called highlands. These cover most of the Moon's surface, especially on the far side. The highland rock is chemically different from the maria rock and lighter in colour. The lunar mountains that line the edges of craters or maria, reach more than 3.5 km (2 miles) in height and are smoother than Earth mountains. The surface is covered in rocks and powdered grey dust several metres deep.

THE FAR SIDE

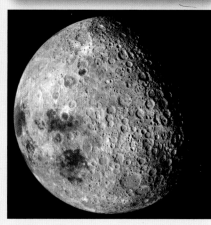

We only ever see one side of the Moon from Earth, so our first view of the far side came from pictures taken by the Soviet probe Luna 3 in 1959. Later NASA Apollo missions took even clearer pictures, such as the one shown here, centred on the boundary between the near and far sides. The far side has few maria and consists mostly of heavily cratered highlands.

Waterless seas

The lunar maria, or "seas", are flat plains of volcanic rock. Astronomers think they formed during the Moon's first 800 million years when molten rock welled up and filled the bottoms of gigantic basins. The lava cooled and solidified to form smooth plains. After the maria formed, the rate of meteorite impacts dropped and so the maria have fewer craters than the much older highlands.

📷 WATCH THIS SPACE

This dusty footprint will remain on the Moon for ever as there is no wind to blow it away. Moon dust is said to smell like gunpowder. The fine dust particles covered the astronauts' space suits and equipment when they stepped outside.

▲ LAVA FLOWS *Snakelike channels were formed by rivers of lava billions of years ago. The top of the cooling lava formed a solid roof. Later, the liquid lava drained away and the roof of the tunnel collapsed, leaving winding channels known as rilles.*

186

Destination Moon

Mankind's dream of space travel became a reality in the 1950s and 1960s when the Russians and Americans set out to be the first to conquer space. In the end, both countries scored space firsts: the USSR with unmanned probes and the first man in space, and the USA with a man on the Moon.

Command module

Quick-escape hatch

Astronauts' seats

Forward heat shield

Instrument panel

Service module

Fuel tanks

Engine nozzle

Helium tanks

Fuel cells

WATCH THIS SPACE

By the 1950s, a lunar mission had become a real possibility due to advances in space technology. Many toys, books, and films from this time are based on space travel.

4. LM lands on lunar surface.

5. Upper stage of LM returns to lunar orbit to dock with CSM.

3. LM separates for landing. CSM stays in lunar orbit with fuel for return to Earth.

6. CSM fires its rockets to return to Earth orbit.

2. Rocket is discarded. CSM and LM proceed into orbit around the Moon.

7. Command module separates from service module and returns crew to Earth.

1. Command and service module (CSM), and lunar module (LM) are sent into Earth orbit.

To the Moon and back

The first mission to land men on the Moon began from Cape Canaveral in Florida, USA, on 16 July 1969, when a Saturn V rocket sent the Apollo 11 spacecraft on its historic journey. Actually, the dream almost didn't happen – the lunar module touched down on the Moon with less than 30 seconds of fuel remaining as its pilot, Neil Armstrong, struggled to find a safe landing site.

READY, STEADY, GO!

Over 100 spacecraft have been sent to the Moon since the first lunar mission in 1959, although many of them were failures. Here are some of the early highlights.

Lunar module upper stage

Docking tunnel

Equipment bay

Oxygen tank

Fuel tank

Rendezvous radar antenna

Control console

Lunar module landing stage

Fuel tank

Lunar surface sensing probe

Scientific experiments package

Exit platform

Landing pad

Apollo 11 exploded

The spacecraft consisted of three modules, the command module (CM) for the astronauts to live, work, and ultimately return to Earth in, the service module (SM) containing fuel and equipment for supplying the astronauts with water, electricity, and oxygen, and the two-stage lunar module (LM) for the all-important Moon landing.

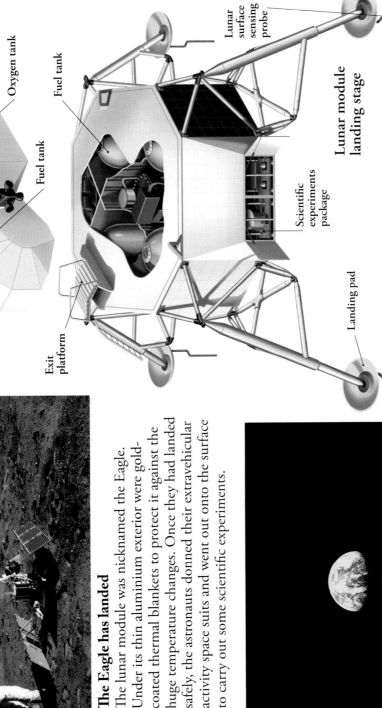

The Eagle has landed

The lunar module was nicknamed the Eagle. Under its thin aluminium exterior were gold-coated thermal blankets to protect it against the huge temperature changes. Once they had landed safely, the astronauts donned their extravehicular activity space suits and went out onto the surface to carry out some scientific experiments.

▲ THIS VIEW *from the Apollo 11 spacecraft shows Earthrise over the Moon's horizon. The lunar landscape is the area of Smyth's Sea on the nearside of the Moon.*

January 1959
Soviet probe Luna 1, the first spacecraft sent to the Moon, malfunctions and misses the Moon by 6,000 km (3,700 miles).

September 1959
Luna 2 makes a deliberate crash-landing, becoming the first craft to touch down on the Moon.

October 1959
Luna 3 becomes the first craft to photograph the far side of the Moon.

July 1964
US probe Ranger 7 takes thousands of photos of the Moon's surface before deliberately crash-landing.

February 1966
Luna 9 becomes the first craft to make a soft landing on the Moon.

April 1967
US probe Surveyor 3 lands on the Moon and photographs the future landing site of the Apollo 12 manned mission.

December 1968
Humans orbit the Moon for the first time during NASA's Apollo 8 mission.

July 1969
Neil Armstrong and Buzz Aldrin are the first people ever to set foot on the Moon as part of NASA's Apollo 11 mission.

November 1970
Lunokhod 1, a Russian rover looking like an 8-wheeled pram, becomes the first vehicle to drive on the Moon.

Man on the Moon

▲ TRANQUILITY BASE *Aldrin and Armstrong's space walk was televised around the world.*

On 20 July 1969, 500 million people watched on TV as Neil Armstrong became the first person to set foot on the lunar surface, announcing, "That's one small step for man, one giant leap for mankind". Altogether, 12 people walked on the Moon between 1969 and 1972 in six successful missions.

Walking on the Moon

The astronauts weighed only one-sixth of their normal weight on the Moon – and so did their life-support backpacks. Too heavy to wear for long on Earth, they were easily carried on the Moon. Walking normally was out of the question. Some used a "kangaroo hop", others a loping walk. Some even enjoyed "skiing" or gliding over the Moon dust, by pushing off with their toes.

That's rubbish!

The Moon is littered with lunar modules, flags, probes, and other pieces of equipment that have been left there or that have crash-landed – planned or unplanned! The unmanned Russian spacecraft Luna 15 crashed into the Moon just hours after Apollo 11's lunar module landed.

Storage for tools, lunar rock and soil samples

Camera

Dish antenna for relaying pictures back to Earth

Moon buggy

Apollo missions 15 to 17 carried a 3 m (10 ft) long, open-topped roving vehicle that was carried, folded up, on the side of the lunar module. The battery-powered rover had a top speed of 18.6 km/h (11.5 mph).

Solid tyres

Rock on

The Apollo astronauts brought back case upon case of rock and soil samples from their six missions. Despite the low gravity, it was hard, dirty work. The astronaut's arm and hand muscles tired very quickly in the restrictive space suits and gloves. Bending over was almost impossible, so the astronauts had special tools to pick up rocks. They also found out that Moon dust was powdery, very abrasive, and extremely clingy, turning space suits grey, scratching visors, and even wearing through the surface layers of their boots.

▲ ROCK SAMPLES *are studied to help scientists piece together the Moon's history. This basalt rock was found by Apollo 15 astronauts and shows that the Moon had a volcanic past.*

▲ TRAINING *missions were carried out on Earth to test tools and manoeuvres. Here the astronauts are practising in a volcanic crater in Arizona, USA.*

📷 **WATCH THIS SPACE**

As a memento of his trip, Apollo 16 pilot Charles Duke left a photo of his family and a medal in a plastic bag on the lunar surface. The back of the photo is signed by his family.

Let it shine

One of the scientific experiments that the Apollo astronauts set up on the lunar surface was a laser reflector. Scientists back on Earth aimed a laser at the Moon and then measured how long it took for the reflection to come back. From these measurements they discovered that the Moon is slowly drifting away from Earth by 3.8 cm (1½ in) a year.

◄ SCIENTISTS *sent the laser beam through an optical telescope at the McDonald Observatory, USA. This experiment determined the distance between Earth and the Moon to an accuracy of 2.5 cm (1 inch).*

▲ SEVERAL *reflectors have been placed on the Moon since 1969. The returning beams from the laser reflectors are too weak to be seen with the human eye and sensitive amplifiers are used to enhance the signal.*

⬧ SPLASHDOWN!

After a fiery re-entry into the Earth's atmosphere, parachutes helped the Apollo command module's descent into the Pacific Ocean. The water cushioned the landing, and once down, floats were activated to keep the capsule upright.

▲ PARACHUTES *ensured a safe landing for the cone-shaped command module.*

▲ FROGMEN *helped the crew from their charred capsule and into life rafts before airlifting them aboard a navy ship.*

HORNET + 3

▲ THE APOLLO 11 *crew spent several weeks quarantined in an airtight container when they returned, to make sure they hadn't picked up any alien bacteria.*

ALMOST THERE
This picture of the Apollo 11 command module was taken by the Eagle lander as it began its descent to the Moon's surface, leaving pilot Michael Collins to orbit alone.

Return to the Moon

After the Apollo programme ended in 1972, and the last Luna probe visited the Moon in 1976, there were no missions until Japan's Hiten in 1990. Today, space agencies around the world are planning future missions to the Moon and beyond.

◀ Japan achieved its first ever lunar flyby, lunar orbiter, and lunar surface impact with Hiten: only the third nation ever to achieve this.

MAPPING MISSIONS

The launch of the Clementine spacecraft in 1994 heralded NASA's return to the Moon. Over the course of its 71-day orbit, Clementine mapped all of the 38 million square kilometres (15 million square miles) of the Moon. NASA followed up this successful mission with the Lunar Prospector in 1998 and the LRO in 2009.

Multi-talented

Clementine not only carried equipment into outer space to test how it coped with a space environment, but it also mapped the topography (height) of the Moon's surface and the thickness of its crust, taking over a million pictures in total. Data provided by Clementine suggested that there may be frozen water in the deep craters near the south pole.

▲ CLEMENTINE *bounced radio waves off the Moon's surface and found the first evidence of water ice.*

▲ CLEMENTINE'S *data guided the Lunar Prospector orbiter to study places that might contain water ice.*

Lunar Prospector

The Lunar Prospector orbited for one year, looking for ice beneath the Moon's poles. It also searched for minerals and gases that could be used on future manned lunar bases and made into fuel for launching spacecraft from the Moon into outer space.

Lunar Reconnaissance Orbiter (LRO)

The unmanned LRO was launched in 2009 to investigate possible sites for setting up a manned base on the Moon. The Lunar Crater Observation and Sensing Satellite (LCROSS) was sent up at the same time. It was crashed into the surface in a search for water ice.

▶ THE LCROSS *mission confirmed that there was a little water ice in at least one of the Moon's craters. LRO's pictures also disproved claims that the Apollo missions were a hoax.*

Flag

Apollo 17 lunar module

Footprint tracks

MOON MISSIONS

SELENE

The new era of lunar exploration included not just the US, but a number of different nations, including the European Space Agency (ESA), Japan, China, and India.

■ **ESA's SMART-1** (2003: orbiter), investigated the theory that the Moon was formed when a smaller planet collided with Earth 4.5 billion years ago.

■ **Japan's Kaguya** (SELENE) (2007: orbiter) released two satellites, Okina and Ouna, into Moon orbit, which helped it to map the gravity of the far side of the Moon.

■ **China's Chang'e-I** (2007: orbiter) spent 494 days orbiting the Moon, creating a 3-D map of its surface, and studying how the Sun affects the space environment.

■ **India's Chandrayaan-1** (2008: orbiter) searched for radioactive matter that would help researchers explain the Moon's history.

INTO THE FUTURE

The space nations have several plans for future lunar exploration.

■ **Chang'e-II** (2010) A Chinese lunar orbiter.

■ **Luna-Glob 1** (2012) A Russian unmanned orbiter.

■ **ESA's ESMO project** (2013/2014) The first ever European Student Moon Orbiter.

ESA's ESMO

■ **Chandrayaan-2** (2013) India plans to land a rover on the Moon.

■ **Luna-Glob 2** (2013) A joint Russian orbiter-rover mission with Chandrayaan-2.

■ **Chang'e III** (2013) A lunar lander and rover are planned.

■ **Luna-Grunt** (2014 and 2015) Two separate lunar orbiters and landers planned.

ESA (2017–2020) A lunar lander, capable of delivering cargo and exploration equipment to the Moon.

■ **India** (2020) India's first manned Moon mission.

The Lunar X competition

Fancy winning the $30 million Google Lunar X Prize? All you have to do is organize the first privately funded team to send a robotic rover to the Moon by the end of 2014. The rover must travel 500 m (1,640 ft) and return images, video, and data to Earth. Twenty teams are currently in the running.

◀ TEAM ITALIA *is aiming to create a reliable and cost-effective robot and is considering many different designs, including this one.*

And on to Mars?

Several nations are keen to be the first to set up a manned base on the Moon, powered by the Sun and using water ice at the poles. Valuable minerals could be mined and sent back to Earth and the base could provide a stepping stone for missions to Mars and other planets. China has already booked a ride for one of its satellites on Russia's Phobos-Grunt robot mission to Mars in 2011 in a joint exploration venture.

▼ SCIENTISTS *believe that the Moon has deposits of an extremely rare form of helium, which could be mined for use as a fuel back on Earth.*

THE SUN

The central star of our solar system is a huge burning ball of gas 150 million km (93 million miles) away from us. It generates huge amounts of energy inside its core.

The Sun

The Sun is our nearest star, located about 150 million kilometres (93 million miles) from Earth. Even though it's made entirely of gas, its mass is 333,000 times greater than that of Earth and 750 times greater than that of all the planets in the solar system put together.

WATCH THIS SPACE

The Sun is studied by a fleet of spacecraft, including the Solar and Heliospheric Observatory (SOHO). Since its launch in 1995, SOHO has revolutionized our knowledge of the Sun. It gives us early warning of solar storms heading towards Earth and has also helped us discover more than 1,500 comets.

▶ SUNSPOTS *are cooler regions of the photosphere, which appear dark against their brighter, hotter surroundings.*

The chromosphere is the layer of atmosphere above the photosphere.

The photosphere is the Sun's visible surface.

The convective zone, through which energy passes in swirls of heated plasma.

The radiative zone, through which energy travels as light.

The core is the centre of the Sun, where nuclear reactions take place.

The spotty Sun

Most of the time the Sun looks like a featureless yellow disc but sometimes dark spots appear on its surface. These are cooler areas of the photosphere and occur when the Sun's magnetic field interrupts the flow of heat through the Sun's layers. Watching the movement of the spots across the surface has shown us that the Sun spins faster at the equator than at the poles (⊙ p202–203).

LAYERED INTERIOR

The Sun is rather like a huge onion, with an interior divided into several layers. At the centre is the super-hot core, where nuclear reactions take place. Energy that escapes from the core rises into the radiative zone. In the convective zone energy is circulated in swirls of plasma called convection cells. The cells that reach the surface – the photosphere – are visible as a bright, grainy pattern.

SUN PROFILE

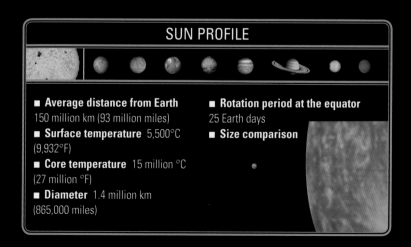

- **Average distance from Earth**
  150 million km (93 million miles)
- **Surface temperature** 5,500°C (9,932°F)
- **Core temperature** 15 million °C (27 million °F)
- **Diameter** 1.4 million km (865,000 miles)

- **Rotation period at the equator**
  25 Earth days
- **Size comparison**

SPICULES *are spikes or jets of super-hot plasma forced up through the Sun's magnetic field.*

CORONAL MASS EJECTIONS *are huge bubbles of plasma ejected from the Sun's corona into space.*

TELL ME MORE...

The Sun is fuelled by nuclear reactions, which take place within the core. During these reactions, atoms are broken down and huge amounts of energy are released. Temperatures in the core reach 15 million °C (27 million °F). The Sun has been shining for more than 4.6 billion years, yet is still less than halfway through its life. Despite burning off around half a billion tonnes of hydrogen every second, it is big enough to continue shining for at least another five billion years.

THE CORONA *is the outer atmosphere, much hotter than the photosphere.*

FACULAE *are hotter, brighter areas of the photosphere that are associated with the formation of sunspots.*

GRANULATION *is the mottling caused by convection cells at the Sun's surface.*

BIRTH AND DEATH OF THE SUN

Like all stars, the Sun was born in a cloud of gas and dust. About 4.6 billion years ago, the cloud collapsed and gravity broke it up into smaller, denser blobs. These grew hotter and hotter until nuclear reactions started and all the new stars in the cloud began to shine. The Sun will continue to get hotter until it runs out of hydrogen. When this happens, the Sun will grow into a red giant, swallowing the planet Mercury. Finally, the dying star will become a white dwarf, shrouded in a glowing cloud called a planetary nebula.

PROMINENCES *are dense clouds of plasma looping out from the Sun along lines in the magnetic field.*

Inside the Sun

The Sun is a gigantic nuclear power station. Vast amounts of energy are generated in its super-hot core. This filters up to the surface and is emitted into space – mainly in the form of visible light and heat. It is this energy that prevents Earth from turning into a ball of ice.

NUCLEAR POWER

The Sun is mainly made of hydrogen gas. Within the core, the crushing pressures and super-hot temperatures force hydrogen atoms together. They undergo nuclear fusion, and are converted into helium. This process releases huge amounts of energy, which leaves the core in the form of high-energy X-rays and gamma rays.

On the move
Hot gas rising towards the surface from deep inside the Sun creates a pattern of bright cells. These granulations measure 1,000–2,000 km (620–1240 miles) across. Larger plumes of rising gas create giant cells called supergranules, which can measure 30,000 km (18,640 miles) across. Individual granules may last for up to 20 minutes, while supergranules may last for a couple of days.

Convective zone

X-rays

Radiative zone

Gamma rays

▲ A SLOW ESCAPE
The radiative zone is so dense that gamma rays and X-rays can take up to one million years to reach the convective zone.

The temperature at the core is 15 million °C (27 million °F) and the pressure is 340 billion times that experienced at sea level here on Earth.

Photosphere

The photosphere is the layer above the convective zone. It is the visible surface of the Sun. The photosphere looks solid but is actually a layer of gas around 500 km (300 miles) thick. It is thin enough to allow light and heat energy to escape out into space. The temperature of this layer is much lower than at the core, around 5,500°C (10,000°F). Light from the photosphere takes around eight minutes to reach Earth.

▲ HOT SPOT *The Sun's magnetic field sometimes creates loops of super-hot plasma. These pass through the cooler photosphere and shoot up into the corona.*

Burning bright

The Sun releases enough energy per second to meet the needs of Earth's population for more than 1,000 years. It does this by changing 550 million tonnes (600 million tons) of hydrogen into helium each second!

The red areas show plasma falling

The blue areas show plasma rising

Noisy Sun

The churning of hot plasma in the convective zone causes sound waves, which travel out through the Sun. At the Sun's surface the waves push the plasma up to 50 km (30 miles) outwards, but sound cannot travel through the vacuum of space (which is why we can't hear the noise it makes). Instead, the waves turn inwards and allow the plasma to sink back down. By studying these wave patterns scientists have learned a lot about the inside of the Sun.

🔍 TAKE A LOOK: CIRCULATION

The Sun spins about an axis. Unlike Earth, which is solid and has a single speed of rotation, the Sun has several speeds of rotation and spins faster at the equator than at the poles. The surface rotation is illustrated on the right, with the faster areas in green and slower areas in blue. The hot plasma also circulates within the Sun, moving between the equator and the poles. Plasma flowing towards the poles moves fairly close to the surface, but the flow returning to the equator is deeper.

North pole

Surface flow from the equator to the poles.

Flow from the poles to the equator.

Hot plasma

South pole

▲ SOLAR MOTION *The faster areas are shown in green, and the slower areas in blue.*

The Sun's atmosphere

The Sun is a huge ball of hot gas. What we see as the surface is the photosphere, the lowest zone of the layered atmosphere, which produces visible light. Above this sit the thin chromosphere and the thick, uneven corona. Each layer is hotter and less dense than the one below it.

THE CORONA

The Sun is surrounded by an extremely hot, wispy atmosphere called the corona. The temperature of the gas here can reach up to 2 million °C (3.6 million °F). Although it is extremely hot, it is not very bright and is usually only seen on Earth during a solar eclipse. However, instruments on spacecraft can now block out the Sun's bright disc so that the corona is visible. The reason for the corona's sizzling temperature is still uncertain, but it seems to be linked to the release of stored magnetic energy.

▲ SOLAR ECLIPSE *The corona appears as a glowing crown around the Moon during a solar eclipse.*

▲ *This image from NASA's TRACE satellite shows the plasma erupting in loops within the corona.*

Coronal loops

Coronal loops are flows of trapped plasma (super-heated gas), which move along channels in the magnetic field of the corona. The plasma flows at up to 320,000 km/h (200,000 mph) in loops that can rise more than a million kilometres (600,000 miles) above the Sun's surface. They show a wide range of temperatures and many will reach several million degrees.

▼ AT LEAST TWO *solar eclipses are visible each year to people on Earth. A total solar eclipse, when the Moon completely covers the Sun, can last for up to eight minutes. This is the only time most humans get to view the Sun's outer atmosphere.*

Ulysses

The Sun's poles are very difficult to observe from Earth. To find out more about them, NASA and the ESA developed the Ulysses spacecraft. Launched in October 1990, Ulysses is the only spacecraft to have explored the Sun's polar regions. It completed three passes before being shut down in 2009, and revealed that the solar wind is weaker at times of low solar activity.

Dish antenna for communicating with Earth, one of four antennas on Ulysses.

Solar filaments

Huge tongues or arches of relatively cool, dense gas often lift off from the chromosphere and into the corona. They may travel out for hundreds of thousands of kilometres, sometimes separating from the Sun and launching billions of tonnes of gas into space. When seen against the brilliant solar disc they appear as dark ribbons (filaments), but are easily visible as prominences against the blackness of space. Shaped by the Sun's magnetic field, they are often linked to sunspots and solar flares. Some will last for many months, others for only a few hours.

⊙ TAKE A LOOK: SOLAR WIND

The Sun releases hot, charged gas particles in a solar wind that blows through space. Particles that escape through holes in the corona create a fast solar wind that blows towards Earth at speeds of up to 900 km a second (560 miles a second). Other areas on the Sun release a solar wind that travels more slowly. These overlapping streams of slow and fast-moving particles create a shock wave when they meet Earth's magnetic field. Some of the solar wind particles move through this shock wave, passing through the magnetic field and down towards Earth's poles, where they cause the glowing auroras (p204–205).

If the magnetic field lines weaken and break, prominences erupt into space

The yellow lines show areas of the magnetic field

The magnetic field shapes the solar filaments and prominences

Other areas of the Sun give rise to a slow, dense solar wind

Holes in the corona release fast streams of solar wind

THE SUN

Solar storms

Breakdowns in the Sun's magnetic field result in violent explosions, which can disable satellites and threaten the lives of astronauts in space. When these eruptions head towards Earth, they can cause dramatic effects in our atmosphere and severe disruptions to our communication systems.

FLARES

Solar flares are huge explosions that occur around sunspots, where the magnetic field is very intense. They last for only a few minutes but release enormous amounts of energy. Flares may erupt several times a day when the Sun is very active but are rare when the Sun has few sunspots. Major flares can trigger coronal mass ejections.

Sunspot cycle
The Sun spins faster at the equator and slower near the poles. This tangles the Sun's magnetic field until, like an over-stretched rubber band, it eventually snaps. The field flips and the poles switch round. This event occurs roughly every 11 years and drives the sunspot cycle, a regular rise and fall in the number of sunspots seen on the Sun.

The heat of a solar flare can exceed 10 million °C (18 million °F).

▲ SOLAR POWERED *Solar flares are the biggest explosions in the solar system. They release ten million times more energy than a volcanic explosion here on Earth.*

TAKE A LOOK: QUAKES

When flares explode they cause quakes inside the Sun, very similar to the earthquakes we experience on Earth. Shock waves from the quake can travel the equivalent of ten Earth diameters before fading into the photosphere, and reach speeds of up to 400,000 km/h (250,000 mph).

▲ SOLAR FLARE photographed by the SOHO spacecraft.

▲ SHOCK WAVES caused by the flare can be seen in rings around the epicentre.

▲ SPREAD The rings spread out over 100,000 km (62,000 miles) across the Sun's surface.

▲ ENERGY released by the solar quake was huge – enough to power the USA for 20 years.

Mass ejections

Sunspots are often linked with enormous eruptions of gas that blast billions of tonnes of material out into the solar system. These huge streamers of gas are called coronal mass ejections (CMEs). They fire electrically charged particles out into space at speeds of up to 1,200 kilometres a second (750 miles a second). Reaching the Earth within two to three days, these particles can cause polar auroras, power cuts, and communication disruptions. Like flares, coronal mass ejections are thought to be caused by the rapid release of magnetic energy and are most common at times of peak sunspot activity.

This image shows the largest solar flare ever recorded, observed by SOHO on 2 April 2001.

The flare triggered this massive coronal mass ejection.

WATCH THIS SPACE

In 2001, a magnetic storm raged around planet Earth. Triggered by a coronal mass ejection associated with a giant sunspot, the storm caused spectacular displays of the aurora australis. In the early hours of April 1, the skies over New Zealand were alive with southern lights. Pictured here, the red aurora hangs above the city of Dunedin.

Particle blitz

Charged particles blasted into space by a solar flare blitzed the SOHO spacecraft only three minutes after the flare erupted on 14 July 2000. The particles created a snowstorm effect on this image taken by the satellite. You can also see a coronal mass ejection blasting a huge cloud of gas into space and the dark circle at the centre where the camera blocked the brilliant light from the Sun.

AMAZING AURORA

Auroras are the dancing curtains of light that hang in the polar night sky. They happen when charged particles in the solar wind are dragged into the upper atmosphere by Earth's magnetic field. Here they collide with oxygen and nitrogen atoms, releasing flashes of red and green light.

The solar cycle

Every day our Sun shines in the sky. Although it always looks the same, it is changing constantly. It goes through cycles of being extremely active followed by periods of quiet. These cycles can have a great effect on our planet.

This sequence of X-ray images shows changes in the Sun's corona over a 10-year cycle, as seen by Japan's Yohkoh spacecraft.

THE CHANGING SUN

Between 2008 and 2010, the Sun became much less active, with fewer flares and active regions. This dip in activity, called the solar minimum, occurs every 11 years or so. Despite appearances, the amount of radiation produced by the Sun at the solar minimum is only about 0.1 per cent lower than at the solar maximum.

This graph shows the number of sunspots seen each year since 1880.

During the 17th century, almost no sunspots were observed. This period, known as the Maunder Minimum, is the longest recorded period of low solar activity. The Maunder Minimum coincided with a long period of cold weather on Earth, referred to as the "Little Ice Age". Scientists strongly suspect there is a link between the two events.

Frost fairs

The northern hemisphere experienced a "Little Ice Age" from the 1400s to the 1700s. During this period, the temperature dropped by a few degrees and the effects were severe. Greenland was largely cut off by ice, the canals in Holland often froze solid, and glaciers advanced in the Alps, destroying villages. There were some fun times though – the frozen rivers were so thick with ice that frost fairs could be held and people could go skating.

The Sun and ozone

Changes in solar activity are most noticeable in the amount of ultraviolet (UV) light that gets through to Earth's surface. UV light is invisible, but we notice it because it causes sunburn. Most UV light is absorbed by the ozone layer 10–50 km (6–30 miles) above the Earth (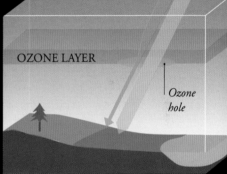 p174). Solar storms can destroy ozone molecules, making it easier for UV to reach the ground. UV can be dangerous to organisms because it damages body cells.

UV-B (shortwave UV) causes sunburn and can trigger skin cancer.

UV-A (longwave UV) can also cause sunburn. It penetrates Earth's atmosphere more easily than UV-B, but is less intense.

SUN

OZONE LAYER

Ozone hole

▶ ULTRAVIOLET LIGHT
Although UV light can be dangerous to life on Earth, it can also be very useful. It helps us make vitamin D, which we need to make strong bones, and helps plants to grow, too.

Butterfly diagram showing the position and occurrence of sunspots

The butterfly effect

English astronomer Edward Walter Maunder (1851–1928) discovered that sunspots do not occur at random over the surface of the Sun. Instead, they follow an 11-year cycle. At the start of each cycle sunspots appear near the poles, but as the cycle progresses they appear closer to the equator. When plotting a graph of the sunspot positions he had observed over many years, Maunder realized that the data revealed a butterfly shape – so diagrams of sunspot locations are known as "butterfly diagrams".

Observing the Sun

People have been watching the Sun for thousands of years, keeping records that are used by modern astronomers to understand more about solar activity and past movements of the Sun, Earth, and Moon. Today the Sun is observed by many amateur astronomers, and by special solar observatories on Earth and in space.

📷 **WHAT A STAR!**

The "father of modern astronomy", Italian astronomer Galileo Galilei (1564–1642) proved that the Sun is at the centre of the solar system.

GALILEO'S SUNSPOTS

Galileo Galilei studied the Sun by projecting its image through a telescope and drawing what he saw. Making his observations at the same time each day, he noted dark spots on the Sun's surface, which had very irregular shapes and would appear and disappear from the Sun's disc. The movement of the spots also proved that the Sun was rotating on an axis.

McMath Pierce Solar Telescope
The largest solar telescope in the world is the McMath Pierce Solar Telescope on Kitt Peak in Arizona, USA. Built in 1962, the telescope uses a 1.6 m (5¼ ft) mirror mounted on top of a 30 m (100 ft) high tower. The mirror directs sunlight down a 60 m (200 ft) long angled tunnel towards the instruments housed underground. The telescope produces detailed images of the Sun and is used to study sunspots and solar activity.

Hinode

Launched in September 2006, the Hinode spacecraft is an orbiting solar observatory created to study the Sun's magnetic activity. It orbits the Earth at an altitude of 600 km (370 miles) and points continuously towards the Sun for nine months of the year. The spacecraft carries three advanced telescopes, which it uses to take X-ray images of the Sun, to measure its magnetic field in 3-D, and to measure the speed of the solar wind.

TAKE A LOOK: THIRTEEN TOWERS OF CHANKILLO, PERU

Located in Peru's coastal desert lies the oldest solar observatory in the Americas. Dating back 2,300 years, the Thirteen Towers of Chankillo are a line of 13 stone blocks running from north to south along a low ridge, forming a "toothed" horizon. The positions of the towers match the points at which the Sun rises and sets over the course of a year. It is likely that the hilltop structure was used as a solar calendar by an ancient Sun cult, helping them to observe the movements of the Sun through the solar year.

June solstice (shortest day)

Equinox

December solstice (longest day)

Observation point

▲ SOLAR CALENDAR *The Thirteen Towers stand like teeth along the ridge, greeting the first and last of the Sun's rays each day.*

Tower telescopes

Close to the ground, heat from the Sun makes the air hot and turbulent. This can distort images received through telescopes, so special tower telescopes are built to observe the Sun. The Richard B. Dunn Solar Telescope at Sacramento Peak in California, USA (right), has a very tall tower, rising 41.5 m (136 ft) above ground level, with another 67 m (220 ft) below ground. Almost all of the air has been removed from the tower to get the clearest possible image of the Sun.

STARS AND STARGAZING

Stars are bright, burning balls of gas that are found all over the Universe. They form patterns in our night sky that have been studied for thousands of years.

The Sun, our nearest star, is only 150 million km (95 million miles) away. In terms of the size of the Universe, it's on our doorstep! But the Sun is just one star – there are trillions of others, all with their own amazing features. The Sun is very average in size and brightness, and enjoying a comfortable middle age. But, like all stars, it will change dramatically as it gets older.

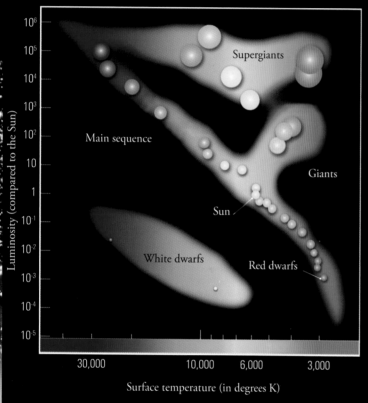

Main sequence

Supergiants

Giants

Sun

White dwarfs

Red dwarfs

Luminosity (compared to the Sun)

Surface temperature (in degrees K)

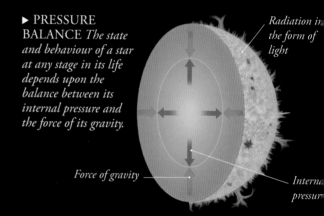

▶ PRESSURE BALANCE *The state and behaviour of a star at any stage in its life depends upon the balance between its internal pressure and the force of its gravity.*

Radiation in the form of light

Force of gravity

Internal pressure

HOT AND BRIGHT

This chart (left), called a Hertzsprung-Russell diagram, shows the temperatures of stars and their brightness, or luminosity. Cool stars are shown in red and hot stars in blue. Most hydrogen-burning stars, including our Sun, lie on the diagonal branch, or "main sequence". Giants that have burned all their fuel leave the main sequence, while faint dwarfs lie near the bottom.

THE LIFE OF A STAR

All stars begin life in a cloud of dust and hydrogen gas, called a nebula. Most average stars take billions of years to burn all their hydrogen fuel. When it runs out, the star expands and becomes a red giant, then sheds its outer layers to end its life as a small, dim white dwarf. Bright, massive stars use up their fuel quickly – in a few million years. When there is nothing left to burn, the star expands to become a red supergiant, then explodes in a supernova to form a neutron star or black hole.

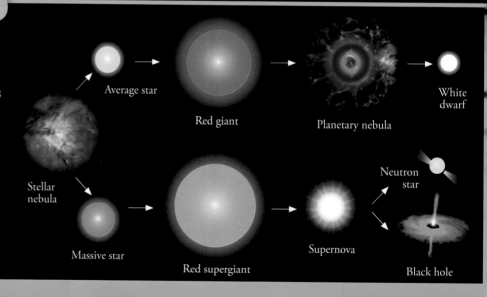

Average star

Red giant

Planetary nebula

White dwarf

Stellar nebula

Massive star

Red supergiant

Supernova

Neutron star

Black hole

TAKE A LOOK: STAR TYPES

Here are some of the types of star found on the Hertzsprung-Russell diagram. All of them are at different stages in their life cycle. Some are young and hot, some are old and cold, and others are about to explode.

◄ WOLF-RAYET STAR *These are very hot, massive stars that are losing mass rapidly and heading towards a supernova explosion.*

▼ MAIN SEQUENCE STAR *Stars like our Sun that lie along the main sequence on the diagram burn hydrogen and turn it into helium.*

▼ BLUE SUPERGIANTS *are the hottest and brightest "ordinary" stars in the Universe. This is Rigel, the brightest star in Orion.*

▲ WHITE DWARF *This is the final stage in the life of an average star like our Sun. A white dwarf is formed from the collapsed core of a red giant and is very dense.*

▲ NEUTRON STAR *Formed when a red supergiant explodes, a neutron star is small, but extremely dense. Its iron crust surrounds a sea of neutrons.*

▲ RED SUPERGIANT *These stars are huge, with a radius 200 to 800 times that of the Sun, but their surface temperature is low, making them look red or orange-yellow in colour.*

Giants and supergiants

When main sequence stars start to run out of fuel they expand and can become truly enormous. These giant and supergiant stars swell up and start to burn helium instead of hydrogen. One day our own Sun will turn into a red giant about 30 times bigger and 1,000 times brighter than it is today.

VV Cephei

Antares

Betelgeuse

▲ TRUE GIANT *Even supergiants like Betelgeuse and Antares are dwarfed by VV Cephei, a star so big that it is known as a hypergiant. It lies in the constellation Cepheus, about 2,400 light years from Earth, and is the second-largest star in the Milky Way.*

Sun (1 pixel)   Sirius   Pollux   Arcturus   Rigel   Aldebaran

Birth of a star

Most stars are born in a huge cloud of gas and dust, called a nebula. The story starts when the nebula begins to shrink, then divides into smaller, swirling clumps. As each clump continues to collapse, the material in it becomes hotter and hotter. When it reaches about 10 million °C (18 million °F), nuclear reactions start and a new star is made.

NEBULAS

Nebulas can be different colours. The colour comes from the dust in the nebula, which can either absorb or reflect the radiation from newborn stars. In a blue nebula, light is reflected by small dust particles. A red nebula is caused by stars heating the dust and gas.

▲ THE TRIFID NEBULA
This cloud of gas and dust lies in the constellation of Sagittarius. The cloud is gradually being eroded by a nearby, massive star. At the top right of the cloud a stellar jet is blasting out from a star buried inside. Jets like these are the exhaust gases from newly forming stars.

▲ THE LAGOON NEBULA
Near the Trifid is the even larger Lagoon Nebula. It gets its name from a dark patch that looks like a lake. Several groups of new stars are forming inside this nebula. At its centre is a very young, hot star whose radiation is evaporating and blowing away the surrounding clouds.

▲ THE HORSEHEAD NEE
*Not all nebulas are colourful. T
Horsehead Nebula is a cloud of
that forms part of the Orion N
head shows up against the red
which is heated by stars. Many
in the Orion Nebula within th*

▲ THE SEVEN SISTERS
*The Pleiades cluster lies in the c
Taurus. It is also known as the
because up to seven of its massi
can be seen with the naked eye.
than 300 young stars in the clu
a thin dust cloud that shows as*

▲ THE EAGLE NEBULA
*This is one of three huge fingers of
cool hydrogen gas and dust. At the
top of this finger, hot young stars
shine brightly among the dark dust.
Eventually these stars will blow the
dust away and become clearly visible
as a new star cluster.*

TAKE A LOOK: CARINA NEBULA

These two images show the Carina Nebula –
a huge pillar of dust and gas where stars are
being born. In the top image, the cloud is
glowing due to radiation from nearby stars.
The infrared image (bottom) allows us to see
some of the stars inside the nebula.

▲ VISIBLE LIGHT *Hidden inside this glowing
nebula are stars that have yet to emerge.*

▲ INFRARED LIGHT *Here, two infant stars
inside the nebula are releasing jets of material.*

A FLASH OF BRILLIANCE

V838 Monocerotis is a red supergiant star, located about 20,000 light years away from Earth. In March 2002, this star suddenly flared to 10,000 times its normal brightness. The series of images below show how a burst of light from the star spread out into space, reflecting off the layers of dust that surround the star. This effect is called a light echo. The images make it look as if the nebula itself is growing, but it isn't. The spectacular effect is caused by light from the stellar flash sweeping outwards and lighting up more of the nebula.

20 May 2002

2 September 2002

28 October 2002

17 December 2002

September 2006
More than four years after the star erupted, the echo of the light is still spreading out through the dust cloud.

The death of a star

The larger a star is, the shorter its life will be. Hot, massive stars only shine for a few million years because they burn up their hydrogen fuel rapidly. Smaller stars are much cooler, so they use their fuel more slowly and can shine for billions of years. But, sooner or later, all stars run out of fuel and die.

BEFORE *This star is about to explode.*

10 DAYS AFTER *This image shows the same star during its supernova explosion. The star is situated in a nearby galaxy called the Large Magellanic Cloud. When it exploded in 1987, it was the first supernova to be visible to the naked eye for almost 400 years.*

Betelgeuse

When a star begins to use up its hydrogen fuel, it balloons outwards to become a huge red giant or supergiant. Betelgeuse, a red supergiant in the constellation of Orion, is more than 1,000 times wider than the Sun. It is also about 14,000 times brighter, because it is burning its fuel at a rate 14,000 times faster than the Sun. A few hundred thousand years from now, Betelgeuse will have exhausted its fuel, and will explode as a supernova. It will then become the brightest star in our sky, second only to the Sun.

Stellar death throes

Eta Carinae is a star that is rapidly reaching the end of its life. It is being torn apart by massive explosions that throw out huge clouds of gas and dust. The star's brightness is also changing dramatically. In 1843 it was the second brightest star in the sky: today it cannot be seen with the naked eye.

SMOKE RINGS

Small or medium-sized stars like our Sun end up as red giants. When a red giant runs out of hydrogen and helium, it is not hot enough to burn other fuels, so it collapses. Its outer layers are puffed out into space like giant smoke rings. These shells of gas are called planetary nebulas, because they looked like planets when first seen through early telescopes. The central star shrinks to form a white dwarf, an extremely hot object about the size of Earth.

▲ THE CAT'S EYE NEBULA
The central bubble of gas was ejected by the dying red giant star about 1,000 years ago. It is expanding outwards into older gas clouds created by previous outbursts.

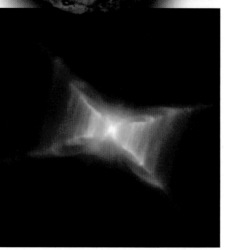

▲ THE RED RECTANGLE NEBULA
At the centre of this nebula is a binary (double) star system. The two stars are surrounded by a ring of thick dust, which has shaped the surrounding gas into four spikes.

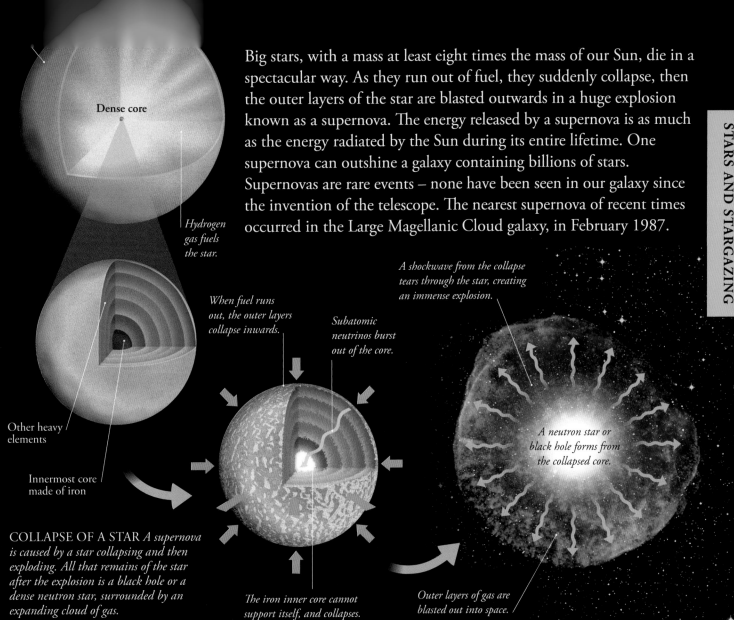

Big stars, with a mass at least eight times the mass of our Sun, die in a spectacular way. As they run out of fuel, they suddenly collapse, then the outer layers of the star are blasted outwards in a huge explosion known as a supernova. The energy released by a supernova is as much as the energy radiated by the Sun during its entire lifetime. One supernova can outshine a galaxy containing billions of stars. Supernovas are rare events – none have been seen in our galaxy since the invention of the telescope. The nearest supernova of recent times occurred in the Large Magellanic Cloud galaxy, in February 1987.

Dense core

Hydrogen gas fuels the star.

Other heavy elements

When fuel runs out, the outer layers collapse inwards.

Innermost core made of iron

Subatomic neutrinos burst out of the core.

A shockwave from the collapse tears through the star, creating an immense explosion.

A neutron star or black hole forms from the collapsed core.

COLLAPSE OF A STAR *A supernova is caused by a star collapsing and then exploding. All that remains of the star after the explosion is a black hole or a dense neutron star, surrounded by an expanding cloud of gas.*

The iron inner core cannot support itself, and collapses.

Outer layers of gas are blasted out into space.

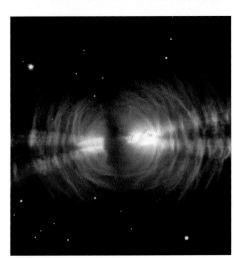

▲ THE EGG NEBULA
Here, the central star is hidden by a dense layer of gas and dust. However, its light illuminates the outer layers of gas, creating a series of bright arcs and circles.

▲ THE BUTTERFLY NEBULA
This nebula consists of two "wings" of gas, thrown out from the dying central star. The butterfly stretches for about two light years – half the distance from our Sun to the next star.

▲ THE ESKIMO NEBULA
The "parka hood" is a ring of comet-shaped objects, with their tails streaming away from the star. The "face" is a bubble of material being blown into space by the star's wind.

Interstellar space

The space between the stars, called interstellar space, is not completely empty – there are scattered molecules of gas and dust everywhere. Over a whole galaxy, this adds up to a huge amount of material.

GLOBULES

Small clouds of gas and dust are called globules. The smallest are known as Bok globules, after the US astronomer Bart Bok, and are often as small as our solar system (about two light years across). The gas in these clouds is mainly molecular hydrogen, with a temperature of around –260°C (–436°F). Globules can contract slowly under the force of their own gravity and form stars.

▶ BOK GLOBULES
These dark Bok globules are silhouetted against a background of hot, glowing hydrogen gas.

Gas and dust

Scientists can detect molecules in space because they absorb or emit radio waves. More than 140 types of molecule have been identified so far. The most common are gases, such as hydrogen. There is enough gas in the Milky Way, for example, to make 20 billion stars like our Sun. Dust particles, water, ammonia, and carbon-based (organic) compounds have also been found in space.

▲ SPACE DUST *Each dust particle is smaller than the width of a human hair.*

Globule with a tail

Looking like an alien monster about to swallow a helpless galaxy, this faint, glowing cloud of dust and gas is being shaped by winds from a nearby, newly born star. The star's strong ultraviolet light makes the cloud's "mouth" glow red. This cloud is an example of a cometary globule, so-called because its long tail resembles the tail of a comet.

▲ DUST CLOUD *This globule contains enough material to make several stars as big as our Sun.*

THE VEIL NEBULA

Dust and gas are continually being added to interstellar space by stellar winds and dying stars. The wispy Veil Nebula is the remains of a massive supernova that exploded about 30,000 to 40,000 years ago. Even today, the Veil Nebula is still expanding outwards at a rate of about 100 km (60 miles) each second.

Birthplace of stars

This cloud, called the Orion Nebula, is so bright that it can easily be seen with the naked eye. It lies about 1,500 light years from Earth, measures about 25 to 30 light years across, and has a mass several hundred times that of the Sun. The Orion Nebula is heated by a group of young stars at its centre, called the Trapezium, and is a place where new stars are being formed.

FAST FACTS

- The ingredients of interstellar space are continually changing as new molecules are created and others are split apart.
- Dust and gas are added by dying stars and removed by the birth of new stars.
- Hydrogen, helium, and carbon monoxide are the most common gases in space.
- Space is bathed with many forms of radiation, such as light, heat, and radio waves.
- Other space ingredients include magnetic fields, cosmic rays, and neutrons.

Solar system on the move

Our solar system is sweeping through interstellar space at high speed. As it moves, the solar wind creates an invisible bubble around it, known as the heliosphere. This bubble pushes against the gas and dust in interstellar space, forcing the gas and dust to flow around it. Scientists once thought that the shape of the solar system as it moved through space was like a comet with a tail, but new observations show that it actually resembles a squashy ball.

◄ THE TRAPEZIUM
The cluster around the Trapezium contains 1,000 hot stars that are less than a million years old.

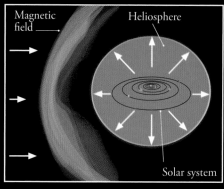

Magnetic field · Heliosphere · Solar system

▲ PUSHING THROUGH SPACE *The interstellar magnetic field bends and parts to let the solar system pass through.*

Multiple stars

Most stars form in clusters inside huge clouds of gas and dust. As time goes by, these stars may drift apart until they are no longer part of the original cluster. Our Sun is fairly rare in being a solitary star. More than half of all stars are in binary systems, while many others are in systems of three or more stars.

BINARY SYSTEMS

A binary system is a group of two companion stars that orbit each other. The first binary to be discovered was Mizar, situated in the "handle" of the Plough. Its companion star was spotted by Giovanni Riccioli in 1650. Since then, many pairs of double stars have been found. Famous binaries include the bright star Acrux in the Southern Cross, which was discovered to be double in 1685, and Mira, a red giant in Cetus (the Whale).

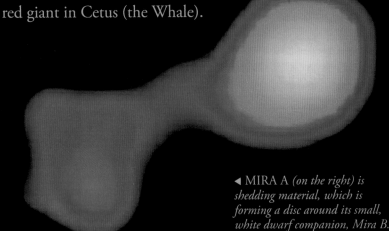

◄ MIRA A (on the right) is shedding material, which is forming a disc around its small, white dwarf companion, Mira B.

Double Dog Star

The brightest star in the night sky is Sirius, nicknamed the Dog Star because it is in the constellation of Canis Major (the Great Dog). The blue-white star Sirius A is hotter than our Sun and 22 times as bright. Its companion, Sirius B, is a faint white dwarf, the dense remnant of a collapsed star.

▲ SIRIUS B (on the right) is so close to Sirius A and so faint, that images of it have only recently been obtained.

Cannibals in space

Sometimes the two stars in a binary system are so close that one is able to steal material from the other. The "cannibal" star then grows in size and mass at the expense of its neighbour. One example of this is the double star system Phi Persei. This contains an elderly star that is shedding its outer layers. The cast-off material has been sucked in by its companion, which has now grown to a hefty nine times the size of our Sun. It is spinning so violently that it is flinging gas from its surface into a ring around its middle. One day it may even start dumping gas back onto the first star.

THE PHI PERSEI DUO

1. THE PAIR OF STARS in Phi Persei have stayed the same for the last 10 million years, orbiting one another and held together by the pull of their gravity.

2. THINGS CHANGE when the bigger star starts to run out of hydrogen – the fuel that powers its nuclear furnace. The now-ageing star begins to swell.

3. AS THE AGEING STAR expands, it begins to dump its mass onto its smaller companion star.

4. THE FIRST STAR sheds practically all of its mass, leaving its bright core exposed.

5. THE SMALLER COMPANION has now captured most of its partner's excess mass. It changes identity from a moderately sized star into a massive, hot, rapidly spinning star.

6. THE SECOND STAR is spinning so fast that its shape is distorted into a flattened sphere. The spinning also causes the star to shed hydrogen gas, which settles into a broad ring around it.

OPEN CLUSTERS

Open clusters are groups of hundreds, or even thousands, of stars. They are held together by their gravity, which attracts them to one another. The stars in an open cluster all formed inside the same large cloud of gas and dust. As a result, they are all the same age and have the same composition, but their masses can vary considerably. Well-known open clusters that are visible with the naked eye include the Pleiades (The Seven Sisters), the Hyades, and the Jewel Box.

Three's a crowd

There is more to the Pole Star (Polaris) than meets the eye – it is actually a triple star. One companion, Polaris B, has been known since 1780. The third star is so close to Polaris A that it wasn't seen until 2005.

▲ NGC 3603 *This giant nebula is one of the biggest clusters of young stars in the Milky Way galaxy. This image shows young stars surrounded by dust and gas.*

Globular clusters

Dense, ball-shaped groups of stars, called globular clusters, orbit the Milky Way and other large galaxies. A single cluster can contain millions of stars, which all formed at the same time and from the same cloud. These stars can stay linked by their gravity for billions of years. Many globulars are very old, and contain some of the oldest surviving stars in the Universe.

FAST FACTS

■ The age of most globular clusters suggests that they formed very early in the history of the Universe, when the first galaxies were being born.

■ Most globulars are full of elderly stars, typically 10 billion years old, and no new stars are forming.

■ However, some globular clusters contain several generations of younger stars, so they must have formed more recently.

■ Young globular clusters may be the left-overs of collisions between large galaxies and dwarf galaxies.

▲ REMAINS OF A DWARF GALAXY?
Omega Centauri is one of the most spectacular sights in the southern night sky. This globular cluster is thought to be around 12 billion years old. Recent observations show that stars near its centre are moving very rapidly, suggesting that the cluster has a medium-sized black hole at its centre. The cluster may be the old heart of a dwarf galaxy that was largely destroyed in an encounter with the Milky Way.

Central bulge

Milky Way

Halo of clusters

▲ GLOBULARS CLOSE TO HOME

There are about 150 globular clusters near the Milky Way. Unlike open clusters, which are always found in the disc of the Milky Way galaxy, many globular clusters are located in a "halo" around the galaxy's central bulge. Scientists can calculate how far away these globulars are from how bright they appear.

▲ WHITE AND RED DWARFS

NGC 6397 is one of the closest globular star clusters to Earth. The Hubble Space Telescope has been able to look right into the centre of this cluster. It found faint white dwarfs that died long ago, as well as faint, cool, red dwarfs that have been slowly burning up their hydrogen fuel for perhaps 12 billion years.

Mega cluster

Omega Centauri is the biggest of all the Milky Way's globular clusters, containing perhaps 10 million stars and measuring about 150 light years across. In the night sky, it appears nearly as large as the full Moon.

▲ M13 *This globular cluster is one of the brightest and best-known in the northern sky. The glittering ball of stars appears to the naked eye as one hazy star and is easily spotted in winter in the constellation Hercules. About 300,000 stars are crowded near its centre, with more scattered further out. M13 measures more than 100 light years across.*

Other solar systems

For centuries, people have wondered whether distant stars had planets orbiting around them. Unfortunately, most stars are so far away that it was impossible to spot any planets. But modern instruments have now made it possible to detect them, and more than 400 have already been found.

BABY PLANETARY SYSTEMS

Out in space, new solar systems are still forming. This is the Orion Nebula, where many stars are being born. Around each new star is a spinning disc of gas and dust. If material in this disc starts to clump together, it eventually forms planets that orbit the star.

A planet situated outside our solar system is called an exoplanet. The first two were discovered in 1992 in orbit around an extreme type of star called a pulsar. These planets cannot be seen, but their existence is known from the way they affect the radio waves emitted by the pulsar (p227).

▲ PULSAR PLANETS *These planets are unlikely to support life, because pulsars emit high levels of harmful radiation.*

▲ PLANETARY NURSERY *Astronomers have found 30 baby solar systems forming in the Orion Nebula.*

Pulling power

The first exoplanet in orbit around a Sun-like star was discovered in 1995. The planet was detected from a tiny wobble in the motion of the star 51 Pegasi. As the planet, called 51 Pegasi b, orbited the star, its gravity sometimes pulled the star towards Earth and sometimes away from it. This wobble showed up as light shifts in the spectrum of the starlight. Since then, hundreds of exoplanets have been found from the wobbles they create in nearby stars.

Unseen planet

▲ COLOUR SHIFTS *The wavelength of a star's light changes as it moves towards or away from Earth. Shifts in the spectrum may show that a planet is present.*

A planet like Earth?

As planetary systems are fairly common, there may be many exoplanets similar to Earth scattered across the Universe. We have not yet found one, but space observatories are expected to do so in the next few years. The system below, called HR 8799, was one of the first multi-planet systems to be recorded. Images like this prove that complex planetary systems do exist – systems that might just contain an Earth-like planet.

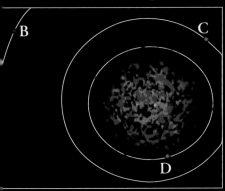

▲ HR 8799 SYSTEM *Three planets (B, C, and D) are orbiting around a central star.*

DUSTY DISCS

Planets form inside huge rotating discs of dust and gas. Even before the first exoplanets were spotted, dust discs were found around many young stars. The first was the disc around a star called Beta Pictoris. In 2008, scientists discovered an object very close to this star. They think it is a giant planet, located somewhere inside the disc.

▶ BETA PICTORIS *is a hot young star in the constellation Pictor. The disc around the star is quite cool, but glows brightly in infrared light.*

55 CANCRI

At present, the planetary system most like our own solar system is called 55 Cancri and lies in the constellation of Cancer. Our solar system has eight planets, while 55 Cancri has at least five — more than any other exoplanet system that has so far been discovered. The inner four planets of 55 Cancri are all closer to the star than Earth is to the Sun, and all five of its planets are larger than Earth. Both systems have a giant gas planet in a distant Jupiter-like orbit. However, this planet lies in the habitable zone for the star, and liquid water could exist on a rocky moon orbiting it.

▲ WATER *might exist on a planet in the gap between the inner and outer planets.*

Extreme stars

The Universe is full of stars that are hotter, colder, more massive, or less massive than our Sun. Some of these extreme stars are at the end of their lives. Some are stars that have suddenly become very active. Others are failed stars that never ignited their nuclear furnaces.

White dwarfs

Any star with a mass less than seven times our Sun is expected to end its life as a small, dim star known as a white dwarf. When a dying star puffs off most of its material and collapses, it becomes extremely small, dense, and hot. The matter in a white dwarf is so densely packed that a teaspoonful of the material would weigh several tonnes.

White dwarf

▲ END OF A STAR *Our Sun will end its life as a white dwarf like these stars, in about seven billion years from now.*

Brown dwarfs

Some stars, known as brown dwarfs, are so small and cool that they are unable to start up nuclear reactions in their core or to burn hydrogen. They are often described as "failed stars". Brown dwarfs do shine, but very faintly, because they produce a little heat as they slowly shrink due to gravity.

▲ TWIN BROWN DWARFS *This artwork shows the dimmest star-like bodies known, called 2M 0939.*

NEUTRON STARS

Neutron stars are small, only about 10 km (6 miles) across, yet they are heavier than the Sun. One teaspoon of material from a neutron star would weigh a billion tonnes. Neutron stars are covered by an iron crust, 10 billion times stronger than steel. Inside, they contain a liquid sea of neutrons – the debris from atoms crushed by a supernova explosion.

Novas

If a white dwarf orbits close to a normal star in a binary system, it can pull large amounts of gas from the other star. This gas gets extremely hot, pressure increases on the white dwarf's surface, and eventually a huge nuclear explosion occurs. The white dwarf then grows dimmer for a period of weeks or months before the same thing happens again. These periodic explosions are called novas.

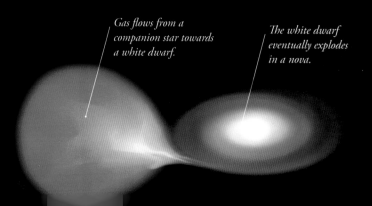

Gas flows from a companion star towards a white dwarf.

The white dwarf eventually explodes in a nova.

PULSARS

A pulsar is a neutron star that emits pulses of radiation as it rotates. When seen from Earth, these pulses appear to sweep across the night sky like the beam from a lighthouse. The radiation from a pulsar can be experienced on Earth as radio signals, or sometimes flashes of visible light, X-rays, and gamma rays.

Magnetic field

Radiation

Neutron star

▲ PULSES OF RADIATION
A neutron star has an intense magnetic field and rotates rapidly, producing high-energy electrons that radiate into space.

Extreme outbursts
Observatories sometimes detect powerful, but short-lived bursts of gamma rays. These flashes are brighter than a billion Suns, yet last only a few milliseconds. They are thought to be caused by a collision, either between a black hole and a neutron star, or between two neutron stars. In the first case, the black hole drags in the neutron star and grows bigger, as shown below. In the second type of impact, the two neutron stars create a black hole.

◄ STELLAR QUAKES
In 2004, one magnetar flared up so brightly that it temporarily blinded all the X-ray satellites in space. The blast of energy came from a giant flare, created by the star's twisting magnetic field.

MAGNETARS

Magnetars are a type of neutron star with magnetic fields up to 1,000 times stronger than those of other neutron stars. They are the strongest known magnets in the Universe, equal to 10 million million hand magnets. Their intense magnetism may result from them spinning very quickly – 300 to 500 times a second – when they are born. This spin, combined with churning neutron fluid in the interior, builds up an enormous magnetic field.

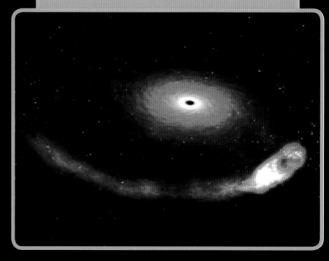

Black holes

A black hole is possibly the strangest object in the Universe. It is a region of space where matter has collapsed in on itself. This results in a huge amount of mass being concentrated in a very small area. The gravitational pull of a black hole is so strong that nothing can escape from it – not even light.

▲ BIG AND SMALL *Black holes come in many sizes. Some are only a few times more massive than our Sun. Others, found at the centres of galaxies, may be millions of times more massive. This is a medium-sized black hole, surrounded by stars in a globular cluster.*

Stellar mass black holes
This type of black hole forms when a heavyweight star – about 10 times heavier than our Sun – ends its life in a supernova explosion. What is left of the star collapses into an area only a few kilometres across. A stellar mass black hole is most easily found when it has a companion star that survives the explosion. Material is often pulled off this star and forms a disc swirling around the black hole. Experts can then calculate the black hole's mass and orbit.

Disc of hot material

▲ JETS OF RADIATION *stream away from the black hole at nearly the speed of light.*

Companion star

▲ TO A CREWMATE *an astronaut looks normal as he starts to be pulled towards the black hole.*

▶ LONG AFTER *the astronaut has fallen into the black hole, crewmates see him, highly stretched and red, on its rim.*

Stretched beyond the limit
Objects that fall into black holes are stretched to just one atom wide. An astronaut who fell in feet first would feel a stronger pull of gravity on his feet than his head. This stretching effect would get worse closer to the hole and eventually he would be crushed by its overpowering gravity. Crewmates watching from a distance would see him turn red, as light struggled to escape from the black hole, appear to hover on the edge of the hole, then disappear.

▲ TWO HOLES *These bright objects are two supermassive black holes orbiting one another. Eventually they may collide to form one enormous black hole. The pink streaks are the jets that they blast out.*

SUPERMASSIVE BLACK HOLES

Most galaxies, including the Milky Way, are believed to contain supermassive black holes at their centres. Some experts think that these black holes are created when a lot of material is squeezed together in the centre of a newly forming galaxy. Another possibility is that supermassive black holes start very small, and then grow gradually by pulling in and swallowing nearby material.

Jet of
radiation

▶ COSMIC JETS
*As gas is drawn into a
black hole it gets very hot.
This energy is released as
jets of radiation (usually
X-rays) that are blasted
far out into space.*

Ring of dust and gas

Jet of
radiation

FAST FACTS

■ All the matter that falls into a black hole piles up at a single point in the centre, called the singularity.

■ If two black holes collided, they would cause gravity waves to ripple through the whole Universe.

■ To turn Earth into a black hole, it would have to be squashed to the size of a marble!

■ There may be as many as 100 billion supermassive black holes in our part of the Universe alone.

■ Black holes are slowly losing all their energy, but it will take billions of years before they evaporate into nothing.

Be a *skygazer*

People have been fascinated by the night sky since prehistoric times. Early civilizations recorded the positions of the Sun, Moon, and planets. Today, light from street lamps and buildings can hide the fainter stars, but there are still plenty of amazing views for skygazers.

▲ ESSENTIAL EQUIPMENT *As well as a star map, take books with you to find out more about what you are looking at. Use a red light to read by; if you use an ordinary torch, it will take longer for your eyes to readjust to the darkness. Finally, don't forget to wear warm clothing!*

SEEING STARS

If you want to see small, faint objects in the sky, you'll need binoculars or a telescope. Binoculars are cheaper than telescopes and are good for looking at star fields, star colours, clusters, and the Moon. Telescopes magnify more and are better for planets, nebulas, and galaxies.

SIGNPOSTS IN THE SKY

At first glance, the night sky seems to be quite evenly scattered with stars, but if you keep looking, patterns begin to emerge. These star patterns, or constellations, were named by early astronomers. One of the most noticeable constellations is Orion (right). It is one of the best signposts in the northern winter sky, and can be used to find other constellations and bright stars.

▲ LONG SHOT *Pictures of very faint objects can be taken by attaching a camera to a telescope and leaving the shutter open for at least half an hour.*

Finder scope

Telescope

Camera

Tripod

The colourful Universe

The colours of planets and stars can be easy to see, but nebulas and galaxies are often disappointing – even in large telescopes, they look like grey or greenish fuzzy patches. This is because their light is not bright enough for the colour-sensing part of your eye to pick up. To see the colours, you need to take pictures of star trails or nebulas with a camera. Hold the camera shutter open for a few minutes, while keeping the camera steady.

TAKE A LOOK: STAR MAPS

The stars in the night sky are so far away that their positions look fixed. You might find it quite easy to remember where the brightest stars and constellations are, but to find the fainter objects, you'll need a star map. There are different types of these. A paper map is useful, but difficult to handle – especially on a breezy night! A planisphere is a disc that you turn to show the exact part of the sky above you. Maps are also available on the Internet.

Line up the numbers and turn the disc to match the time and date.

The area revealed in the window shows what's in the sky above you.

▲ GUIDING STAR *A planisphere will help you find your way around the stars.*

SUNGAZING

▲ *Looking directly at a solar eclipse can damage your eyes.*

The Sun is fascinating to watch – but it's so bright, it can cause blindness. The safest way to look for sunspots or study a solar eclipse is to project an image of the Sun onto a piece of card. You can use a telescope or one lens of binoculars to shine an image of the Sun onto paper (shown here). Or you can make a pinhole projector. Cover a piece of card with foil and pierce a tiny hole in it. Though this, you can project a small image of the Sun onto another card.

Cardboard shade collar

REMEMBER: NEVER LOOK DIRECTLY AT THE SUN, EVEN THROUGH SUNGLASSES.

Telescope or binoculars

Paper with magnified image of the Sun

The night sky

If you look up into the sky on a clear night, you will see thousands of stars, but how do you know which star is which? Luckily, the stars form groups known as constellations, which can help you find your way around the heavens.

Southern constellations

Northern constellations

WHO DREW THE CONSTELLATIONS?

Early astronomers noticed that the stars formed groups and that these groups moved in a regular way across the heavens. They began to use characters, animals, and objects from their myths and legends to remember these groups. Most of the constellation names we use today date from Greek and Roman times, but some go back even further to the Egyptians, Babylonians, and Sumerians.

STAR CATALOGUES

Early astronomers drew up catalogues of the constellations. At first, only 48 constellations were known because much of the southern hemisphere had not been explored by Europeans, so the southern constellations had not been seen. As sailors began to venture further south, more and more constellations were added. It was not until 1922 that the International Astronomical Union decided on the 88 constellations we know today, and defined their shapes.

▶ ASTRONOMERS *looking through a telescope, as illustrated on a page in* The Celestial Atlas, *an early star catalogue.*

TAKE A LOOK: PLANETS

Venus

Moon

Stars are not the only things that are visible in the night sky – you can also spot planets. Mercury, Venus, Mars, Jupiter, and Saturn are all visible to the naked eye. Mercury and Venus are known as the morning and evening stars, because the best times to see them are just before sunrise or after sunset.

Finding the Pole Star

The Pole Star sits almost directly above the North Pole, which makes it an excellent way to find due north. It is visible all year in the northern hemisphere at the tip of a constellation called Ursa Minor (the Little Bear). To find it, you can use another constellation called Ursa Major (the Great Bear). Seven of its stars form a shape that is known as the Plough or the Big Dipper. The two stars that form the front of this shape point to the Pole Star, which is the next bright star you see.

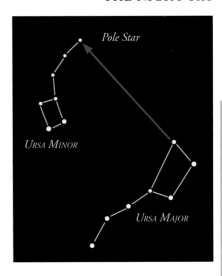

Pole Star

URSA MINOR

URSA MAJOR

THE ZODIAC

A group of 12 constellations can be seen in both hemispheres. The ancients called them the zodiac, from the Greek word for animals. Most of them are named after animals, but some are human and one is an object. The zodiac runs along a path in the sky called the ecliptic, which is at an angle of 23 degrees to the equator. The Sun, Moon, and planets also move on paths close to the ecliptic.

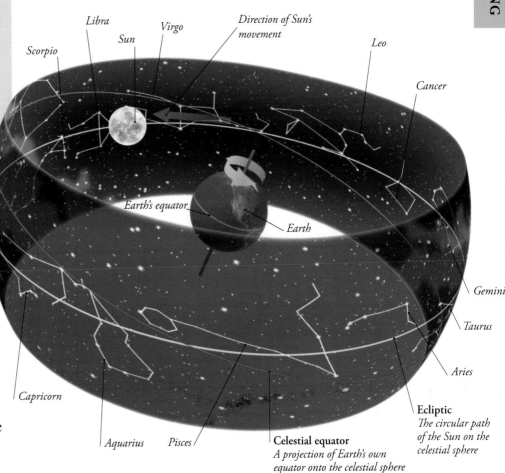

Libra

Sun

Virgo

Direction of Sun's movement

Leo

Scorpio

Cancer

Sagittarius

Earth's equator

Earth

Gemini

Taurus

Capricorn

Aries

Aquarius

Pisces

Celestial equator
A projection of Earth's own equator onto the celestial sphere

Ecliptic
The circular path of the Sun on the celestial sphere

CONSTELLATIONS ON THE MOVE

The stars that we see in a constellation look as if they are grouped together, but in fact some are much closer to us than others. They appear to be flat against the sky because our eyes can't determine the distances between them. Each star is also moving in space. In a few hundreds of thousands of years time, the stars will all be in different positions and the constellations will have changed shape from how we know them today.

The Plough 100,000 years ago...

as it is today...

and in 100,000 years time.

The northern sky

To spot constellations, you need a star chart and a place with a wide view of the sky. The chart on the right shows the constellations visible from the northern hemisphere. You will not be able to see all of them at once – the Earth's tilt and orbital motion mean that some can only be seen at certain times of year.

▲ FLAME NEBULA
This is situated just below the lowest star on Orion's belt.

▼ ORION NEBULA *(M42) is a huge area of star formation, situated in the "sword" that hangs from Orion's belt.*

Betelgeuse

Rigel

Star names

Some stars, such as Betelgeuse and Rigel in the constellation Orion, were named in ancient times. Today, astronomers rank the stars in a constellation in order of brightness, beginning with the brightest. They use Greek letters and the constellation name, so Betelgeuse and Rigel are alpha Orionis and beta Orionis, respectively.

Orion
The Hunter

Orion is one of the most easily recognizable constellations in both the northern and southern skies. It depicts a hunter, armed with a club and a sword that hangs from the three diagonal stars making up his belt. He is holding the head of a lion. The Orion constellation contains two very bright stars – **Rigel**, a blue supergiant at the bottom right, and **Betelgeuse**, a red supergiant

Orion

Cygnus
The Swan

Cygnus is is a major constellation of the northern hemisphere, sometimes called the **Northern Cross.** It can also be seen close to the horizon in the southern hemisphere in winter. At the base of the swan's tail is the bright star **Deneb**, a blue-white supergiant 160,000 times brighter than the Sun. The beak of the swan contains a binary star, **Albireo**, whose two stars can be seen with binoculars

Cygnus

▼ **USING THE CHART** *Turn the book until the current month is in front of you. You may find it easier to photocopy the page, stick it onto some card, and cut it out. Then face south and look for the stars as they appear on the map. If you are not sure which direction is south, make a note of where the Sun is at noon. That direction is always south.*

JULY

AUGUST

SEPTEMBER

OCTOBER

NOVEMBER

DECEMBER

JANUARY

FEBRUARY

MARCH

APRIL

MAY

JUNE

Milky Way

CYGNUS

Ursa Major

Ursa Minor

Pole Star

CASSIOPEIA

TAURUS

ORION

Pole Star
This lies over the North Pole.

Ursa Major
The stars in this constellation point to the Pole Star (see dotted line).

Taurus
The Bull

Just above Orion is Taurus. This constellation features two famous star clusters called the **Hyades** and the **Pleiades**, both of which contain stars that are visible with the naked eye. A prominent red star called Aldebaran forms the eye of the bull, while just above the star that marks the tip of the bull's lower horn is the Crab Nebula (M1). This supernova remnant is all that remains of an exploding star, first spotted in 1054.

Taurus

Cassiopeia
The Queen

Another easily recognizable constellation is Cassiopeia. It is named after a mythical queen who was notoriously vain, which is why she is shown with a mirror in her hand. The five main stars in this constellation form a distinctive W shape. The centre star of the W points towards the Pole Star.

Cassiopeia

The *southern* sky

Stargazing is much easier in the southern hemisphere than in the northern. There is less light pollution, which makes it easier to see fainter stars. The Milky Way also appears brighter and more full of stars than in the north. Here are some of the most interesting things to look for.

▲ TRIFID NEBULA *This colourful nebula is divided into three lobes and contains some very young, hot stars.*

Milky Way

▲ LAGOON NEBULA *This huge nebula, visible with the naked eye, appears pink in images taken by space telescopes.*

CENTRE OF THE GALAXY

When we look at the night sky we can see other parts of our galaxy, the Milky Way. It is at its most dense in the constellation of Sagittarius, because here we are looking right into the centre of the galaxy. Sagittarius contains more star clusters and nebulas than any other constellation.

Sagittarius
The Archer

Sagittarius is depicted as a centaur, a mythical half-man, half-horse creature, firing an arrow. This constellation contains a radio source, thought to be a black hole, which marks the centre of the **Milky Way** galaxy. Sagittarius also contains the **Lagoon**, **Trifid**, and **Omega** nebulas and the globular cluster **M22**.

Sagittarius

Hydra
The Water Snake

The biggest of all the 88 constellations, Hydra spreads across nearly a quarter of the sky. Most of the stars it contains are very faint. The brightest star in this constellation is a double star called **Alphard**. Hydra also contains two star clusters and a planetary nebula.

Hydra

TELL ME MORE...

These websites have more information about the monthly or weekly night sky:

■ www.astronomynow.com/sky_chart.shtml
■ www.nightskyinfo.com/

▼ USING THE CHART *Turn the book until the current month is in front of you. Then face north and look for the stars as they appear on the map. If you don't have a compass to find north, make a note of the direction of the Sun at noon, which is always north in the southern hemisphere.*

JUNE
JULY
MAY
AUGUST
APRIL
SEPTEMBER
MARCH
OCTOBER
FEBRUARY
NOVEMBER
JANUARY
DECEMBER

Cygnus
Milky Way
SAGITTARIUS
CRUX
HYDRA
Large Magellanic Cloud
Small Magellanic Cloud
CANIS MAJOR
Orion
Taurus

Magellanic Clouds *These two galaxies lie close to the Milky Way.*

Crux
The Southern Cross

There is no easily visible star over the South Pole, so navigators use the Crux constellation, which lies close to the pole. The stars in the long arm of the cross point towards the pole's position. Although Crux is the smallest of the constellations, it contains four very bright stars, one of which is a red giant. Lying close to the left arm of the cross is the **Jewel Box** cluster of stars, just visible with the naked eye.

Crux

Canis Major
The Greater Dog

Canis Major is one of the two hunting dogs following **Orion.** (Canis Minor, the Lesser Dog, is nearby but fainter.) It contains **Sirius,** the brightest star in the sky, also known as the Dog Star. Sirius has a companion white dwarf star, but this can only be seen with a powerful telescope. Sirius was important in the Egyptian calendar, as it heralded the annual flooding of the Nile and the start of the new year.

Canis Major

Space *in time*

People have been fascinated by the night sky for hundreds of years. Observations from astronomers throughout the centuries have greatly expanded our knowledge of how the Universe works.

▼ **1845** *Jean Foucault and Armand Fizeau take the first detailed photographs of the Sun's surface through a telescope – the first space photographs ever taken.*

▼ **1781** *William Herschel discovers Uranus while using one of his telescopes. He first thought it was a comet.*

▼ **1846** *Johann Gottfried Galle identifies Neptune.*

▲ **1609** *Galileo Galilei builds his own telescope to study the stars. His discoveries helped to prove that the Sun is at the centre of the solar system.*

▲ **2300** BCE *Stonehenge is built. Thought to be a giant stone astronomical calendar.*

3000 BCE |————————| 1600 CE |————| 1700 |—| 1800 |————

▼ **1801** *Giuseppe Piazzi discovers Ceres, the first asteroid. William Herschel is first to use the term "asteroid" in 1802.*

▲ **164** BCE *Astronomers from Babylon in the Middle East record the earliest known sighting of Halley's comet. It is seen again in 1066 CE and recorded on the Bayeux Tapestry (above).*

▼ **1655** *Christiaan Huygens observes Saturn and discovers its rings.*

▲ **1895** *Konstantin Tsiolkovsky is the first to suggest that rockets can work in a vacuum, making space flight possible.*

▲ **320–250** BCE *The Greek astronomer Aristarchus of Samos is the first to suggest that the Earth travels around the Sun. It took 18 centuries before people agreed with this idea.*

▲ **1916** *German physicist Karl Schwarzschild works out theories that lead to the idea of black holes.*

▼ **1931** *Georges Lemaitre suggests the theory that the Universe started from a single atom. His "cosmic egg" idea later becomes known as the "The Big Bang Theory".*

▲ **1959** *Russia's moon probe Luna 2 is the first spacecraft to land on the Moon, and Luna 3 sends the first photographs of the far side of the Moon back to Earth.*

▼ **1926** *The first liquid-fuel rocket is launched by Robert Goddard.*

▲ **1961** *Yuri Gagarin is the first person in space, orbiting Earth for 108 minutes!*

⊢ **1900** ⊢ ⊢ **1950** ⊢

▼ **1957** *Sputnik 1 is launched into orbit by Russia. It is the first man-made satellite in space.*

▼ **1962** *NASA's Mariner 2 is the first space probe to reach a planet as it flies past Venus. This is the start of many more space flights by the USA and Russia in the 1960s and 1970s.*

▲ **1930** *Subrahmanyan Chandrasekhar predicts the idea of supernovas, caused by large white dwarf stars collapsing in on themselves.*

▲ **1945** *Arthur C. Clarke, a science-fiction writer, suggests that a satellite can be used for transmitting telephone and TV signals around Earth. His ideas become reality 20 years later.*

▲ **1925** *Edwin Hubble announces the discovery of galaxies beyond our own.*

241

▲ **1965** *Russian Alexei Leonov was the first person to space walk. He spent 12 minutes floating up to 5 m (17½ ft) from Voskhod 2.*

◄ **1986** *Mir is the first permanent space station in orbit. It enables people to live in space for extended periods of time.*

▲ **1969** *Neil Armstrong flies into space on Apollo 11 and is the first person to walk on the Moon.*

▼ **1976** *NASA's Viking 1 is the first spacecraft to land on, and explore, Mars.*

▼ **1981** *The first of NASA's reusable space shuttles, Columbia, is flown into space.*

| 1970 | 1980 |

▶ **1971** *Lunokhod 1 finishes its mission as the first remote-controlled lander on the Moon.*

▲ **1977** *NASA launches the Voyager probes to explore deep space.*

▼ **1986** *The European Space Agency's Giotto probe takes the first ever close-up photographs of a comet nucleus as it flies through Halley's comet.*

▼ **1971** *Russia's Salyut 1, the world's first space station, is launched into orbit.*

▲ **1982** *Rings discovered around Neptune.*

▼ **2001** *Genesis probe is launched to collect samples of atoms from the solar wind.*

▼ **1994** *Hubble Space Telescope uncovers evidence of a black hole in the M87 galaxy.*

▲ **2004** *SpaceShipOne is the first privately built spacecraft to reach outer space.*

▼ **2001** *NEAR is the first spacecraft to orbit and land on an asteroid (Eros).*

▼ **2010** *NASA announces plans to retire all its space shuttles. Last flight scheduled for September 2010.*

1990 2000

▼ **2001** *The first space tourist, Dennis Tito, spends six days on the International Space Station.*

▲ **2006** *Stardust mission uses aerogel to bring back samples of comet dust.*

THE FUTURE? *There are still many discoveries to be made. The biggest challenges include finding ways to explore further afield in space, and finding life on other planets.*

▲ **1990** *The Hubble Space Telescope is the first large optical telescope in orbit. After its mirror is fixed, it returns amazing pictures of distant stars and galaxies.*

▶ **1998** *The first modules of the International Space Station are launched.*

▲ **2010** *Tranquility, the last non-Russian part of the International Space Station, is launched on the space shuttle Endeavour.*

Glossary

GLOSSARY

Absorption line A dark line or band on a spectrum that corresponds to the absorption of light at a particular wavelength.

Aerogel A lightweight substance used to collect space dust.

Antenna A type of aerial used on spacecraft and telescopes to send and receive signals.

Aphelion The point in the orbit of a planet, comet, or asteroid, when it is furthest away from the Sun.

Asteroid A giant rock that orbits the Sun.

Asteroid belt The area of space that has the highest number of orbiting asteroids in it, between the orbits of Mars and Jupiter.

Astrolabe An ancient instrument used to calculate the position of stars in the sky.

Astronaut A person trained to travel in a spacecraft.

Atmosphere The layer of gas that surrounds a planet.

Atom The smallest particle of matter that can exist on its own. It is made up of neutrons, protons, and electrons.

Aurora Curtains of light that appear near the poles of planets. Solar wind particles are trapped by a magnetic field and are drawn into the planet's atmosphere. Here they collide with atoms and give off light.

Axis The imaginary line that goes through the centre of a planet or star, and around which it rotates.

Background radiation A faint radio signal that is given out by the entire sky; leftover radiation from the Big Bang.

Big Bang The cosmic explosion that scientists believe created the Universe billions of years ago.

Billion One thousand million.

Binary stars Two stars that orbit each other. It is also called a binary system.

Black hole An area of space with such a strong gravitational pull that it sucks in anything that comes too close, even light.

Blazar An active galaxy that has a supermassive black hole at its centre and sends high-speed jets of gas towards Earth.

Brown dwarf An object that is smaller than a star, but larger than a planet. It produces heat, but little to no light at all.

Celestial object Any object that is seen in the sky.

Charged particle A particle that has a positive or negative electrical charge.

Chromosphere The region of the Sun's atmosphere above the photosphere.

Comet A large solid object made of dust and ice that orbits the Sun. As it gets near the Sun, the ice starts to vaporize, creating a tail of dust and gas.

Constellation A pattern of stars in the sky that represent mythical people or objects.

Coriolis effect An effect of Earth's rotation that makes winds and ocean currents swirl to the right in the northern hemisphere and to the left in the southern hemisphere.

Corona The Sun's hot upper atmosphere. It is seen as a white halo during a solar eclipse.

Cosmonaut A Russian astronaut.

Cosmos Another word for the Universe.

Crater A hollow or basin made by a meteorite crashing into a planet, or the Moon.

Crust The thin outer layer of rock of a planet or moon.

Dark energy The energy that scientists believe is responsible for the expansion of the Universe.

Dark matter Invisible matter that can bend starlight with its gravity.

Density The amount of matter that occupies a certain volume.

Drag The force that opposes the forward movement of something through the air.

Dust Tiny bits of "soot" from stars that absorb starlight. Also fine material on the surfaces of planets and moons.

Dwarf planet A planet that is big enough to have become spherical but has not managed to clear all the debris from its orbital path.

Eclipse The blocking of light from an object when another object passes in front of it. A lunar eclipse is when the shadow of Earth falls on the Moon. A solar eclipse is when the shadow of the Moon falls on Earth.

Electromagnetic radiation Energy waves that can travel through space and matter.

Electromagnetic spectrum The complete range of energy waves in order of wavelength, from radio waves to gamma rays.

Electron A subatomic particle with a negative electrical charge.

Elliptical Oval-shaped.

Equator The imaginary line around the centre of a planet.

Escape velocity The speed at which an object has to travel to escape the gravity of another object.

EVA Short for "extra-vehicular activity", which means activity by an astronaut outside of his or her spacecraft in space.

Exoplanet A planet outside our solar system.

Exosphere The top layer of Earth's atmosphere, where most spacecraft fly.

Extraterrestrial Not belonging to Earth.

False-colour image A picture of an object where different colours are used to show up matter or features that we can't normally see in visible light. Images from non-optical telescopes are shown in false colour.

Filament A string of galaxy superclusters that stretches out across space. Also name for a huge tongue of gas released into space from the surface of the Sun.

Flyby When a spacecraft flies past a planet, comet, or asteroid without landing or orbiting it.

Free-fall A state of weightlessness that occurs when an object is not affected by gravity, or any opposing force, for example, in orbit around Earth.

Galaxy A collection of millions of stars, gas, and dust held together by gravity and separated from other galaxies by empty space.

Gamma ray An energy wave that has a very short wavelength.

Geostationary orbit The orbit of a satellite that moves around Earth at the same speed as Earth, so that it looks as if it is not moving across the sky.

Geyser A jet of liquid that escapes through cracks in rock.

Globular clusters Ball-shaped groups of stars that orbit large galaxies.

Globules Small clouds of gas and dust in space.

Granulation Mottling on the surface of the Sun.

Gravity The force that pulls objects towards one another.

Habitable If a place is habitable, it is suitable for living in, or on.

Heliopause The boundary between the heliosphere and interstellar space.

Heliosphere A large area that contains the solar system, the solar wind, and the solar magnetic field.

Hemisphere Half of a sphere. The division of Earth into two halves, usually by the equator, which creates a northern hemisphere and a southern hemisphere.

Hertzsprung-Russell diagram A diagram that shows a star's temperature, brightness, size, and colour in relation to other stars.

Hydrothermal Relating to heated water inside Earth's crust.

Hypersonic Relating to the speed of something that is equal to or more than five times the speed of sound.

Infrared Waves of heat energy that can't be seen.

Intergalactic Between galaxies.

Interstellar Between the stars.

Ionosphere A region of Earth's atmosphere 50–600 km (31–373 miles) above the surface.

K Stands for degrees Kelvin, a measurement of temperature. 0 Kelvin (absolute zero) is –273°C (–459°F).

Launch vehicle A rocket-powered vehicle that is used to send spacecraft or satellites into space.

Light Waves of energy that we can see.

Light year The distance that light travels in one year.

Low Earth orbit An orbit close to Earth.

Luminosity The brightness of something.

Magnetar A type of neutron star with an incredibly strong magnetic field.

Magnetic field An area of magnetism created by a planet, star, or galaxy, which surrounds it and extends into space.

Magnetometer An instrument that is used to measure magnetic forces.

Magnetosphere The area around a planet where the magnetic field is strong enough to keep out the solar wind.

Magnitude The brightness of an object in space shown as a number. Bright objects have low or negative numbers and dim objects have high numbers.

Mantle A thick layer of hot rock underneath the crust of a moon or planet.

Mare A large, flat area of the Moon that looks dark when viewed from Earth. They were originally thought to be lakes or seas, but are now known to be floods of lava. The plural is maria.

Matter Something that exists as a solid, liquid, or gas.

Mesosphere The layer of atmosphere 50–80 km (30–50 miles) above the Earth, where shooting stars are seen.

Meteor A bit of rock or dust that burns up as it enters Earth's atmosphere. They are also called "shooting stars".

Meteorite A rocky object that lands on Earth.

Microgravity When the force of gravity is present, but its effect is minimal.

Microwave A type of energy wave with a short wavelength.

Milky Way The name of the galaxy where we live.

Module A portion of a spacecraft.

Multiverse Universes that are parallel to our own.

Nebula A cloud of gas and dust in space from which stars are born.

Neutrino A particle smaller than an atom that is produced by nuclear fusion in stars and by the Big Bang. It is very common, but extremely hard to detect.

Neutron A subatomic particle that does not have an electrical charge.

Neutron star A dense, collapsed star that is mainly made of neutrons.

Nucleus The centre of something.

Observatory A building, spacecraft, or satellite containing a telescope that is used for observing objects in space.

Orbit The path an object travels around another object while being affected by its gravity.

Orbiter A spacecraft that is designed to orbit an object, but not land on it.

Ozone Colourless gas that forms a layer in Earth's atmosphere, absorbing some of the harmful ultraviolet radiation in sunlight.

Particle An extremely small part of a solid, liquid, or gas.

Payload Cargo that is carried into space by a launch vehicle or on an artificial satellite.

Perihelion The point in the orbit of a planet, comet, or asteroid, when it is closest to the Sun.

Phase The amount of the Moon or a planet's surface that is seen to be lit up by the Sun.

Photosphere The part of the Sun's lower atmosphere where its light and heat come from.

Planet A celestial object that orbits a star.

Planetary nebula A glowing cloud of gas and plasma around a star at the end of its life.

Planetesimals Small rocky or icy objects that are pulled together by gravity to form planets.

Planisphere A moveable disc that shows the position of the stars in the night sky

Plasma A highly energized form of gas.

Probe An unmanned spacecraft that is designed to explore objects in space and transmit information back to Earth.

Prominence Large flame-like plume of plasma that comes out of the Sun.

Proton A subatomic particle with a positive electrical charge.

Pulsar A neutron star that sends out pulses of radiation as it spins.

Quasars Short for quasi-stellar objects, which means a very luminous, distant object that looks like a star.

Radiation Energy released by an object.

Radiometer A piece of equipment used for detecting or measuring radiation.

Red giant A very bright, but very cool huge star.

Rille A narrow channel or crack on the Moon's surface.

Rover A vehicle that is driven over the surface of a planet or moon, usually by remote control.

Satellite A naturally-occurring or man-made object that orbits another object larger than itself.

Seyfert galaxy An active galaxy, often a spiral, powered by a supermassive black hole at its centre.

Shock wave A wave of energy that is produced by an explosion or by something travelling at supersonic speed.

Silicate A type of mineral containing silicon and oxygen.

Solar radiation Energy from the Sun.

Solar wind A flow of charged particles from the Sun.

Space–time The combination of all three dimensions of space together with time.

Stratosphere The layer of atmosphere 8–50 km (5–30 miles) above Earth where aeroplanes fly.

Subatomic particles A particle that is smaller than an atom and that makes up an atom.

Suborbital A type of orbit where a spacecraft flies to the top of Earth's atmosphere (100 km, 60 miles) and weightlessness occurs.

Supernova The bright explosion that occurs as a star collapses.

Thermosphere The layer of atmosphere 80–600 km (50–375 miles) above the Earth, where auroras occur.

Thrust The force produced by a jet or rocket engine that pushes something forward.

Transit The passage of a planet or star across the face of another.

Troposphere The layer of Earth's atmosphere 6–20 km (4–12 miles) above the ground, where our weather occurs.

Ultraviolet ray A type of energy wave. It is an important part of sunlight, but exposure to it can burn people's skin.

Umbra The dark, central area of the Moon's shadow or of a sunspot.

White dwarf A small, dim star. Our Sun will eventually become a white dwarf.

X-ray A type of energy wave that can pass through objects that visible light cannot penetrate.

Zero gravity This is not actually a lack of gravity, but an apparent lack of gravity experienced by astronauts in free-fall or in orbit.

Index

Acknowledgements

The publisher would like to thank the following for their kind permission to reproduce their photographs:

(Key: a-above; b-below/bottom; c-centre; f-far; l-left; r-right; t-top)

Jacket images: *Front:* **Alamy Images:** Brand X Pictures bl; **HubbleSite:** NASA, ESA, and A. Zezas (Harvard-Smithsonian Center for Astrophysics); GALEX data: NASA, JPL-Caltech, GALEX Team, J. Huchra et al. (Harvard-Smithsonian Center for Astrophysics); Spitzer data: NASA/JPL/Caltech/Harvard-Smithsonian Center for Astrophysics fbr; **NASA:** JPL-Caltech br; JSC fbl; MSFC bc; **Science Photo Library:** Lynette Cook. *Back:* **ESA:** bl; NASA, ESO and Danny LaCrue cr; JPL-Caltech/STScI/CXC/UofA/ESA/AURA/JHU fbr; **NRAO / AUI / NSF:** bc; **Science Photo Library:** Henning Dalhoff / Bonnier Publications br; Larry Landolfi t. *Front Flaps:* **Getty Images:** AFP/ Jim Watson. *Back Flaps:* **NASA:** JPL-Caltech/R. Hurt (SSC)

1 Getty Images: Purestock. **2 Corbis:** Mark M. Lawrence (tr); Douglas Peebles (cra/Volcano). **Dorling Kindersley:** NASA (br). **NASA:** ESA (crb/Huygens); JPL (crb); JPL/ University of Arizona (cra). **Science Photo Library:** CCI Archives (cra/Herschel). **SOHO/EIT (ESA & NASA) :** (cr). **3 Corbis:** Bettmann (ca/Chimps). **HubbleSite:** NASA, ESA, M. Wong and I. de Pater (University of California, Berkeley) (ca) (cb/ Discovery space shuttle). **NASA:** (cb/Boot print) (br); A.Caulet St-ECF, ESA (cb); ESA, and H. Richer (University of British Columbia) (tc); ESA, and the Hubble Heritage (STScI/AURA) -ESA/Hubble Collaboration (cra); ESA, and The Hubble Heritage Team STScI/AURA (bc); GSFC (crb/Moon crater); MSFC (cr); Voyager 2 (crb) (cra/Antenna). **NRAO / AUI / NSF:** (c). **Reuters:** NASA (crb/Telescope). **SST, Royal Swedish Academy of Sciences, LMSAL:** (tr). **4 Corbis:**

Bettmann (cra); NASA/ Science Faction (ca); NOAA (cla); Seth Resnick/ Science Faction (fcla). **SOHO/EIT (ESA & NASA) :** (fcra). **4-5 Getty Images:** Stockbyte (Background). **5 Corbis:** Ed Darack/ Science Faction (fcla). **Getty Images:** Robert Gendler/Visuals Unlimited, Inc. (cla). **NASA:** MSFC (ca). **6-34 Chandra X-Ray Observatory:** X-ray: NASA/CXC/SAO; Optical: NASA/STScI; Infrared: NASA/JPL-Caltech/ Steward/O.Krause et al. (l). **6-7 Science Photo Library:** David Nunuk (Background). **7 Alamy Images:** Dennis Hallinan (fcla). **Chandra X-Ray Observatory:** X-ray: NASA/CXC/SAO; Optical: NASA/STScI; Infrared: NASA/JPL-Caltech/ Steward/O.Krause et al. (c). **Corbis:** Mark M. Lawrence (cl). **8 Alamy Images:** Dennis Hallinan (cl). **8-9 Alamy Images:** Dennis Hallinan (Background). **9 Corbis:** Mark M. Lawrence (l). **HubbleSite:** NASA / ESA / CXC / STScI / B. McNamara (University of Waterloo) (cr). **NASA:** (c); STS-51A (tr). **10 Getty Images:** (cl); Rob Atkins (clb); Jeremy Horner (fclb). **NASA:** JPL-Caltech/R. Hurt (SSC) (cr). **10-11 NASA:** JPL-Caltech/C. Lonsdale (Caltech/IPAC) and the SWIRE Team (Background). **11 Science Photo Library:** Mark Garlick (c). **12-13 Science Photo Library:** Kaj R. Svensson. **14 Corbis:** Stapleton Collection (c). **15 Corbis:** Paul Almasy (cl); Bettmann (tr) (c); Jose Fuste Raga (bc); Rob Matheson (t/Background); Seth Resnick/ Science Faction (c). **SOHO/EIT (ESA & NASA) :** (tc). **16 Corbis:** Roger Ressmeyer (tr) (b). **16-17 Getty Images:** Stattmayer (t/Background). **17 Corbis:** Bettmann (cr) (clb); Roger Ressmeyer (cla); Jim Sugar (br). **18 Science Photo Library:** John Sanford. **19 Corbis:** Ed Darack/ Science Faction (tr); Roger Ressmeyer (crb). **European Southern Observatory (ESO) :** (bl). **Getty Images:** Joe McNally (clb). **Large Binocular Telescope Corporation :** (c). **Reuters:** NASA (cla). **TMT Observatory Corporation:** (br). **20 Corbis:** Matthias Kulka (ca); Mehau Kulyk/ Science Photo Library (bl); NASA/ JPL/ Science Faction (br). **NASA:** JPL-Caltech/Las Campanas (br). **21 Corbis:** Markus Altmann (fbl); NASA-CAL /Handout /Reuters (bl); NASA, ESA and The Hubble Heritage Team/ Handout/ Reuters (tc). **Science Photo Library:** David A. Hardy (c); NASA (br); NRAO / AUI / NSF (fbr); JPL/ Caltech/Harvard-Smithsonian Center for Astrophysics (bc). **22 NASA:** JPL (bl). **22-23 NASA:** JPL-Caltech/ University of Arizona (c); JPL-Caltech/ IRAS / H. McCallon (br). **23 NASA:** JPL-Caltech/ K. Su (Univ. of Arizona) (tc). **Science Photo Library:** CCI Archives (tr); Robert Gendler (clb). **24 Courtesy of the NAIC - Arecibo Observatory, a facility of the NSF:** (cl). **24-25 NRAO / AUI / NSF:** (b). **25 NRAO / AUI / NSF:** (cla) (tr). **Science Photo Library:** Paul Wootton (tc). **26 (c) University Corporation for Atmospheric Research (UCAR) :** 2007 Copyright/ Carlye Calvin (cl).

ESA: ECF (crb). **Max Planck Institute for Solar System Research:** SUNRISE project/ P. Barthol (bl). **NASA:** Swift/ Stefan Immler, et al. (tr). **27 Chandra X-Ray Observatory:** Optical: Robert Gendler; X-ray: NASA/CXC/SAO/J.Drake et al. (clb). **ESA:** (ca). **NASA:** ESA (tl); SDO (tr); Courtesy of SOHO / MDI, SOHO / EIT & SOHO / LASCO consortia. SOHO is a project of international cooperation between ESA and NASA. (crb/Sun rays). **28 Getty Images:** NASA (l). **HubbleSite:** (br). **Science Photo Library:** Emilio Segre Visual Archives / American Institute Of Physics (cla). **29 Alamy Images:** Dennis Hallinan (b/Earth). **Chris Hansen:** (br). **NASA:** (c); ESA and the Hubble SM4 ERO Team (tr). **NRAO / AUI / NSF:** (cb). **Science Photo Library:** Emilio Segre Visual Archives / American Institute Of Physics (crb). **30 NASA:** STScI Digitized Sky Survey/Noel Carboni; NASA and The Hubble Heritage Team (STScI/AURA) (bl); NASA, ESA, and J. Maíz Apellániz (Instituto de Astrofísica de Andalucía, Spain) (tr). **31 HubbleSite:** NASA, ESA and The Hubble Heritage Team (STScI/AURA) (cl). **NASA:** Courtesy NASA/JPL-Caltech (tl) (cr); JPL-Caltech/J. Bally (Univ. of Colo.) (br). **32 Chandra X-Ray Observatory:** NGST (bl). **ESA:** (bc); D. Ducros (tr). **Science Photo Library:** NASA (br). **32-33 Alamy Images:** Dennis Hallinan (Background). **33 Chandra X-Ray Observatory:** NASA/ CXC/ SAO (cra); X-ray: NASA/CXC/SAO; Optical: NASA/STScI; Infrared: NASA/JPL-Caltech/Steward/O.Krause et al. (fcra). **ESA:** D. Ducros, 2009 (bc). **HubbleSite:** NASA, ESA, and the Hubble Heritage Team (STScI/AURA) -ESA/ Hubble Collaboration (fcla). **NASA:** (bl) (br); JPL-Caltech (cla). **34 Global Oscillation Network Group (GONG) :** NSO/ AURA/ NSF/ MLSO/ HAO (cla). **Laser Interferometer Gravitational Wave Observatory (LIGO) :** (c). **National Science Foundation, USA:** Glenn Grant (br). **35 ALMA:** ESO/ NAOJ/ NRAO (crb) (clb). **NASA:** SOFIA (tl); Carla Thomas (cla). **The Sudbury Neutrino Observatory Institute (SNOI) :** Lawrence Berkeley National Laboratory for the SNO Collaboration (cr). **36-37 HubbleSite:** NASA, ESA, J. Hester and A. Loll (Arizona State University) (Background). **36-62 HubbleSite:** NASA, ESA, J. Hester and A. Loll (Arizona State University) (l). **37 HubbleSite:** (c); NASA, ESA, CXC, and JPL-Caltech (fcl). **NASA:** JPL-Caltech/R. Hurt (SSC) (cl). **38 Corbis:** Moodboard (clb). **38-39 HubbleSite:** NASA, ESA, and the Hubble Heritage Team (STScI/ AURA) - ESA/Hubble Collaboration (c). **39 Alamy Images:** George Kelvin / PHOTOTAKE (cr) (crb) (fcrb). **Science Photo Library:** Detlev Van Ravenswaay (br). **40 Chandra X-Ray Observatory:** NASA/ CXC/ SAO/ P.Slane, et al. (bl). **43 © CERN :** Maximilien Brice (crb). **Corbis:** NASA/ epa (Background). **Getty Images:** Rob Atkins (fcra); Jeremy Horner (cra). **NASA:** WMAP Science Team (clb). **44-45 Science Photo Library:** NASA / ESA / STSCI / R.WILLIAMS, HDF TEAM (Background). **45 Anglo Australian Observatory:** David Malin (br). **HubbleSite:** NASA, ESA, Y. Izotov (Main Astronomical Observatory, Kyiv, UA) and T. Thuan (University of Virginia) (crb). **NASA:** X-ray: CXC/Wesleyan

Univ./R.Kilgard et al; UV: JPL-Caltech; Optical: ESA/S. Beckwith & Hubble Heritage Team (STScI/AURA); IR: JPL-Caltech/ Univ. of AZ/R. Kennicutt) (tc). **Science Photo Library:** (c); JPL-Caltech/CTIO (bc). **46 NASA:** JPL-Caltech (bl) (br). **Science Photo Library:** Volker Springel / Max Planck Institute For Astrophysics (cl). **46-47 NASA:** JPL-Caltech/STScI/CXC/UofA/ESA/AURA/ JHU (c). **47 European Southern Observatory (ESO) :** (bl). **NASA:** Al Kelly (JSCAS/NASA) & Arne Henden (Flagstaff/USNO) (bc); ESA, A. Aloisi (STScI / ESA), Hubble Heritage (STScI / AURA) - ESA/Hubble Collaboration (fbl); The Hubble Heritage Team (STScI/AURA) / Ray A. Lucas (ca). **48-49 HubbleSite:** NASA and The Hubble Heritage Team (STScI/AURA, x). **50 European Southern Observatory (ESO) :** Yuri Beletsky (cl). **Science Photo Library:** Chris Butler (bl). **50-51 NASA:** JPL-Caltech/R. Hurt (SSC) (c); CXC/ MIT/ Frederick K. Baganoff et al. (crb). **51 NASA:** CXC/ UMass/ D. Wang et al. (tr); JPL-Caltech/ R. Hurt (SSC) (bc); JPL-Caltech/ S. V. Ramirez (NExScI/ Caltech) , D. An (IPAC/Caltech) , K. Sellgren (OSU) (clb); NASA/ CXC/ M.Weiss (cra). **52 Chandra X-Ray Observatory:** NASA/ SAO/ CXC (crb). **NASA:** JPL-Caltech /M. Meixner (STScI) & the SAGE Legacy Team (bl). **53 CSIRO:** Dallas Parr (br). **ESA:** Hubble and Digitized Sky Survey 2 (tl); NASA, ESO and Danny LaCrue (cra). **NASA:** ESA, and the Hubble Heritage Team (STScI/ AURA) (tr). **54 Science Photo Library:** Mark Garlick (br); MPIA-HD, BIRKLE, SLAWIK (c). **55 NASA:** Adam Block/ NOAO/ AURA/ NSF (c); JPL-Caltech/D. Block (Anglo American Cosmic Dust Lab, SA) (tr); JPL-Caltech/Univ. of Ariz. (cl); Paul Mortfield, Stefano Cancelli (br); UMass/Z.Li & Q.D.Wang (cb). **56-57 NASA:** JPL-Caltech/ ESA/ CXC/ STScI. **58 NASA:** X-ray: NASA /CXC/ CfA/E. O'Sullivan Optical: Canada-France-Hawaii-Telescope/ Coelum (c). **58-59 Courtesy of Dr Stelios Kazantzidis (Center for Cosmology and Astro-Particle Physics, The Ohio State University) :** (b/Spiral galaxy collision); NASA, ESA, and the Hubble Heritage Team (STScI/ AURA) (tr); NASA, ESA, and the Hubble Heritage Team (STScI/ AURA) -ESA/ Hubble Collaboration (crb); NASA, ESA, Richard Ellis (Caltech) and Jean-Paul Kneib (Observatoire Midi-Pyrenees, France) (clb); NASA, H. Ford (JHU) , G. Illingworth (UCSC/ LO) , M.Clampin (STScI) , G. Hartig (STScI) , the ACS Science Team, and ESA (cr). **59 HubbleSite:** NASA, ESA, CXC, C. Ma, H. Ebeling, and E. Barrett (University of Hawaii/ IfA) , et al., and STScI (tl). **60 Corbis:** STScI/ NASA (crb). **Till Credner , Allthesky.com:** (Background). **HubbleSite:** (bl). **Science Photo Library:** NRAO / AUI / NSF (cr). **61 Chandra X-Ray Observatory:** X-ray: NASA/CXC/Univ.

of Maryland/A.S. Wilson et al.; Optical: Pal.Obs. DSS; IR: NASA/JPL-Caltech; VLA: NRAO/ AUI/NSF (bl). **HubbleSite:** John Hutchings (Dominion Astrophysical Observatory) , Bruce Woodgate (GSFC/NASA), Mary Beth Kaiser (Johns Hopkins University), Steven Kraemer (Catholic University of America), the STIS Team., and NASA (tl). **NRAO / AUI / NSF:** Image courtesy of National Radio Astronomy Observatory / Associated Universities, Inc. / National Science Foundation (cra). **Science Photo Library:** NASA / ESA / STSCI / J. BAHCALL, PRINCETON IAS (crb).

62 Science Photo Library: Mike Agliolo (crb); Volker Springel / Max Planck Institute For Astrophysics (cl). **62-63 Science Photo Library:** Lynette Cook. **63 HubbleSite:** NASA, ESA, M.J. Jee and H. Ford (Johns Hopkins University) (br). **Science Photo Library:** M. Markevitch/ CXC/ CFA/ NASA (bl). **64-65 Getty Images:** AFP/ Jim Watson (Background). **64-88 Dorling Kindersley:** ESA - ESTEC (l). **65 Corbis:** Bettmann (fcl). **ESA:** (c). **US Geological Survey:** Astrogeology Team (c). **66 Getty Images:** Sir Godfrey Kneller (c). **NASA:** KSC (l); United Launch Alliance/ Pat Corkery (r). **67 NASA:** Bill Ingalls (c); Pratt & Whitney Rocketdyne (tr). **68-69 NASA:** Bill Ingalls. **70 Alamy Images:** Linda Sikes (br). **Corbis:** NASA/CNP (c). **Science Photo Library:** Mark Garlick (cl). **71 Alamy Images:** Stock Connection Blue (c). **Corbis:** (cra); Bettmann (tl). **Getty Images:** NASA (clb). **Science Photo Library:** NASA (cr) (crb). **72 NASA:** (tr); KSC (crb); MSFC / KSC (cl). **73 ESA:** (cra). **EUROCKOT Launch Services GmbH:** (cra). **Getty Images:** Space Imaging (bl). **NASA:** Victor Zelentsov (tl). **Courtesy Sea Launch:** (br). **74 ESA:** CNES/ Arianespace/ Photo optique video du CSG (cb); Service Optique CSG (cl). **74-75 ESA:** CNES/ Arianespace/ Photo optique video du CSG (t). **75 ESA:** CNES/ Arianespace/ Photo optique video du CSG (bc) (cr); Service Optique CSG (clb). **76 Corbis:** Alain Nogues/ Sygma (br). **NASA:** JPL (c). **77 NASA:** b. **78 Corbis:** Bettmann (b). **ESA:** D. Ducros (cl). **NASA:** Goddard Space Flight Center/ MODIS Rapid Response Team/ Jeff Schmaltz (cr). **79 CNES:** Illustration P.Carril - Mars 2003 (clb). © **EADS :** Astrium (crb); J. Huart (cra). **80-81 USGS:** Courtesy of the U.S. Geological Survey. **82 Getty Images:** Ludek Pesek (b). **NASA:** NSSDC (tl). **Science Photo Library:** Detlev Van Ravenswaay (c). **83 NASA:** Ames Research Center (cra); JPL (tl); NSSDC (clb). **Science Photo Library:** NASA / JPL (bc). **US Geological Survey:** Astrogeology Team (fclb). **Wikimedia Commons:** Daderot (br). **84 ESA:** (c). **NASA:** (crb). **85 CNES:** Illustration D. Ducros - 1998 (cr). **ESA:** NASA (r) (cb) (bc) (br). **86 NASA:** ISRO/ JPL-Caltech/ USGS/ Brown Univ. (bl). **Science Photo Library:** Indian Space Research Organisation (r). **87 CBERS:** INPE (cra). **Corbis:** Li Gang/ Xinhua Press (tc). **Getty Images:** ChinaFotoPress (cl). **Courtesy of JAXA:** NHK (b/Background) (cb). **88 ESA:** AOES Medialab/ ESA 2002 (cb). **Science Photo Library:** David A. Hardy, Futures: 50 Years In Space (ca). **89 Courtesy of JAXA:** (crb). **Science Photo Library:** David A. Hardy (clb); NASA (tl) (cla). **90-114 Dorling Kindersley:** NASA (l). **90-91 Getty Images:** NASA/ National Geographic (Background). **91 Corbis:** Bettmann (cl). **NASA:** (fcl). **SpaceX:** NASA (c). **92 Corbis:** Bettmann (cl) (cr); NASA - digital version copyright/Science Faction (bl). **NASA:** 5909731 / MSFC-5909731 (cra). **92-93 Corbis:** Bettmann (Background). **93 Corbis:** Bettmann (cla) (bc) (cr); Karl Weatherly (cb). **Dorling Kindersley:** Bob Gathany (tl). **NASA:** (clb); MSFC (tr). **94 NASA:** ESA (r); Robert Markowitz/ Mark Sowa (bc). **95 ESA:** (cla) (cra);

ASI-Star City (crb). **NASA:** (cl) (br) (clb); Bill Ingalls (tl). **Science Photo Library:** NASA (cr). **96 NASA:** JSC (clb) (b) (tr). **97 Dorling Kindersley:** NASA (clb). **NASA:** JSC (crb) (br) (fbr). **Science Photo Library:** NASA (t). **98 NASA:** (cl) (bc). **Science Photo Library:** NASA (crb) (br). **99 NASA:** (tl) (bc) (tr). **Wikimedia Commons:** Aliazimi (bl). **100 Alamy Images:** RIA Novosti (cl). **Corbis:** Bettmann (c); Hulton-Deutsch Collection (tr). **Getty Images:** Hulton Archive (ca). **NASA:** 5909731 / MSFC-5909731 (br). **101 Corbis:** Roger Ressmeyer (tr). **NASA:** Kennedy Space Center (bl). **Press Association Images:** (fbr). **Science Photo Library:** Power And Syred (crb). **102-103 NASA:** (Background). **104 Alamy Images:** RIA Novosti (cla). **The Kobal Collection:** MGM (crb). **NASA:** (clb). **104-105 Science Photo Library:** NASA (b). **105 NASA:** (tl) (cla). **106 NASA:** (cl) (br). **107 Courtesy of JAXA:** (br). **NASA:** (cla) (cr) (tr). **108 NASA:** (cra) (cb) (crb). **109 Corbis:** Bettmann (cr). **NASA:** (br); MSFC (tl) (cla). **Science Photo Library:** NASA (cra). **110 Alamy Images:** Detlev van Ravenswaay / Picture Press (br). **Corbis:** Jim Sugar (bl). **NASA:** Scaled Composites (ca). **110-111 Corbis:** Ed Darack/ Science Faction (Background). **111 Bigelow Aerospace :** (crb). **Getty Images:** Daniel Berehulak (b). **NASA:** KSC (bl). **Science Photo Library:** Take 27 Ltd (br). **courtesy Virgin Galactic:** (tl) (cra). **112 Reaction Engines Limited / Adrian Mann:** Reaction Engines Ltd develops SKYLON, a space plane which evolved from the HOTOL project (b). **Science Photo Library:** Richard Bizley (cra). **113 Agence France Presse:** (crb). **Corbis:** (cl). **NASA:** DFRC/ Illustration by Steve Lighthill (b). **SpaceX:** NASA (tr). **114 Alamy Images:** Pat Eyre (crb). **Corbis:** James Marshall (bl). **ESA:** S. Corvaja (bl). **Science Photo Library:** Sinclair Stammers (cra). **115 Alamy Images:** Photos 12 (cr). **NASA:** MSFC (clb). **PA Photos:** AP/ NASA (br). **Science Photo Library:** Victor Habbick Visions (t). **116-117 NASA:** JPL/ University of Arizona (Background). **116-162 Dorling Kindersley:** NASA /Finley Holiday Films (l). **117 Corbis:** Dennis di Cicco (c). **HubbleSite:** M. Wong and I. de Pater (University of California, Berkeley) (cl). **118 NASA:** JPL-Caltech / T. Pyle (SSC) (c). **Science Photo Library:** Detlev Van Ravenswaay (crb). **119 David A. Hardy :** PPARC (br). **Julian Baum:** (clb). **120 HubbleSite:** Reta Beebe (New Mexico State University) / NASA (cb); NASA, ESA, L. Sromovsky and P. Fry (University of Wisconsin) , H. Hammel (Space Science Institute) , and K. Rages (SETI Institute) (crb). **NASA:** (clb/Earth). **120-121 NASA:** JPL-Caltech (solar system planets). **121 Dorling Kindersley:** NASA /Finley Holiday Films (cb). **122 Science Photo Library:** NASA (r). **123 Getty Images:** Dieter Spannknebel (tl); NSSDC (clb). **NASA:** NSSDC/ GSFC (ca). **Science Photo Library:** M. Ledlow Et Al / NRAO / AUI / NSF (cb). **SOHO/EIT (ESA & NASA) :** (cr). **124-125 Science Photo Library:** NASA (tc). **125 NASA:** MPS/ Katlenburg-Lindau (cr). **NASA:** NSSDC (bl) (bc). **126 NASA:** JPL (cra) (b) (clb). **127 ESA:** (crb). **NASA:** Ames Research Center (tr); JPL (tl); JPL-Caltech (cra) (c) (cl). **Science Photo Library:** David P.Anderson, SMU/ Nasa (cb). **128 ESA:** DLR/ FU Berlin (G. Neukum) (bc). **NASA:** (cra); ESA (cr); JPL (cb); JPL/ Malin Space Science Systems (br); NSSDC (bl). **129 Getty Images:** Time & Life Pictures (clb). **NASA:** GSFC (r); JPL /MSSS (tl); JPL/ Malin Space Science Systems (br). **130 Corbis:** Lowell Georgia (br); JPL / USGS (bl); JPL /MSSS (c). **NASA:** JPL/ Cornell (t) (bl) (br) (cr). **Science Photo Library:** NASA (fbl). **132-133

NASA:** HiRISE/ JPL/ University of Arizona. **134 Alamy Images:** Mary Evans Picture Library (tr). **Science Photo Library:** Chris Butler (cb) (br). **135 NASA:** JPL / USGS (t). **Science Photo Library:** Henning Dalhoff / Bonnier Publications (crb); D. Van Ravenswaay (br). **136 HubbleSite:** NASA/ESA, John Clarke (University of Michigan) (tr); M. Wong and I. de Pater (University of California, Berkeley) (br). **137 Corbis:** NASA-JPL-Caltech - digital versi/Science Faction (r). **HubbleSite:** NASA, ESA, IRTF, and A. Sánchez-Lavega and R. Hueso (Universidad del País Vasco, Spain) (clb). **NASA:** JPL/ Cornell University (cla). **138 Corbis:** Bettmann (tr); JPL / USGS (b). **NASA:** JPL/ University of Arizona (c); JPL/ Brown University (bl); JPL/ DLR (tr); JPL/ University of Arizona (cr). **139 NASA:** JPL (cla) (bc) (cl) (clb). **140 NASA:** JPL-Caltech (crb); MSFC (bl). **141 NASA:** Walt Feimer (c); JPL (clb); JPL-Caltech (cl) (br); MSFC (cra); JPL/ Space Science Institute (clb). **142 NASA:** JPL/ STScI (cr). **Science Photo Library:** D. Van Ravenswaay (crb); NASA, ESA, J. Clarke (Boston University) , and Z. Levay (STScI) (c). **143 Corbis:** NASA - digital version copyright/ Science Faction (tc); STScI/ NASA (r) (bc). **Science Photo Library:** NASA/ JPL/ University Of Arizona (tl). **144 Alamy Images:** The Print Collector (r); JPL / USGS (bc). **NASA:** JPL/ Space Science Institute (clb) (cl) (crb). **NRAO / AUI / NSF:** (cr). **144-145 NASA:** JPL/ Space Science Institute (tc). **145 ESA:** (br); NASA/ JPL/ University of Arizona (tr) (cb) (crb). **NASA:** (cla); JPL (bl); JPL/ GSFC/ Space Science Institute (clb); JPL/ University of Arizona (ca). **146-147 NASA:** JPL/ Space Science Institute. **148 Getty Images:** John Russell (cl). **W.M. Keck Observatory:** Lawrence Sromovsky, (Univ. Wisconsin-Madison) (cla). **NASA:** JPL (br); NSSDC (l). **149 NASA:** GSFC (br); JPL (c); JPL / USGS (bl); JPL-Caltech (cla) (cr) (fcr); NSSDC (cra). **150 NASA:** (bl); Voyager 2 (c). **151 NASA:** (cra); JPL (bl); JPL / USGS (cla). **Science Photo Library:** Royal Astronomical Society (r). **152 HubbleSite:** NASA, ESA, and M. Buie (Southwest Research Institute) (tr). **NASA:** Dr. R. Albrecht, ESA/ ESO Space Telescope European Coordinating Facility (cla). **152-153 NASA:** ESA and G. Bacon (STScI) (b). **153 HubbleSite:** ESA, H. Weaver (JHU/APL) , A. Stern (SwRI) , and the HST Pluto Companion Search Team (cb). **154 Corbis:** Dennis di Cicco (b). **155 Corbis:** Jonathan Blair (bl); Gianni Dagli Orti (cla). **HubbleSite:** NASA / ESA / M. Wong (Space Telescope Science Institute, Baltimore, Md.) / H. B. Hammel (Space Science Institute, Boulder, Colo.) / Jupiter Impact Team (cr). **Science Photo Library:** Mark Garlick (br); Gordon Garradd (tr); NASA / ESA / STSCI / H. Weaver & T. Smith (cb). **156 Corbis:** Roger Ressmeyer (cr). **Dorling Kindersley:** ESA (cra). **ESA:** SOHO (clb). **NASA:** JPL (br). **157 HubbleSite:** NASA, ESA, P. Feldman (Johns Hopkins University) and H. Weaver (Johns Hopkins University Applied Physics Laboratory) (tr); JPL/ UMD (cla). **NASA:** JPL (tl); MSFC (cl). **Science Photo Library:** Erik Viktor (b). **158 ICSTARS Astronomy:** Vic & Jen Winter. **159 Corbis:** Tony Hallas/ Science Faction (br). **HubbleSite:** John Caldwell (York University, Ontario) , Alex Storrs (STScI) , (tr). **Kwon, O Chul:** (cr). **Jimmy Westlake:** (cla). **160 Corbis:** Hans Schmied (ca). **Science Photo Library:** Mark Garlick (cla). **160-161 Corbis:** Bryan Allen (b). **161 Dorling Kindersley:** The Natural History Museum, London (cl). **Galaxy Picture Library:** UWO/ University of Calgary/ Galax (tr). **NASA:** Ted Bunch/ JPL (fcra); M. Elhassan/ M. H. Shaddad/ P. Jenniskens (crb); Michael Farmer/ JPL (cr); JPL/ Cornell (cl). **162 Selden E. Ball:** Cornell University (ca). **Corbis:** NASA/ Roger Ressmeyer (cr). **NASA:** JPL/ University of

Arizona (fcr). **Science Photo Library:** Christian Darkin (b); NASA (cl); T. Stevens & P. Mckinley, Pacific Northwest Laboratory (br). **163 NASA:** (tc) (bl); JPL / USGS (bc); JPL/ University of Arizona (cl); JPL/ University of Arizona/ University of Colorado (tr); NOAA (cr). **Science Photo Library:** Mark Garlick / US Geological Survey (cb). **164-165 Science Photo Library:** Planet Observer (Background). **164-176 Dorling Kindersley:** NASA (l). **165 Corbis:** Momatiuk - Eastcott (fcl); Douglas Peebles (c). **Getty Images:** Barcroft Media (cl). **166 Dorling Kindersley:** Planetary Visions Ltd (cla). **166-167 NASA:** (c). **167 NASA:** (tr/Earth); MSFC (bc). **168-169 Alamy Images:** Rolf Nussbaumer Photography. **170 Alamy Images:** Alaska Stock LLC (b). **NASA:** JPL (cl). **171 iStockphoto.com:** Janrysavy (cl) (cb) (cr) (fcrb). **NASA:** GSFC (bl); MODIS Ocean Science Team (br). **Science Photo Library:** European Space Agency (c). **172 Corbis:** Douglas Peebles (crb). **172-173 Corbis:** Galen Rowell (b). **173 Corbis:** Momatiuk - Eastcott (cla). **Science Photo Library:** Bernhard Edmaier (crb); David Parker (br); Ron Sanford (tr). **174 Corbis:** Bryan Allen (clb); Hinrich Baesemann / DPA (cla). **NASA:** (tr). **Science Photo Library:** Detlev Van Ravenswaay (br). **175 Corbis:** (br); Mike Hollingshead / Science Faction (bl); Gerolf Kalt (clb); NOAA (cr). **Science Photo Library:** David R. Frazier (cl). **176 Dorling Kindersley:** The Royal Museum of Scotland, Edinburgh (br). **Science Photo Library:** Lynette Cook (Volcanoes); Henning Dalhoff / Bonnier Publications (clb). **177 Alamy Images:** Amberstock (tl). **Dorling Kindersley:** Jon Hughes (bl) (bc). **ESA:** (crb). **imagequestmarine.com:** Peter Batson (cb). **NOAA:** Office of Ocean Exploration; Dr. Bob Embley, NOAA PMEL, Chief Scientist (ca). **Science Photo Library:** Victor Habbick Visions (tr); P. Rona/ OAR/ National Undersea Research Program/ NOAA (cl). **178-179 Alamy Images:** Melba Photo Agency (Background). **179 NASA:** (cl) (b). **180 Alamy Images:** Patrick Eden (b). **Science Photo Library:** Andrew J. Martinez (cra) (fcra). **181 Corbis:** William Radcliffe/ Science Faction (cr). **Science Photo Library:** Planetary Visions Ltd (bc). **182 Getty Images:** VGL/ amanaimagesRF (fcra). **NASA:** Image courtesy of the Image Science & Analysis Laboratory, NASA Johnson Space Center (cra). **Science Photo Library:** Dr Fred Espenak (ca); NOAO (tc); David Nunuk (crb). **182-192 Dorling Kindersley:** NASA (l). **183 Corbis:** Tom Fox/ Dallas Morning News (cb); Reuters (tl). **Getty Images:** VGL/ amanaimagesRF (tr). **NASA:** Image courtesy of the Image Science & Analysis Laboratory, NASA Johnson Space Center (fcr). **Science Photo Library:** NOAO (c). **184 NASA:** JSC (cb). **184-185 Getty Images:** Stocktrek RF (c). **Moonpans.com:** (b). **185 Getty Images:** SSPL (crb). **NASA:** JSC (cb); MSFC (cla);